INVESTMENT STRATEGIES AFTER THE NEW TAX ACT

MARTIN M. SHENKMAN, J.D., CPA

John Wiley & Sons, Inc.

New York • Chichester • Brisbane • Toronto • Singapore

This text is printed on acid-free paper.

Copyright © 1994 by Martin M. Shenkman
Published by John Wiley & Sons, Inc.

Library of Congress Cataloging in Publication Data:

Shenkman, Martin M.
    Investment strategies after the new tax act / by
    Martin M. Shenkman.
        p.   cm.
    Includes index.
    ISBN 0-471-01703-5 (cloth; acid-free)
    ISBN 0-471-01699-3 (paper; acid-free)
    1. Taxation—United States.   2. Investments—United States.
    3. United States—Economic policy—1993–   I. Title.
    HJ2381.S52   1994
    336.2'00973—dc20   93-38727

Printed in the United States of America

10 9 8 7 6 5 4 3 2 1

To my wife, Shelly,
and my three sons:
Yoni, Dovi, and Daniel

DISCLAIMER

In the preparation of this book, effort has been made to offer current, correct, and clearly expressed information. Nonetheless, inadvertent errors can occur, and tax rules and regulations often change.

Further, the information in the text is intended to afford general guidelines on matters of interest to taxpayers. The application and impact of tax laws can vary widely from case to case, however, based on the specific or unique facts involved. Accordingly, the information in this book is not intended to serve as legal, accounting, or tax advice. Readers are encouraged to consult with professional advisers concerning specific matters before making any decision, and the author and publisher disclaim any responsibility for positions taken by taxpayers in their individual cases or for any misunderstanding on the part of readers. The information in this book is based on the Omnibus Budget Reconciliation Act of 1993 (Public Law 103-66), signed into law August 10, 1993. It was completed prior to the issuance of any regulations, rulings, or notices interpreting the new tax act. Therefore, current tax advice must be obtained prior to taking any actions based on the discussions herein.

ACKNOWLEDGMENTS

I would like to thank a number of people who were of considerable assistance in the preparation of this book: Michael Hamilton of John Wiley & Sons, whose support and encouragement were outstanding, as usual; Steven Subelsk, of Sidney Noveck & Company, CPAs, Southfield, Michigan, for his review of the manuscript; Richard Feldand, Jay Levine, of Feld Marks & Co., Teaneck, New Jersey, for their review of the manuscript; Mark A. Goldsmith of Herrick, Feinstein, New York, New York, for his review of the manuscript; Kramer, Regen, Benz & Zitolo, CPAs, PC, New York, for their preparation of the tables illustrating the tax effects of the Clinton Tax Act; and Gary M. Hoffman, CPA, of Nardone & Hoffman, PC, New York, for his review of the manuscript. Any errors or omissions are my own.

MARTIN M. SHENKMAN

Teaneck, New Jersey
December 1993

CONTENTS

PART ONE

INTRODUCTION

1 A Perspective on the Clinton Tax Act

THE CLINTON TAX ACT

Few investors will escape the effects of the Revenue Reconciliation Act of 1993, Title XIII of the Omnibus Budget Reconciliation Act (OBRA) 1993, passed by Congress on August 6, 1993 (the Clinton Tax Act). President Clinton's February 17, 1993, speech promised the most sweeping tax bill since the Tax Reform Act of 1986. The changes finally enacted in fact affect large corporations, closely held or smaller businesses, wealthy taxpayers, middle-income and low-income taxpayers, employees, investors of all types, retired persons, and other taxpayers.

The nature of the changes represent a dramatic departure from the Tax Reform Act of 1986 philosophy of simplification (maybe only by comparison with the Clinton Tax Act), lower rates (those are gone), and the goal of removing tax considerations from investment planning (only at your own peril). Tax rates are higher, incentives for certain types of investments will affect investment strategies, and complexity is back. With such dramatic changes, affecting almost every taxpayer, the 1993 tax bill is important for every investor to understand. The effects can be substantial. The changes in tax planning as compared with the years after the Tax Reform Act of 1986 and before 1993 are substantial. Great caution and diligence should be exercised.

This book explains how every investor will be affected by the Clinton Tax Act. It provides practical advice about revising your investments to profit from opportunities created and to minimize the cost of rate increases and other changes. Tips and traps are highlighted to help guide you through post-Clinton investing. Examples and other materials that you can use in your tax planning are included to help illustrate the new rules. A glossary will help you through the maze.

3

WHAT HAPPENED TO "TAX SIMPLIFICATION?"

The death knell has been sounded for the principles underlying the
Tax Reform Act of 1986. Taxes will again assume their common historic role of stimulating investment; tax rate disparities will encourage tax-oriented investment strategies (although tax shelters may still
be a dirty word, many investors will be looking for them); and the
progressive tax rates have been enhanced so the more you make, the
more you pay. Any thought of a flat tax or tax simplification is gone.

THEMES THAT AFFECTED TAX ACT

President Clinton stressed several principles underlying his tax pack-
age. Whether or not the Clinton Tax Act achieves the stated goals,
these principles can help you anticipate and understand many of the
tax changes described in later chapters.

Investment and Not Consumption

A major theme was to promote investment. Therefore, numerous
consumption-oriented spending deductions have been further limited. For example, business entertainment deductions, club dues, and
travel expenses for spouses have all been severely restricted. These
changes highlight a trend that will have a much harsher effect on investors than many realize. The Clinton Tax Act, like several tax acts
before it, has severely restricted a broad range of deductions. These
restrictions often affect legitimate business and investment deductions that you have incurred and have paid for. The result is that the
top tax rates you read about are really much worse than they sound
because the deductions you can claim before applying those tax rates
are so limited. Thus, not only have rates increased, but the income
that will be taxed has increased as well. The result is a much higher
actual tax bite.

The objective of stimulating investment utilizes job incentives, various tax deductions to encourage investment in hard assets (equipment
and fixtures), and credits to encourage investment in special areas.
Tax implications of investments have reassumed their historically important role.

Small Business

Several investment incentives have been targeted for small businesses where, historically, the most jobs have been created. President Clinton stated that the changes will contain the most significant benefits for small business in history. Whether they are that significant is doubtful, but every investor in a small business should pay careful attention since proper planning will be necessary to take the most advantage of the new benefits. For example, certain tax incentives are available to businesses investing in other qualified small businesses. The deduction for investments in equipment has been increased. But, as you will see in this book, not only are the incentives extremely complicated, they are often not nearly as generous as they may have sounded initially.

Commitment to Children and Strengthening of Families

The President promised several broad programs to benefit children and families. Increases in the earned income credit to help lower income workers is an example of the changes made to achieve this objective. Since these incentives generally do not affect investors, they are not discussed in any detail.

Job Creation

The President made job creation incentives an important part of the Tax Act. Job tax credits for creating new jobs as well as the various investment incentives should encourage job creation.

Closing Loopholes

The President has promised to further close tax "loopholes." Many of these relate to business entertainment and travel deductions. This has long been a favorite loophole to attack.

HOW TO BEGIN PLANNING

The first step in planning your investments following the Clinton Tax Act is to begin to understand the changes that were made. This process cannot stop, however, with this book. For many years to come, the Internal Revenue Service (IRS) will be issuing rulings and regulations that interpret and apply the Clinton Tax Act changes. You must then assess how the changes are likely to affect your personal investment strategies so that you can plan the steps you will take to achieve your goals. The Tips highlighted throughout this book should give you ideas for beginning this process. Where your income is sizable, or your situation complex, your next step should be to discuss your plan with your tax adviser. Like all major tax acts, the Clinton Tax Act is full of complex rules, exceptions, and special provisions, so professional help is always advisable.

WHAT THE GOVERNMENT SHOULD REALLY BE DOING

The approach taken in the Clinton Tax Act is wrong. What is most needed to achieve growth is consistency, savings incentives, and simplicity. Even in an unfavorable tax environment, business can grow if it knows the rules of the game. Unfortunately, Congress has changed the tax rules so often that the only certainty is that the rules will change again. When evaluating an investment, a common step is to project the net of tax return over the life of the investment, discount it back to present dollars, and evaluate the merits of the investment compared with its cost. Since the tax rules change significantly every few years, business must discount projected returns at a higher rate to reflect the increased risk. This does not bode well for investment. The Clinton Tax Act, with its about-face from many of the principles of the 1986 Tax Reform Act, will only exacerbate this problem.

Savings and investment incentives are critical to the rebuilding of the economy. But the Clinton Tax Act, with increased tax rates and more restrictions on pensions and other similar changes, really does not promote savings to the extent that it should.

Finally, as the rest of this book will demonstrate, simplicity is not a word to use to describe the Clinton Tax Act.

CONCLUSION

The Clinton Tax Act has affected hundreds of provisions in the Internal Revenue Code. This chapter has highlighted several miscellaneous changes that will affect a broad cross section of investors. The key point is that the changes are numerous and complex, and can have costly results. Caution must be exercised in any tax planning.

Like all too many tax acts, the Omnibus Budget Reconciliation Act of 1993 means that you must face the daunting tasks of understanding the new rules, adjusting your investment, business, and financial plans accordingly, and bearing additional tax costs and professional fees. About the only solace is that those who are diligent will reap the benefits of lower tax costs and better net of tax investment returns. Be cautious, however; as is true of any tax legislation, the interpretation of these new laws will require future rulings, regulations, and court cases. Be certain to consult with your tax, investment, legal, pension, insurance, and other advisers before making any decision. Good luck.

PART TWO

CHANGES
AFFECTING
ALL INVESTORS

2 Higher Tax Rates Take a Bigger Bite

OVERVIEW OF HOW INDIVIDUAL TAXPAYERS ARE TAXED

The Clinton Tax Act made scores of tax changes that affect how you may be taxed. To understand how the various changes fit together, you must understand the general sequence of the tax calculation. This overview of the 11 major steps in the individual tax calculation provides a framework for much of the following discussion, helps define many of the tax terms that you will confront, and highlights several of the tax changes. Table 2.1 provides a schematic of these 11 steps.

These steps in the tax calculation (except Step 11, which is the subject of Chapter 4) are explained in greater detail in the following sections.

Gross Income

Gross income is all cash proceeds, revenues, and income from all sources. Many of the items that have to be included in your gross income are obvious: wages (Form W-2), consulting fees (Form 1099-NEC); dividends, interest, and royalty incomes (Form 1099); alimony; rental income (net of expenses); unemployment compensation; tips; and so forth. Some of the items that may have to be included are not as obvious: the value of any prizes and most awards; certain payments resulting from a divorce that you may have thought were tax-free property distributions but which are treated as taxable alimony instead; your share of income from an S corporation, partnership, or limited liability company even if you did not receive any cash distributions; certain distributions from trusts and estates; and so forth. The Clinton Tax Act made several changes to the determination of your gross income. The amount of Social Security that you must report as income may have increased (Chapter 18). The increased tax rates on trusts and estates may encourage more distributions to be made to

TABLE 2.1 Individual Tax Calculation Steps

1. Gross income: wages, interest, dividends, rents

—

2. Adjustments from gross income: alimony, IRA, KEOGH

=

3. Adjusted gross income (AGI)
4. Modified adjusted gross income: special changes required for many tax calculations, such as determining taxable Social Security

—

5. Itemized deduction: taxes, medical, casualty; or standard deduction, $6,000 (1992 Joint)

—

6. Personal exemptions: $2,450 (1994 est.) for you, spouse, dependents subject to phaseout

=

7. Taxable income

×

8. Tax rates: 15% to 39.6% as increased by Clinton Tax Act; Capital gains 28%

=

9. Tax liability: new rules for when estimated taxes must be paid

—

10. Tax credits: low income housing; research and experimentation; as amended by Clinton Tax Act

= Tax Due

11. Alternative Minimum Tax (AMT): Compare with regular tax and pay greater amount. Clinton Tax Act has made many changes to AMT.

you as a beneficiary than under prior law (Chapter 5). Gains on investments in certain qualifying businesses called Qualified Specialized Small Business Investment Companies and Qualifying Small Business Stock may be excluded from your income (Chapter 15).

Adjustments to Gross Income

A number of items may be deducted from your gross income to arrive at Step 3, your adjusted gross income (AGI). These deductions are called *adjustments*. They include certain employee business expenses, deductions on rental property (deducted on Form 1040, Schedule E), alimony payments (where they are not recharacterized as a nondeductible property settlement payment), contributions to individual retirement accounts (where neither you or your spouse are active participants in an employer retirement plan), interest forfeited on premature withdrawals from savings accounts or certificates of deposit, and so forth. The Clinton Tax Act made several changes to the adjustments to gross income. The deduction for self-employed taxpayers for 25 percent of their health insurance premiums has been retroactively reinstated (Chapter 16). Certain moving expense deductions that are still permitted will be deductible after 1994 as adjustments to gross income rather than as itemized deductions (Chapter 8).

Adjusted Gross Income

When the adjustments for gross income are deducted from your total gross income, you obtain adjusted gross income, or AGI. AGI is important for many different tax calculations. The starting point for calculating the alternative minimum tax is AGI (Chapter 4). Miscellaneous itemized deductions are reduced by 2 percent of AGI to determine the amount deductible. Medical expenses are generally only deductible if they exceed 7.5 percent of AGI. Casualty losses are deductible only if they exceed 10 percent of AGI. The Clinton Tax Act has changed many of the rules affecting casualty losses (Chapter 9). Personal exemptions are phased out based on AGI, as are itemized deductions. The Clinton Tax Act has made permanent these last two limitations and has made certain other adjustments to them (Chapter 7).

Modified Adjusted Gross Income

This is not really part of the general tax calculation. However, it is important to many different tax calculations so it has been noted separately to highlight it. Many tax rules are based on AGI subject to various adjustments. The required adjustments vary somewhat from rule to rule so generalizations could be misleading. Under prior law, estimated tax rules were based on a concept of modified adjusted gross income. The Clinton Tax Act changed these rules simplifying the calculations of estimated taxes to be paid by individuals (Chapter 7). The Clinton Tax Act increased the portion of Social Security benefits that you may have to include in income. The calculations depend on a modified version of your AGI, which consists of adding tax-exempt income and a portion of your Social Security benefits to your AGI (Chapter 18). The passive loss limitations have several calculations based on modified versions of AGI. Determining whether the special exception for active participation in rental real estate applies to you will depend on a modified version of your AGI. Tax credit phaseouts are also based on modified AGI (Chapter 12).

Itemized Deductions or Standard Deduction

Itemized deductions may be permitted for various expenses, including medical expenses, property taxes, state and local income taxes, certain employee business expenses, charitable contributions, and moving expenses. The Clinton Tax Act has made numerous changes that directly or indirectly affect your calculation of itemized deductions. The rules for charitable contributions have been changed in several respects, including increased reporting requirements (Chapter 6). The rules for moving expenses have been restricted in many ways; some are now deductible for AGI (Step 2; see Chapter 8).

TIP: The rules for calculating your regular tax and alternative minimum tax (AMT) itemized deductions have changed. For AMT purposes, important itemized deductions allowed for calculating your regular tax are not permitted. The changes in the relationship of these two tax systems, regular and AMT, complicate planning for itemized deductions. You must first determine which tax system you are going to be subject to for a particular tax year and then determine which planning steps to take.

If your itemized deductions, after giving effect to the new Clinton Tax Act rules, do not exceed a certain minimum amount, called the "standard deduction," you are entitled to claim the standard deduction instead.

Personal Exemptions

You are permitted a deduction for an amount for yourself, your spouse, each of your dependent children, and certain other dependents. For someone other than a child to qualify as a dependent, the person must meet several requirements, including the following: generally be a relative, such as a brother, sister, mother, father; have an income below specified amounts; and have more than half of his or her support for the year provided by the taxpayer.

Where the parents are divorced, separated, or living apart at all times during the last 6 months of the calendar year, special rules apply to determine which parent is entitled to the exemption. The parent having actual custody over the particular child for the greater part of the year will generally be entitled to claim the exemption for that child. For this rule to apply, the parents must together have custody of the child for more than half of the year and must together provide over half of the child's support. If the custodial parent expressly waives or releases the right to claim a dependency exemption for a child, the other (noncustodial) parent may claim the exemption. The custodial parent must file Form 8332 declaring that he or she will not claim the exemption for one or more calendar years. The noncustodial parent can attach this form to his or her tax return and can then claim the exemption for that year.

The Clinton Tax Act makes permanent the phaseout of the personal exemptions at certain income levels (Chapter 7). For higher income taxpayers, the exemptions are effectively eliminated.

Taxable Income

The result of the preceding calculations is your taxable income to which you apply the tax rates to calculate the tax.

Tax Rates

When you've determined your taxable income, you multiply it by the appropriate tax rates to determine your tax. Most taxpayers will simply look up the tax in tax tables provided by the IRS for each filing status (e.g. single, married, etc.) and each income level. The Clinton Tax Act, as discussed later in this chapter, has increased tax rates, increased the relative tax advantage of capital gains, and made other changes that substantially complicate the tax-planning process. You may also have to add your self-employment tax to your regular tax.

Tax Liability

The tax you have calculated, subject to credits and the alternative minimum tax noted in the final two steps, is the amount you must pay in tax. The timing of the payments, in particular when you may have to make estimated tax payments, has been changed in several respects by the Clinton Tax Act (Chapter 7).

Tax Credits

There are several tax credits you may be able to use advantageously. These include the rehabilitation tax credit, the low-income housing tax credit, and the research and experimentation tax credit. The Clinton Tax Act made several changes to the low-income housing credit (Chapter 10) and the research and experimentation credit (Chapter 17).

Alternative Minimum Tax

If you are subject to the AMT, you must calculate the AMT and then compare it with your regular tax liability. You have to pay the larger of the two (Chapter 4).

With this overview of the tax calculation, the changes made by the Clinton Tax Act can be reviewed.

HIGHER TAX RATES

The Clinton Tax Act includes several large, and important, tax rate increases.

> **TIP:**   Although the 39.6 percent tax rate has been stated to be the new top tax rate, some taxpayers, as a result of the numerous phaseouts and other complications, could face a marginal federal tax rate of more than 45 percent. When this is combined with state and local taxes, some taxpayers will face marginal tax costs that exceed 50 percent.

Individuals face the increased tax rates shown in Table 2.2.

To understand which rate in Table 2.2 applies to you, the following definitions will be helpful:

- *Married Taxpayer.* Married taxpayers who file a single tax return reporting both their incomes (jointly). Taxpayers who are legally separated cannot file a joint tax return.
- *Married Filing Separately.* Married taxpayers who report their income on two separate tax returns. Couples planning a divorce often use this filing status to avoid liability for acts of the soon-to-be ex-spouse. Many tax deductions are limited based on a percentage of gross income so filing a joint return can still be more expensive for some taxpayers than filing separate returns. Exercise caution in making this election because many exemptions and tax benefits are reduced by one-half for married taxpayers filing on separate tax returns.
- *Surviving Spouse.* Where your spouse has died and you have not remarried, you may file using this special status. You may file using this advantageous status for two tax years following the year of your spouse's death.

- *Head of Household.* This special tax rate gives a portion of the favorable tax treatment afforded married taxpayers to a taxpayer who, while unmarried, maintains a home that for more than one-half the year is the principal place of residence of a child, other relative, or other qualifying dependent person.

The 39.6 percent rate is the result of applying a 10 percent surtax on taxable income above a specified amount.

Although the increases in the top individual federal income tax rates were to be from the present 31 percent to 36 percent on incomes above $180,000, budget requirements resulted in these higher rates applying at lower income levels. The surcharge on wealthier taxpayers was supposed to be 10 percent for those with incomes of $250,000 and greater. President Clinton had promised that 98.8 percent of American families would have no increase in their income tax rates. Unfortunately, the higher rates will reach many more taxpayers than originally promised.

The income levels at which the new 36 percent tax bracket applies will be indexed for inflation for tax years beginning after 1994.

Tables 2.3 and 2.4 illustrate the new tax rates by indicating how you may be affected at various levels of taxable income. The comparisons show gross income and taxable income. Taxable income is gross income less the itemized deductions for a New York state and city resident (or the standard deduction, if greater). Only one exemption is used for single taxpayers. For married taxpayers, four exemptions were assumed.

Increased tax rates applicable to trusts and estates are discussed in Chapter 15.

TABLE 2.2   Tax Rates for Individuals

Taxpayer Affected	Taxable Income When New Rate Effective	New Tax Rate (%)
Married filing jointly	$140,000	36.0
Surviving spouses	140,000	36.0
Head of household	127,500	36.0
Married filing separately	70,000	36.0
Single individuals	115,000	36.0
All taxpayers (except married filing separately)	250,000	39.6
Married filing separately	125,000	39.6

TABLE 2.3   Comparison of Tax Rates for a Single Taxpayer*

Gross Income	Taxable Income	Tax before Act	Tax after Act
$ 50,000	$ 42,826	$ 9,118	$ 9,118
75,000	64,755	15,602	15,602
100,000	86,671	22,391	22,391
150,000	132,191	36,501	37,361
200,000	178,463	50,846	54,019
250,000	224,407	65,088	70,589
350,000	315,072	93,194	105,541
500,000	451,069	135,353	159,395
750,000	677,732	205,619	249,154
1,000,000	944,394	275,884	338,912

*Calculations and analysis prepared by Kramer, Regen, Benz & Zitolo, CPAs, PC, New York, NY.

WHAT THE NEW RATES MEAN TO INVESTORS

The increased tax rates have a number of far-reaching consequences for investors. Wealthy Americans, particularly those affected by the higher 39.6 percent tax rate, will find that many of the tax-planning concepts prevalent prior to the limitations imposed by the Tax Reform Act of 1986 will again become important considerations. These include taking advantage of lower tax on capital gains, different tax brackets of family members, tax credits, and other tax-oriented planning.

Wealthy investors will again benefit from aggressively seeking out new tax shelter investments and strategies. However, the presence of the passive loss limitation rules enacted in 1986 will result in different

TABLE 2.4   Comparison of Tax Rates for Married Taxpayers Filing Joint Return*

Gross Income	Taxable Income	Tax before Act	Tax after Act
$ 50,000	$ 34,400	$ 5,164	$ 5,164
75,000	58,913	11,702	11,702
100,000	80,844	17,834	17,834
150,000	125,221	31,347	31,347
200,000	173,374	46,274	47,944
250,000	222,466	61,493	65,617
350,000	315,951	90,473	101,646
500,000	451,949	132,633	155,501
750,000	678,611	202,898	245,259
1,000,000	905,274	273,163	335,018

*Calculations and analysis prepared by Kramer, Regen, Benz & Zitolo, CPAs, PC, New York, NY.

types of tax-favored investments than the real estate syndications and other tax-favored investments of the pre-1986 era. The fact that the Clinton Tax Act loosened the passive loss rules for active real estate professionals will not bring back the pre-1986 tax shelters since these benefits will not be available to the armchair investor (see Chapter 12).

Investments geared to producing capital gains taxed at a maximum 28 percent rate should receive more attention. The rules affecting capital gains are discussed in detail in Chapter 3.

Investments in tax-free municipal bonds will be more favored. Tax-free municipal bonds have been and will remain a mainstay investment option for taxpayers in higher tax brackets. The new higher marginal tax rates will make the returns of tax-free bonds, relatively more favorable than they had been prior to the Clinton Tax Act.

> **TIP:** Most wealthy taxpayers already favored tax-free municipal bonds in their portfolio before the Clinton Tax Act. The basic effect of the act is to increase the relative advantage of municipal bonds to taxable bonds as a result of the increase in the top marginal tax rate.

> **TRAP:** Don't fall prey to the lazy strategy of simply buying tax-free bond funds. Diversification of your investment portfolio should provide better returns and will provide less risk even if the initial "gut" tax-planning reaction is to favor tax-free bonds. Also, if your portfolio is large enough, consider, at minimum, "laddering" your bonds so that you have bonds of varying maturities. This lessens the risk of being forced to sell in a bad interest rate environment and provides yet another level of diversification within the tax-exempt bond fund component of your portfolio.

Investment strategies and products are discussed in greater detail in Chapter 19.

In addition to tax-free investing, tax-deferred investing is more important as a result of higher tax rates. Tax deferral is a planning strategy to put off paying tax on certain income to a later tax year. The longer you put off the tax, the greater the benefit, since your investments will continue to compound tax free. Tax-deferred investing strategies include taking maximum advantage of retirement plans and other planning opportunities:

- Keogh plans and other retirement plans (subject to new limitations of the Clinton Tax Act) are more important for deferring taxes because of new higher rates.

- The 401(k) plans offer savings opportunities. If your employer sponsors a 401(k) plan, the new higher tax rates offer a greater incentive for you to make the maximum contribution.
- Individual Retirement Accounts (IRAs) defer taxes until you begin distributions of your retirement funds. The new higher income tax rates make the maximum use of IRA plans more important. Even non-deductible IRA contributions will make more sense for many investors.
- SEP-IRAs are simplified employee pension plans. An employer makes contributions to IRA accounts of his or her employees. The higher Clinton tax rates make the consideration of SEP-IRAs more important for small businesses. Employers can establish SEP-IRAs and contribute up to 15 percent of income up to a maximum of $30,000. A SEP is generally simpler and less burdensome administratively than many other pension programs. An employer can also set up a SEP following the end of the tax year.

TIP: Before setting up a SEP, keep in mind that the Clinton Tax Act has reduced to $150,000 the maximum compensation eligible for consideration in making plan contributions (Chapter 16). In many situations, a money purchase or other type of pension plan that permits you to contribute more than 15 percent of compensation may be preferable.

- Insurance investment products, where appropriate, can provide more advantages than they did prior to the Clinton Tax Act. Increases in cash surrender value inside a properly structured insurance product can avoid taxation under the new higher Clinton Tax Act rates so long as you maintain the insurance in force. Insurance products should be considered as investment options for your portfolio, not only to meet survivors needs and to pay estate taxes. The compounding on a tax-free basis inside a policy can provide many investors, even those of advanced age, an improved return when compared to alternative investments.
- The installment method of selling assets should be considered more frequently. Installment sales defer payments on a sale (such as where you sell your house and take back a purchase money mortgage from the buyer) over several tax years. The gain is generally reported as a proportionate amount of the cash proceeds received in each year. Spreading out the gain could push you down into a lower tax bracket, avoid the alternative minimum tax, and defer the tax.

TIP: If you're subject to the investment interest limitation, you may benefit from negotiating a higher interest rate on the sale instead of negotiating a higher purchase price. This is because the gain on the sale is no longer included in investment income, while the interest income could be offset by otherwise unusable investment interest deductions.

- Tax-deferred annuities offer an opportunity to defer taxes so your investments can grow faster.

TRAP: Don't jump blindly into annuities simply because they are one of the last remaining tax deferral investments available. Be sure to investigate the quality of the annuity, the fees, investment performance, and all the factors that you would analyze in rating any other type of investment. And if you do jump, diversify. Too many investors have put large portions of their portfolios into annuities that are from the same issuer, or that are invested in the same types of funds. Be certain your investment horizon is long enough to make the annuities viable investments. As a result of fees, too short a holding period can dramatically reduce your anticipated return. Ask the broker or agent the commission they earn on each type of annuity so you will know if they have an incentive to push a particular product which may not be the best choice for you.

Tax planning for gifts and transfers to children over age 14 and other lower bracket taxpayers will have a renewed importance. Gifts to children under age 14 will not generally be effective for income tax planning because of the Kiddie Tax (children pay tax at their parents' rate) (Chapter 5). This is a significant change from planning that you have done following the compression of federal income tax rates by the Tax Reform Act of 1986. Following 1986, the modest differences between the highest (28 percent) and the lowest (15 percent) tax rates minimized this type of planning. With the maximum tax rates now at 39.6 percent and the lowest tax rates at 15 percent, the Clinton Tax Act has created a 25 percent differential between the rates at which a high-income parent and a low-income child pay tax [39.6% − 15%]. This restores the incentive to transfer income-producing assets to family members in lower income tax brackets that prevailed before the Tax Reform Act of 1986 compressed the marginal tax rates.

Many wealthy taxpayers prefer the security and control of a trust when holding investments for their children rather than making outright gifts to the child or gifts under the Uniform Gifts to Minors Act (UGMA). This is because a trustee can be designated to manage the assets for the child's benefit, and the monies can be retained in the trust past the child's reaching age 18 (UGMA monies belong to the child at the age of majority, 18 in many states). Unfortunately, the Clinton Tax Act makes tax planning with trusts more expensive and difficult (see Chapter 5). These changes, however, do not decrease the importance of using trusts in your planning.

MARRIAGE PENALTY: MORE COSTLY TO TIE THE KNOT

An unfortunate consequence of the tax system is that when two single people marry, their tax burden, in many cases, increases. This increased tax burden of marriage, called the "marriage penalty" has become worse under the Clinton Tax Act. The marriage penalty exists on both the high and low ends of the tax spectrum. It can affect low-end taxpayers as a result of the effect on the earned income credit. Two unmarried taxpayers may each have qualified for the earned income tax credit. If they marry, they may no longer qualify for the credit as a result of combining their two incomes.

On the high end of the income scales, the penalty becomes substantial and can be many times greater than the marriage penalty under prior law. Two single people can avoid the high tax surcharge when they file separate tax returns. However, if they marry and file a joint tax return, a large portion of their combined income may be subject to the surcharge.

> **EXAMPLE:**   Two single people, after the Clinton Tax Act, each have taxable income of $200,000. Their marginal tax rate based on Table 2.2 is 36 percent. If they marry, their marginal tax bracket would jump to 39.6 percent on the $150,000 taxable income above $250,000 (($200,000 + $200,000) − $250,000).

The application of the new surcharge tax rate on all income above $250,000 for single or married taxpayers creates a substantial penalty for any high-income single taxpayers who marry.

> **TIP:**   Let Uncle Sam pay for your wedding! If you're in a high tax bracket and have planned a December wedding, postponing the date until January of the following year could save you more than $10,000!

> **TRAP:**   Don't assume that avoiding a formal marriage is the best answer from a tax perspective. The estate tax is extremely biased in favor of married couples where the estate is more than $600,000. Anyone can

leave a spouse an unlimited amount of assets without any estate tax cost. However, a non-married couple, or partners in an alternative arrangement, could only leave the surviving partner up to $600,000 in assets without incurring a substantial tax cost. Non-married couples should consider using an insurance trust to fund this tax cost (Chapter 5).

ENERGY TAX

The promised broad-base energy tax never made it into the new law. A BTU tax assessed on the heat content of energy was to provide revenues to lower the deficit and to promote energy independence of the country as well as environmental responsibility. Instead, a much simpler 4.3-cents-per-gallon gasoline tax was imposed. This presumably will be the biggest portion of the tax burden that the middle and lower classes will share. This tax became effective October 1, 1993.

The 2.5-cents-per-gallon tax on diesel fuels, special motor fuels, and gasoline, which was to expire on October 1, 1995, was extended for 4 years to October 1, 1999. The tax applicable to diesel fuel for use by railroads will only be 1.95 cents per gallon.

Exemptions from the new taxes are provided for home heating oil, fuels used in farming, and certain other exceptions.

A floor stocks tax of 4.3 cents per gallon will be assessed on supplies of gasoline and diesel fuel.

CONCLUSION

Higher tax rates may initially seem to be a simple change—expensive, but simple. Unfortunately, the increased tax rates, the spread in marginal tax rates from highest to lowest, the change in the relationship between corporate and individual tax rates (Chapter 14), and the spread in tax rates on ordinary income and capital gains (Chapter 3) create tremendous complexity. Tax planning is essential for almost any type of transaction. A simple change has opened a huge Pandora's box.

3 Capital Gains Tax Benefits Are Back

CAPITAL GAINS TAXED AT FAVORABLE RATE UNDER NEW RULES

The Clinton Tax Act has not directly made many changes to the capital gains tax rules. However, by increasing the marginal individual tax rate to 39.6 percent while holding the maximum tax on capital gains to 28 percent, it has created an incentive to structure investment and business transactions in a manner that will be characterized as capital gains instead of ordinary income. The advantages of capital gains are the result of capping the tax rate at 28 percent and not subjecting capital gains to the 10 percent surcharge applicable to high-income taxpayers.

> **TIP:** The actual tax rate on capital gains, however, can exceed 28 percent as a result of the complex interplay of different tax rules. For example, if your adjusted gross income exceeds a threshold amount, certain of your itemized deductions are reduced by 3 percent of the excess. You are also entitled to a personal exemption for yourself and each of your dependents. For 1993, this amount was $2,350 (it is increased annually to reflect inflation). However, when your income exceeds certain thresholds, your personal exemptions are reduced by 2 percent for each $2,500 (or fractional amount) by which your adjusted gross income exceeds the threshold amount. The threshold amounts are adjusted for inflation and vary depending on your filing status. These limitations, depending on your circumstances, can add 2 percent, or even more, to the effective tax rate you pay on capital gains income. In general, it will be assumed that capital gains will enjoy a net tax advantage of nearly 11.6 percent over ordinary income.

The 11.6 percent advantage of capital gains will undoubtedly influence the handling of investment and business transactions. This was the very tax-oriented planning that the Tax Reform Act of 1986 sought to minimize. To understand the planning opportunities for capital gains, background on the general tax rules affecting capital gains is necessary.

BASIC RULES FOR CAPITAL GAINS

What Are "Capital Gains and Losses"?

Capital gains and losses are the gains or losses realized on the sale (or certain other transfers or events that are treated like sales by the tax laws) of capital assets. An asset is simply anything of value that you own. Capital assets include stocks and bonds (for anyone except a stockbroker or dealer), your house, a piece of raw land you hold as an investment, and so forth.

The more technical definition that the tax laws provide for capital assets is as follows. A capital asset is any property held by a taxpayer except:

1. Inventory (stock in the taxpayer's trade), generally property held for sale to customers in the ordinary course of business. Examples include the goods a retail store holds for sale, such as clothing, or lots in a subdivision that a developer is holding for sale. For real estate, security brokerage firms, and other dealers, the key test is whether the developer held the property primarily for sale to customers in the ordinary course of his business. It is necessary to look at all the facts and circumstances surrounding the transaction, such as the taxpayer's intent, the amount of advertising done, other sales of similar property to customers, the portion of the income earned from such sales compared with the taxpayer's other sources of income, the time devoted to the project, and the period for which the asset was held (investments tend to be held longer than inventory).
2. Depreciable property and land used in the taxpayer's trade or business.

TIP: Gains on the sale of these assets can often qualify for treatment as capital gains. This will be explained in the following discussion. An example would be a warehouse building a contractor owns for storing his equipment.

3. A note or accounts receivable that arose in the ordinary course of business.
4. Copyright; literary, musical, or artistic composition; letter or memorandum if the taxpayer created it, or if the taxpayer's investment (tax basis) is determined by reference to the person who created it.

EXAMPLE: If your father painted a picture and gave it to you, the picture would not be a capital asset and you would not realize capital gains when you sell it. If you purchased a picture at auction and sold it several years later, you would realize capital gains assuming you were not an art dealer.

What are capital gains and losses? They are income realized or investment lost when selling capital assets. Generally, this gain or loss is calculated by subtracting your cost or investment in an asset (your tax basis) from what you received on selling the asset (the amount realized).

EXAMPLE: An investor buys a parcel of raw land on January 1, 1995, for $50,000 in cash—no loans, no mortgages, and no other fees. This is his tax basis in the land. On March 15, 1996, the investor sells his land to a buyer for $75,000 in cash. Again, there are no loans, mortgages, or fees. The investor realized $75,000 on the sale. His gain is $25,000 (the $75,000 realized minus his $50,000 tax basis). Is the gain a capital gain? If this is the only land he owned, and he had no intention of developing it, he would be considered an investor rather than a dealer so that the gain realized on its sale will be a capital gain.

In most real estate transactions, these two concepts of "tax basis" and "amount realized" are somewhat more complicated. The tax basis

TABLE 3.1 Tax Adjustments

Tax Basis

+	Purchase price
+	Cost of any capital improvements (lasting improvements, such as a new roof or an addition)
+	Ancillary costs to acquire the property (such as legal fees, title insurance, recording fees)
−	Any losses (such as from fire, theft, or condemnation)
−	Depreciation claimed on the property

Amount Realized

+	Cash received on the sale
+	Fair value of any other property received (e.g., the investor could have sold his land for $70,000 in cash and a U.S. government bond worth $5,000)
+	The amount of debt that the buyer assumes.

and the amount realized must be adjusted for a number of items. Table 3.1 highlights some of the more common adjustments your tax adviser will make for you.

CAPITAL GAINS AND LOSSES

Sales of capital assets qualify for favorable treatment. Gains recognized on the sale of these assets would qualify for a maximum capital gains tax rate of 28 percent, instead of the 39.6 percent maximum individual tax rate.

> **EXAMPLE:** An investor purchased an antique for $50,000 in 1994. He sold it for $75,000 in 1997. The tax results are as follows:
>
> | | |
> |---|---:|
> | Selling price (amount realized) | $75,000 |
> | Purchase price (tax basis) | − 50,000 |
> | Capital gain | $25,000 |
> | Tax rate | × 28% |
> | Tax | $ 7,000 |
>
> Without the benefit of this lower tax rate on capital gains, the investor might have had to pay $9,225 in tax ($25,000 gain times 39.6% tax rate), so the favorable treatment afforded capital gains by the Clinton Tax Act provided the investor an additional $2,225 in savings [$9,225 − 7,000]. This represents almost 9 percent of the appreciation realized ($2,225/$25,000).

The gains recognized on assets held for more than one year are called long-term capital gains. Gains recognized on the sale of capital assets not held for this minimum period are called short-term capital gains.

> **TRAP:** The return of meaningful capital gains tax advantages as a result of the Clinton Tax Act means that investors must now pay careful attention to the period for which they hold an asset in order to obtain the capital gains tax benefit desired.

Netting Short- and Long-Term Capital Gains

When a taxpayer has both long-term and short-term capital gains and losses, the following rules should generally be followed:

1. Separate all capital gains and losses into two groups—the long- and short-term gains and losses.
2. Net all the long-term transactions with each other (add them up). Net all the short-term transactions with each other.
3. Look up the appropriate procedure in Table 3.2.

The combination of net short-term gains or losses, and net long-term gains or losses is your net capital loss for the year.

If your taxable income is taxed at rates of 28 percent or less, then your net capital gains are taxed at the same rates as ordinary income. If any portion of your taxable income is taxed at rates greater than 28 percent then a special calculation is made to assure that your net long-term capital gains are not taxed at rates above 28 percent, even if your non-capital income is. This calculation is made on Schedule D of your Form 1040 tax return. If your net long-term capital gains or losses and your net short-term gains or losses are a net loss, this net capital loss may only be used to offset up to $3,000 of ordinary income in any tax year. Capital losses in excess of $3,000 are carried forward to the

TABLE 3.2   Procedures for Netting Capital Gains and Losses

S/T*	L/T**	Result
+	+	S/T taxed at ordinary rates; L/T may benefit from the 28 percent rate; S/T and L/T not mixed.
+	−	If the net is a S/T capital gain, it is taxed at ordinary rates. If the net is a L/T capital loss, it is used to reduce ordinary income up to $3,000 per year. This can provide a tax savings at the maximum 39.6 percent rate.
−	−	The total capital loss is applied to reduce ordinary income. The maximum net capital losses that can be applied to reduce ordinary income in any year for individuals is $3,000. Any unused losses are carried over for use in future years (a "carry forward").
−	+	S/T loss is first applied to reduce the L/T gain—a spoiler effect since the S/T loss would otherwise be deductible against ordinary income up to $3,000 per year but now acts to reduce the L/T gain available for the favorable 28 percent rate.

*S/T = Short term (held one year or less).
**L/T = Long term (held more than one year).
"−" = Loss.
"+" = Gain.

next tax year where they are subject to the same limitation. For net capital losses there is a distinction between long-term or short-term.

One final twist needs to be mentioned. The preceding discussion of the definition of capital assets excluded depreciable assets and land used in a trade or business. Thus, the building of a warehouse used by a man in his storage business would not qualify for favorable capital gains 28 percent maximum tax rate. A special rule may help the warehouse owner, as explained in the following section.

Certain Trade or Business Assets

If depreciable assets and land used in a trade or business are held for the period required for long-term capital gains (more than one year), they could qualify for the favorable treatment available to other capital assets, as shown in Table 3.2.

Net all the gains and losses realized on the sale of qualifying trade or business assets (known as "Code Section 1231 assets" because that section of the Internal Revenue Code contains the rules affecting them). If the net amount is a loss, then that loss can be used to offset ordinary income in full. The $3,000 limitation previously described will not apply. If the net amount is a gain, it gets thrown into the preceding analysis (treat it like any other capital gain and apply the rules described above. With this background, the changes made by the Clinton Tax Act can now be reviewed.

> **TIP:**   The media has focused on the preferential treatment afforded capital gains. The limitations on deducting capital losses still exist and should not be ignored in the planning process. Coordinate the sale of your capital assets with your tax adviser to minimize the harsh effects of this limitation. Perhaps you have been thinking about selling other assets that have appreciated considerably. If you sell all these gain and loss assets in the same tax year, the gains and losses can be used to offset each other. Not only can this approach help avoid the limitations of the $3,000 rule, but it will shelter the gain on the appreciated assets from tax. You won't always want to offset short term losses and long term gains. Timing is key— consult with your tax adviser before signing any deal.

CAPITAL GAINS EFFECT ON AN INVESTMENT AND BUSINESS TRANSACTIONS

The seemingly innocuous change of creating an 11.6 percent lower tax rate for capital gains has far-reaching implications for the entire tax-planning process. Capital gains benefits reintroduce an opportunity for tax savings in a broad range of investment, business, and other transactions.

Sublet or Assignment of a Lease

Where a tenant sublets the interest in a leased property, the income received will be taxed as ordinary rental income at rates up to 39.6 percent. However, where a tenant assigns interest in the lease to another person, the income realized will be capital gains taxed at a maximum 28 percent rate. In an assignment, the tenant relinquishes all interests in the property and does not retain any reversionary interest (the right to have the leased property back at the end of the period). Prior to the Clinton Tax Act, the difference in tax result between ordinary income and capital gains was not as significant, so planning for the distinction between a lease and an assignment was frequently ignored when transactions were negotiated. For proper implementation of this type of planning, it is necessary to understand additional details and tax rules.

For tax purposes, an assignment is treated as a sale of all the tenant's interests in the leased premises. As such, the payments that a tenant receives on assignment of a lease will be taxed as proceeds from the sale of the lease. Where the lease is characterized as a capital asset, the assignor/tenant will realize capital gains to the extent that the proceeds received as a result of the assignment exceed the tenant's investment (adjusted tax basis) in the leased premises. The tenant's basis should include any amount that the tenant paid to acquire the leasehold interest, any unamortized leasehold acquisition costs (brokerage commissions) and any remaining undepreciated basis in leasehold improvements (fixtures, carpeting, tiling, and so forth) transferred as part of the assignment.

Where a lease is assigned, the transaction is analogous to a sale and any expenses are treated accordingly. Thus, the costs of assigning a lease should be treated as a reduction in the amount realized on the sale, or an increase in the investment in the lease being assigned resulting in the same net effect to the assignor, a lower taxable gain from the transaction.

The prerequisite to understanding and planning for the income tax implications of an assignment or sublet is to distinguish between an assignment and sublet. This distinction, and the following tax analysis, will be easier with these definitions:

- *Landlord.* The original landlord who leased the premises to the original tenant pursuant to the original lease agreement (the "Lease"). The landlord is also referred to as the "lessor."
- *Tenant.* The original tenant who leased the premises from the Landlord pursuant to the Lease. When the original tenant subleases or assigns the premises to another tenant the original tenant is called the OverTenant. This arrangement is governed by a lease agreement called the UnderLease, or the "sublease." The OverTenant is also referred to as the "sublessor," since he or she is the lessor for the sublease transaction. An OverTenant who participates in a transaction characterized as an assignment is also called the "assignor."
- *UnderTenant.* The tenant who subleases the premises from the original tenant (the OverTenant) pursuant to a lease agreement called the UnderLease. The UnderTenant is also called the "sublessee." Where the transaction is characterized as an assignment, the UnderTenant is referred to as the "assignee."

Where the OverTenant enters into a sublease with the Under-Tenant, the OverTenant will retain some reversionary right to the leased premises. One approach is for the OverTenant to structure the contractual arrangements with the UnderTenant so that the Under-Lease ends at least one day prior to the termination of the OverLease. This assures the OverTenant of a reversionary interest in the leased premises. Where the OverTenant retains such a reversionary right, the relationship between the OverTenant and UnderTenant is one of a sublease. Where there is no reversionary right in the OverTenant, the OverTenant is deemed to have assigned his entire interest in the lease to the UnderTenant (more properly referred to as the assignee). Although there can be important legal implications to the use of an assignment as opposed to a sublease, the practical implications may not be as material because landlords often reserve the right to approve any assignment or sublease. As part of the approval process, the landlord can insist on legal steps from the UnderTenant to protect its rights, for example, by signing of an attornment agreement. The tax implications, however, can be significant.

For tax purposes, the mere fact that the assignor remains contingently liable for the performance of the lease obligations may not prevent characterization of the transaction as a valid assignment so long as the tenant has transferred all interests in the leasehold. Where the assignor retains certain interests or title in the lease as a security interest, this may not cause the attempted assignment to be treated as a sublease. For example, where a taxpayer assigned a leasehold interest in certain real property for a royalty based on the materials extracted from that property, the court found that the taxpayer had retained too great an interest in the property for the transaction to have the tax benefits of being characterized as an assignment. Care must be exercised by an OverTenant hoping to structure an assignment where that OverTenant remains liable on the OverLease. This is because as the scope of the OverTenant's liability and rights expands, the relationship begins to look more and more like a sublease. Where the OverTenant has any rights of re-entry, or rights to future extensions or renewals of the lease, classification as an assignment will become questionable.

The proper characterization of a transaction as either an assignment or a sublease can be problematic because business and economic considerations may conflict with the requirements of achieving the desired tax characterization of the transaction. For example, in many situations, the landlord, as a prerequisite to approving an assignment, will insist that the original tenant remain secondarily liable on the lease in the event that the assignee defaults. As previously noted, this alone may not taint the attempted assignment as a sublease. However, where a tenant is forced to remain secondarily (contingently) liable on a lease, that tenant may insist on the right to re-enter the premises when the liability is triggered. Without this right, the tenant could be agreeing to make payments on leased premises that he or she cannot occupy.

A lease should be characterized as a Code Section 1231 asset where it is used in the taxpayer's trade or business and meets the other requirements of Code Section 1231. Based on the netting of a taxpayer's Code Section 1231 transactions for the tax year, the gain from the assignment of a lease interest could be characterized as a capital gain.

An assignor of a leasehold interest may also be precluded from realizing capital gains treatment where a five-year look-back rule applies to the extent of net Code Section 1231 losses during the look-back period. This is a complex requirement that you should review with your tax adviser.

Where the assignor and the assignee are related, the assignor may not have realized capital gains treatment since the tax laws tend to be more stringent in such cases. For example, you and a corporation, more than 50 percent of the value of the outstanding stock of which is owned by or for you, are related for tax purposes. Where there is a sale or exchange of leasehold interests, between related persons, any gain recognized by the assignor is characterized as ordinary income.

Depreciation Recapture Rules Still Applicable to Sales of Business Assets

Where you sell depreciable real estate used for rental or depreciable business equipment used in your business, the gain realized will be capital gains to the extent not attributable to accelerated depreciation deductions. Therefore, in making depreciation elections, you will again have to consider potential capital gains consequences. Since the Tax Reform Act of 1986, this had not been an issue.

Investor versus Dealer Status

For investors and businesspersons who sell property as dealers, such as a real estate developer who subdivides land and sells lots, the Clinton Tax Act has increased the importance of the distinction between an investor versus a dealer. If you are a dealer, any gain you realized would be taxed as ordinary income at rates up to 39.6 percent. Dealer status could occur for example, where you subdivided real estate and sold and/or developed lots on a regular basis (real estate is not the only example of dealer versus investor status). If, however, you maintained investor status, the gain you recognized on the sale of your investment could be treated as a capital gain and thus would be taxed at the maximum capital gains tax rate of 28 percent. Prior to the Clinton Tax Act, the spread between the 31 percent maximum tax rate on ordinary income and the 28 percent maximum capital gains tax rate was not sufficient to influence the structure of many transactions. The Clinton Tax Act has changed this scenario. With an 11.6 percent tax differential in favor of capital gains, taxpayers will again go to great lengths to structure their activities and transactions in order to avoid dealer status. For dealers in securities, additional complications of dealer status will affect tax planning (see Chapter 19).

The determination whether you are a dealer or a mere investor is not simple. It depends on the facts in each particular situation. Some of the following comments can help you identify how a particular situation may be treated. If you are involved on a regular basis in the development, improvement, and advertisement of property for sale, your activities will probably be characterized as those of a dealer. Where the activities concerning the property rise to the level of a trade or business and the property is held as more than a mere investment property for passive income, dealer status is more likely. Development activities will not always rise to the level of a trade or business.

The determination whether a taxpayer's real estate activities rise to the level of a trade or business is a factual one, subject to a number of tests including the nature and purpose of the acquisition of the property, the duration of ownership, the continuity of sales and sales-related activities over a period of time, the volume and frequency of sales, the extent of development or improvement of the property, the extent of soliciting customers and advertising, and the substantiality of sales compared with other sources of the taxpayer's income.

Even if you're a dealer for some properties, it doesn't mean that you will automatically be treated as a dealer for all properties. You may have, for example, an active real estate development firm and own a separate parcel of property as a mere passive investment. The best approach when you wear two hats is to isolate investment assets in separate entities from those that conduct active businesses. For example, your real estate development activities could be conducted in an S corporation while your investment property could be held in a separate partnership with different investors. Suppose you have been lax in maintaining a clear distinction between dealer and nondealer activities and properties. Can you change your status from dealer to mere investor? In limited situations, you may be able to. The task is not an easy one and will almost assuredly invite IRS scrutiny.

> **TIP:**   A taxpayer is characterized as a dealer and the partners wish to change its status to an investor. Generally, there should be a substantial and definite change in the intent of the general partners and the partnership to change its status. Courts will require an external and tangible reason evidencing the change. Courts have noted a change in zoning, change in profitability, and condemnation as evidence of a change in intent as to dealer status. The requirement is quite difficult to meet. One court refused to recognize condemnation as a factor.

Allocation of Sale Price on the Purchase or Sale of Your Business

An investor who sought to sell a business prior to the Clinton Tax Act may have been indifferent as to how the purchase price of the business was allocated among the various assets the buyer was purchasing. Often, the buyer's desires for the allocations, as long as they were within reason, were accepted. This will no longer be the case. The seller will benefit to the extent that the purchase price can be allocated to assets, such as land, that produce capital gains income, rather than to assets that generate ordinary income, such as inventory.

EXAMPLE: Assume a business owns two assets worth a total of $100,000, land and inventory. Further, assume the seller has a zero tax basis (investment or cost) in each. If the price were to be allocated $80,000 to inventory and $20,000 to land, the gain would be $80,000 ordinary income taxed at 39.6 percent (= $31,680) and $20,000 capital gains taxed at 28 percent (= $5,600), for a total tax of $37,280. If the seller were able to negotiate the opposite allocation, $80,000 to land and $20,000 to inventory, the tax results would be far more favorable to the seller. The tax cost on the land would be $22,400 ($80,000 × 28%) and on the inventory $7,920 ($20,000 × 39.6%) for a total cost of $30,320. Thus the mere negotiation of a better allocation of the purchase price would net the seller, after tax, an additional $6,960. State and local taxes would make this benefit even greater.

The issues of allocation of purchase price on the acquisition or sale of a business must also consider the new rules permitting the amortization of the cost of intangible assets over 15 years (see Chapter 17). The different tax rates of the buyer and seller, capital versus ordinary nature of different assets, longer depreciation periods for commercial real estate, amortization of intangibles will all serve to make the negotiation of the sale of any business more complex and adversarial.

Advantages of Employees' Requests for Incentive Stock Options Instead of Other Forms of Bonuses

If your employer is offering you stock options, the benefits have increased for you to encourage your employer to structure the stock options as Incentive Stock Options (ISOs) rather than as a nonqualified option. ISOs can generate capital gains income effectively converting ordinary compensation income into favorably taxed capital gains income, which the Clinton Tax Act has made more important. An overview of the requirements and benefits of ISOs will highlight this and help you understand the planning opportunity involved.

An option is a right or privilege you are given to purchase stock from a corporation by virtue of an offer of the corporation continuing for a stated period of time, at a stated price, where you are under no obligation to purchase. The option must be granted for any reason connected with your employment, such as to compensate you as an employee.

To qualify as an ISO, options must be granted pursuant to a plan that specifies the total number of shares that may be issued under the option plan and the employees or class of employees who are eligible to participate. The shareholders of the corporation must approve the plan within 12 months before or after the date the plan was adopted. The maximum number of shares that may be issued in the plan may be stated as a fixed number of shares of stock or as a percentage of the authorized and outstanding shares on the date the plan is adopted. There are limits on the duration of the plan and options to be granted. An ISO must be granted within 10 years from either the date the plan is adopted or the date it is approved by the shareholders, whichever is earlier. This limit does not restrict your ability to exercise an ISO more than 10 years after the plan adoption date, provided the ISO is exercised within 10 years from the date of grant (the date the ISO is awarded). Thus, no ISO may, by its terms, be exercisable more than 10 years after the date on which it is granted.

There are a number of requirements concerning the price at which an option may be exercised. An ISO must have an option price generally equal to the fair market value of the stock on the date the option is granted. The fair market value is a facts-and-circumstances test. A special requirement for certain shareholder/employees receiving ISOs is discussed later in this chapter. This is important for many closely held businesses using ISOs.

An ISO may not be granted to an employee who owns, at the time of the grant, stock possessing more than 10 percent of the total combined voting power of the stock of the employer corporation, or of its parent or subsidiary. However, an exception to this rule provides that an ISO may be granted to a 10 percent or greater shareholder if the option price equals 110 percent of the fair market value of the stock on the date the option is granted, and the option by its terms may not be exercisable more than 5 years after the date of the grant.

An ISO must, by its terms, be nontransferable other than by will or the laws of descent (where you die without a will). It must be exercisable during the employee's lifetime only by the employee.

There is no limitation on the amount of options that you can be granted to purchase stock in any year. However, options shall not be treated as ISOs to the extent that the aggregate fair market value (determined at the time the option is granted) of stock with respect to which options are exercisable for the first time by any individual during any calendar year (under all plans of the individual's employer corporation and its parent and subsidiary corporations) exceeds $100,000. This rule is applied by taking options that are exercisable for the first time in the calendar year into account in the order granted.

A number of holding period requirements have important tax significance with respect to ISOs. To qualify for the preferential ISO treatment, the shares acquired on the exercise of an option must not be disposed of within 2 years from the date of grant nor within 1 year from the transfer of the shares by the corporation to the employee. The term *disposition* is broadly defined to include a sale, exchange, gift, or transfer of legal title. There are limited exceptions to this rule.

If you receive an ISO, you must, in order to qualify for the preferential tax treatment afforded ISOs, be an employee of the corporation at all times during the period beginning on the date of option grant and ending on the date 3 months prior to the exercise of the ISO. There are exceptions for disability so that the ISO may be exercised within 12 months of leaving employment, leave of absence, and so forth.

If you satisfy the various holding periods and all other previously noted requirements, your taxable gain on the ultimate sale of the stock acquired on the exercise of ISOs will be taxed as capital gain. As a result of the Clinton Tax Act changes, there is now an 11.6 percent tax advantage of capital gains over ordinary income. This benefit now exists for the first time since the Tax Reform Act of 1986. Further, if you have excess capital losses, the capital gains income realized from the sale of stock obtained by the exercise of ISOs could be applied to offset those losses. Otherwise, the $3,000 per year limitation on deducting capital losses could prevent their use. If the holding periods are not satisfied, ordinary income taxes at rates of up to 39.6 percent will apply.

The tax deferral benefits are an additional advantage afforded by an ISO as compared with a nonqualified stock option plan (and other types of currently taxed compensation). Upon both the grant and the exercise of an ISO, there are generally no income tax consequences (other than possible alternative minimum tax (AMT) consequences). If you do not satisfy the employment or other requirements of the ISOs at the time the ISOs are exercised, you will generally realize ordinary income in the year of exercise equal to the difference between the fair market value of the stock and the option price. The exercise of an ISO may have AMT implications to the employee.

The AMT is effectively a second tax system under which many taxpayers will have to calculate their tax (see Chapter 4). AMT is computed with the addition of certain tax preference items and adjustments. ISOs can create an adjustment for the AMT calculations. ISOs are taxed for AMT purposes as if the ISOs were governed by the principles of compensation subject to a substantial risk of forfeiture, and not the general ISO rules previously discussed. The result is that you will generally report the excess fair market value of the option over the price paid for the option. This amount is treated as an AMT adjustment when your rights in the stock are freely transferable or not subject to a substantial risk of forfeiture.

Your investment (adjusted tax basis) of any stock acquired will be determined based on the same treatment. If you acquire stock pursuant to the exercise of an ISO and dispose of the stock in the same taxable year, the tax treatment under the regular tax and AMT will be identical.

From the corporation/employer perspective, no tax deduction is permitted on the grant or exercise of an ISO. The corporation/employer will generally only be entitled to a tax deduction with respect to an ISO plan where your actions cause the option to be nonqualified as an ISO. The employer then may deduct, in the year you realize income, an amount equal to the income recognized by the employee.

Although these rules may sound complicated, the Clinton Tax Act has again made ISOs a valuable tax planning tool for employers and employees.

Planning Sale of Corporate Stock to Avoid Ordinary Income

Where you sell stock in a corporation, the initial assumption is that the gain will all be taxed as capital gains because stock (except for a securities dealer, for example) is a capital asset. The answer, unfortunately, is not always so simple. If some of the more complex rules of the Internal Revenue Code apply, you may realize ordinary income instead of the expected capital gains. These complex rules, called collapsible corporation rules, can apply where the tax laws treat a corporation as having been formed for the purpose of avoiding tax on the gain that should be realized on property manufactured, constructed, or produced by the corporation. For example, if you form a corporation to build widgets, which comprise the primary corporate asset, the completed widgets are worth much more than what it cost your corporation to produce them. If the corporation sold the widgets, it would report ordinary income on the sales. Instead, you sell the stock, a capital asset, in hopes of realizing capital gains income. The collapsible corporation rules may apply to recharacterize your gain as ordinary income.

The collapsible corporation rules are based on several mechanical tests. The fair value of certain types of assets must constitute at least half of the total assets of the corporation. In addition, the fair value of these assets must be at least 120 percent of the cost (adjusted tax basis) of those assets.

As a result of the Clinton Tax Act, corporations should consider these complex rules when planning for transactions.

SPECIAL RULES LIMITING ABILITY TO REALIZE CAPITAL GAINS ON SALES OF PARTNERSHIP INTERESTS

The Clinton Tax Act has made several changes that will make it more difficult to realize capital gains on the sale of an interest in a partnership. For example, payments made to the extent of unrealized receivables can require that a portion of your gain be taxed as ordinary income instead of capital gains under conditions that would have generated capital gains under prior law (see Chapter 14).

NEW RULES TO PREVENT IMPROPER CONVERSION OF ORDINARY INCOME INTO CAPITAL GAINS

The reintroduction of significant tax savings for capital gains brings back all the conceptual issues that the Tax Reform Act of 1986 had tried to eliminate. There is now an incentive of an 11.6 percent tax savings to convert ordinary income into favorably taxed capital gains income, the modern-day tax alchemy. Restrictions to prevent the arbitrary or improper conversion are again required. The Clinton Tax Act has several of these complex anticonversion rules that affect transactions after April 30, 1993.

- Investors who purchase stripped preferred stock will be treated in a manner similar to that of investors who purchase stripped bonds. This change will apply the original issue discount rules to these transactions, thus assuring that some portion of the gain will be taxed as ordinary income. With a stripped preferred stock, the dividend component of a preferred stock is sold separately from the underlying stock rights.

- Gains on the sale of a bond discounted at market are taxed as ordinary income to the extent of the market discount that has accrued. Under prior law, there were exceptions for tax-exempt bonds and for certain bonds issued on or before July 18, 1984. These exceptions are eliminated effective April 30, 1993.
- Gains from complex financial transactions, such as hedges and straddles, after April 30, 1993, may be taxed at least in part as ordinary income.

These rules, however, are only in addition to the many existing rules, such as those concerning collapsible corporations, to prevent improper conversion of ordinary income into capital gains. Because these rules affect primarily investors in stocks, bonds, and other marketable securities, they are discussed in Chapter 19.

CONCLUSION

Capital gains are back. Your business and investment strategies must again consider the opportunities to structure transactions to achieve capital gains rather than ordinary income. The result will be more tax planning, more tax-oriented investment products, and a return to many of the approaches commonly used before the Tax Reform Act of 1986.

4 The Alternative Minimum Tax Tougher and More Complex Than Ever

The Clinton Tax Act has increased the rate and added a host of additional complications. However, to understand the changes, and how they will affect your investment strategies and tax planning, a basic overview of the alternative minimum tax (AMT) is first necessary.

WHAT IS THE AMT AND HOW DID THE CLINTON TAX ACT CHANGE IT?

The alternative minimum tax is effectively a second tax system to be considered as an essential component of every tax-planning strategy to the same extent that the "regular" tax is considered. The concept of the AMT is that everyone should at least pay some minimal amount of tax. The wealthy should not be permitted to shelter their income from tax excessively even by taking advantage of permitted tax deductions.

The mechanics of the minimum tax are such that you only pay minimum tax when your minimum tax liability exceeds your regular tax liability. Thus the AMT due is the excess of your tentative minimum tax over your regular tax. The calculations are reported on Form 6251 and filed with your regular federal tax return.

> **TIP:** The safest approach is always to prepare the calculations on Form 6251 if there is even a likelihood of being subject to the AMT. The AMT has become so complicated that relying on intuition as to whether it affects you could be a costly mistake. Also, the changes in the composition of your income and deductions from year to year could result in your being subject to the AMT in some years, but not in others.

Under prior law, the alternative minimum tax was calculated at only a 24 percent rate. The new rates are 26 percent on alternative minimum taxable income (AMTI) that is not more than $175,000, and

28 percent on income above this level. The AMT rate increases are effective January 1, 1993. Unfortunately, the installment method of making up extra tax cost that is provided for the regular tax (Chapter 7) is not made available for the AMT.

> **TIP:** It is usually assumed that taxpayers in the highest bracket are most subject to the risk of the AMT. It may turn out, however, that the increase in the AMT rates could make some taxpayers in the 31 or 36 percent brackets more likely to trigger AMT than the highest-bracket (39.6 percent) taxpayers. This could occur since the spread between the AMT rate and the regular tax rate can be less at these levels.

For corporations, the AMT rate remains at the current 20 percent level.

HOW THE AMT IS CALCULATED

To calculate your AMT, the following steps are necessary:

Step 1. Your tax preference items (TPIs) are added back to your regular taxable income. Certain other adjustments are added or subtracted from your regular taxable income. This increased taxable income figure is known as your alternative minimum taxable income, or AMTI.

Step 2. You then subtract an exemption amount from your AMTI to arrive at your income subject to the AMT. The new AMT exemption amounts are discussed later in this chapter.

Step 3. The difference is multiplied by the appropriate new AMT tax rate.

Step 4. A foreign tax credit may be allowed against the AMT.

Step 5. The excess of the calculated AMT, over your regular tax, is the amount of AMT due.

Table 4.1 provides a schematic for calculating the alternative minimum tax. The following discussion will elaborate on this summary.

PREFERENCE ITEMS AND ADJUSTMENTS THAT INCREASE YOUR AMT INCOME

Preference and adjustment items added back or adjusted for purposes of the AMT calculation are intended to limit the tax savings available

**TABLE 4.1   Alternative Minimum
Tax—Simplified Overview**

Adjusted gross income (AGI) from your Form 1040
+
Tax preference items (TPIs) and ± adjustments
(modified by the Clinton Tax Act)
−
Itemized deductions allowed for AMT
=
Alternative minimum taxable income (AMTI)
−
Exemption amount (increased by Clinton Tax Act)
=
Amount subject to the AMT
×
AMT tax rates (increased by the Clinton Tax Act)
=
Alternative minimum tax (AMT), which is paid to
the extent it exceeds your regular tax

from deductions that Congress deemed particularly favorable. There
are really two types. Some tax preference items (TPIs) are merely
added back. Others must be adjusted. The adjustments reflect the difference between a tax benefit calculated using the rules applicable for
the regular tax calculation and the tax benefit permitted where the
special AMT rules are used. The result is that you must have two com-
plete sets of tax records (books): one for the regular tax and the second for the AMT. Many of these items are highly technical. Rather
than attempting to provide a detailed explanation of each, the following list simply alerts you to the TPIs and adjustments involved so that
you can discuss them in greater depth with your tax adviser:

1. Itemized deductions must be recalculated for AMT purposes
using only the deductions that Congress deemed more essential (such
as medical and casualty deductions), or that Congress did not want to
limit for policy reasons (certain contributions). Qualified interest on
home mortgages is deductible for purposes of the AMT. Itemized deductions for the AMT include medical expenses (in excess of 10 percent of adjusted gross income), casualty losses (less a $100 floor
amount and then less 10 percent of adjusted gross income), qualified
housing interest (which may differ from the interest you can deduct
for your regular tax) and certain other interest expense.

Miscellaneous itemized deductions subject to a special rule limiting
their deduction to the amount over 2 percent of your adjusted gross

income (AGI) are added back for AMT purposes. There is no deduction for any other itemized deductions. You will therefore receive no benefit, for example, for payments of state and local taxes (similarly refunds of these taxes are not taxable for AMT purposes even if taxable for regular tax purposes).

> **TIP:** This rule can make it difficult to guess your effective tax rate on, for example, capital gains. If the sale of a highly appreciated stock will increase your AMTI above the AMT exemptions and trigger the tax, the effective tax cost on your capital gain may exceed the 28 percent marginal rate as a result of this one transaction.

Investment interest is also allowed to a certain extent for the AMT (see Chapter 7). The computation for determining the allowable investment interest expense excludes interest subject to the passive loss limitation rules and interest expense incurred in connection with an active trade or business. Interest expense is allowed to the extent it does not exceed net investment income. Net investment income is generally income from the investments reduced by the expenses directly connected with those investments. The investment expenses used in the AMT version of the investment interest limitation calculation must be adjusted for any tax preference items or other minimum tax adjustments (Chapter 7).

2. No deduction is permitted for your personal exemption or standard deduction (Chapter 7).

3. Incentive stock options (ISOs) can generate a TPI equal to the excess of the fair market value of the option over the amount the executive paid to receive the option (Chapter 3).

> **TIP:** Plan the timing of your ISOs. If you spread options over several tax years, you may be able to keep your regular tax in a lower bracket and avoid the AMT by keeping your income lower.

4. Depreciation deductions can create a TPI to the extent that depreciation deductions exceed the depreciation deductions allowable under the alternative depreciation system (ADS). Thus, for residential real estate, the TPI is the excess of the deduction claimed using a 31.5 year period over the deduction that would have been allowed had a 40-year period been used.

5. Tax-exempt interest on certain bonds classified as private activity bonds issued after August 7, 1986 is treated as a TPI.

TRAP: In your zeal to acquire tax-exempt bonds, be careful not to find yourself acquiring bonds that are taxable for AMT purposes if you are, or may become, subject to the AMT.

6. In many instances, the installment method of accounting for profit as payments are received is not allowable for purposes of the AMT by a dealer. Thus all gain on an asset sold by a dealer on the installment method must be recognized in the year of sale.

7. Appreciation in the value of capital gains property for which you claimed a charitable contribution deduction had been treated, in some instances, as a TPI for AMT purposes. The Clinton Tax Act changed this rule (see Chapter 6).

TIP: If the elimination of this TPI results in your making charitable gifts you had previously deferred, be certain to amend your will if you had provided for the contributions to be made there instead.

8. Passive losses incurred in rental real estate activities, investments made as a limited partner, and other investments in which the taxpayer does not materially participate are subject to similar disallowance rules as for the regular tax. The requirements for AMT purposes, however, are quite complex since the passive loss calculated for regular tax purposes must properly reflect all TPIs and other adjustments.

9. Depreciation deductions may have to be recalculated using less favorable AMT rules. The difference between the AMT and regular tax depreciation deduction must be adjusted against AMT income. The excess of accelerated depreciation deductions on nonrecovery real property over straight-line depreciation is adjusted. For most depreciable property placed in service after 1986, the excess of the depreciation deductions claimed under the Modified Accelerated Cost Recovery System (MACRS) over the depreciation deduction that would have been permitted where the alternative depreciation system (ADS) had been used instead is adjusted. MACRS is, in simple terms, the general depreciation rules provided for deducting the cost of equipment, fixtures, buildings, and so forth. The ADS is an alternative depreciation system with longer deduction periods. Many taxpayers have simplified their calculations by using the ADS for both regular and AMT purposes to avoid calculating this adjustment.

Because the rules for calculating the depreciation deduction for AMT and regular tax differ, the gain or loss on the sale must be calculated separately for both purposes when the depreciated property is sold.

10. Mining exploration and development costs that are deducted as incurred for regular tax purposes must be deducted (amortized) in equal amounts over a 10-year period for AMT purposes.

11. Where a taxpayer has a net operating loss deduction, the amount must be separately calculated for AMT purposes to reflect all the adjustments and TPIs in the determination of a special AMT net operating loss deduction.

12. The amount by which the excess of intangible drilling costs exceeds 65 percent of your net income from gas, oil, and geothermal properties. Excess intangible drilling costs are defined as the excess of your intangible drilling cost deduction over the deduction that you would have had if the costs had instead been deducted in equal amounts over a 10-year period.

13. The excess depletion deduction for an interest in a mineral deposit over the adjusted tax basis of your investment in the deposit must be added back.

Corporations have special additional adjustments which they must make:

14. Adjusted current earnings (ACE) is a special adjustment that regular C corporations (not S corporations) may have to make in determining their minimum tax liability. In deterring the AMT, 75 percent of the difference between the corporation's alternative minimum tax income (AMTI) and its ACE is a tax preference item (TPI) that must be added back to its income. The objective of this TPI is to force payment of some tax by corporations reporting significant profits to shareholders in their financial statements. The calculation of the corporate AMT, and the change made by the Clinton Tax Act, is illustrated in Chapter 17.

EXEMPTION AMOUNT

To calculate the AMT, you subtract the minimum tax exemption amount from your AMTI. The exemption amounts, as changed by the Clinton Tax Act, are shown in Table 4.2. The table illustrates yet another form of marriage penalty. Two single individuals would be

TABLE 4.2   Tax Exemption Amounts

Tax Filing Status	AMT Exemption Amount
Married Filing Jointly	$45,000
Surviving Spouses	45,000
Single Taxpayer	33,750
Married Filing Separately	22,500
Trusts and Estates	22,500

entitled to an exemption from the AMT of $67,500 ($33,750 × 2). If the same two people married, the maximum exemption for AMT would be $45,000, or a reduction of $22,500. At a 28 percent AMT rate, this could be worth $6,300.

> **TIP:**   The removal of the preference item for charitable contributions of certain appreciated property, the higher regular tax rates (since AMT is only payable where it exceeds your regular tax), and the higher exemption amounts all make the likelihood of your paying AMT less. However, this is offset by the increased AMT tax rates, which make the tax more likely to apply. Therefore, the AMT continues to be complex and difficult to predict without "what-if" projections by your accountant.

Once all the preceding steps have been completed, you will have the actual base on which to calculate a tentative AMT. Multiply the result by the applicable 26 or 28 percent AMT rate. This amount, to the extent it exceeds your regular tax liability, is the tax due. The minimum tax cannot generally be offset by nonrefundable tax credits, such as the credit for low-income housing, research and experimentation, or rehabilitation of older or historic buildings. Two final adjustments that may affect your minimum tax liability are foreign tax credits and net operating losses.

AMT CREDIT

An AMT tax credit may be available to offset some of the AMT tax. A portion of the AMT you pay in excess of your regular tax liability will generate a tax credit you can use in later years to offset your regular tax when it exceeds your AMT.

What if you are subject to the minimum tax in the year you sell an asset on the installment method? Then all the gain would be taxed in that year if you are a dealer. Assume that all the money due you is paid in the next year, so the entire gain is recognized for purposes of the regular tax in the second year (for the regular tax a dealer can defer gain or the installment method). If you pay regular tax in the second year, you could be taxed on the same amount you had just paid minimum tax on in the preceding year. The minimum tax credit is designed to mitigate this inherent unfairness. Thus, the AMT attributable to timing type preferences and adjustments enters into the minimum tax credit.

PLANNING FOR THE AMT

Planning for the AMT will be tougher than ever before. With the higher AMT rates, planning—to the extent possible—is also more important then ever. Consider the following suggestions:

- Comprehensive AMT planning is essential. This will generally require that both the regular and AMT be projected and reviewed for a period of several years. Planning for a single tax year at a time can result in errors. Given the many complex interrelationships that must be considered, one of the best planning approaches will be to conduct various computer "what it?" projections. Project your regular tax and AMT for at least a 3-year period under various scenarios. Then review the results with your advisers to choose an optimal strategy. Don't be led into making AMT decisions that are uneconomic or detrimental from a business standpoint unless the benefits are worthwhile. Timing will be key to all planning scenarios.

- Maximize the amount of depreciable property that can be treated as personal property rather than real property. Even though you may have a minimum tax adjustment, it will still compare very favorably with the adjustment you otherwise would have had.

- Time elective medical expenses to maximize the expenses in any one year to attempt to exceed the percentage of adjusted gross income hurdle.

- Maximize your use of home mortgage interest compared with nondeductible consumer interest.

- To the extent possible, structure and plan activities to avoid the passive activity taint that could subject the losses to strict limitations.

- Carefully screen municipal bond investments in order not to inadvertently buy private activity bonds whose income is subject to the minimum tax.
- Consider the merits of investing in insurance type products that are treated favorably under both tax systems, such as annuities.
- Take maximum advantage of pension and retirement plans.
- In some instances, it may prove beneficial to accelerate income into a year in which you are subject to the AMT. You can accelerate income to the point at which your regular tax would equal your AMT. Assume that in year 1 you're subject to the AMT, but in year 2 you won't be. It may be advantageous to accelerate certain income items into year 1 to be taxed at a maximum 26 percent (or 28 percent) percent AMT rate rather than to be taxed in year 2 at a maximum regular rate of 39.6 percent.
- Time the receipt of income to the year in which you will be in the lowest tax bracket considering both AMT and regular tax consequences. This could include timing a bonus; recognizing gain on an investment; paying a dividend from a close corporation; redeeming government savings bonds; recognizing additional investment income where you have investment interest expense in excess of income.
- To the extent possible, try to accelerate or defer deductions that can be used for regular tax purposes but not for the AMT to an earlier or later year when you can get the benefit from them. If you're subject to the minimum tax, you will not get any benefit from many itemized deductions such as state and local taxes.
- Consider special elections to capitalize (add to your investment or tax basis rather than deduct) certain carrying costs for land.
- Time above-the-line investment expenses for a nonminimum tax year when they will be more valuable.
- Certain preference items can be deducted over elective longer periods. This election can sometimes be used to save deductions for later years when the AMT won't limit them. For example, circulation expenses, intangible drilling expenses, and so forth can be written off over longer periods (what is called a normative election). For depreciation, the election to use the alternative depreciation system can provide a similar result. For commercial real estate, the longer post-Clinton Tax Act depreciation period of 39 years makes this election appropriate for a large number of taxpayers.

- Time your controllable tax preferences to avoid the minimum tax. Many of the preference items can be timed to tax years when they won't trigger the minimum tax. Time the exercise of incentive stock options (ISOs). Elect out of the installment sale if it will provide you with a loss that can be advantageously used. Defer an installment sale if its inclusion would trigger the minimum tax in a given year.
- Plan to use any minimum tax credits as soon as possible.

CONCLUSION

The AMT is tougher than ever. Awareness of the increased AMT rates must be incorporated into every tax-planning analysis. The complex record-keeping requirements make it imperative that you regularly review your record-keeping practices with your accountant.

5 Estate and Gift Taxes: It's Harder To Give Your Children What You've Managed To Keep

In trying to raise revenues from wealthier taxpayers, the Clinton Tax Act has made several important changes to the estate and gift tax laws. A brief overview of the transfer tax rules will help you understand how these laws can affect your financial planning. Three taxes can be assessed when you transfer property: (1) the estate tax, (2) the gift tax, and (3) the generation skipping transfer tax. The following sections discuss each of these taxes. Then the effects of the Clinton Tax Act changes are analyzed. Finally, planning possibilities are discussed.

ESTATE TAX

The estate tax is a charge assessed on property owned by you on your death. The actual tax however, is much broader and more complicated than this simple explanation indicates. There are a number of exclusions and deductions. Also, the definition of property you own at your death includes items that many people find surprising.

The estate tax is assessed on all property and property interests included in what is called your gross estate. Once these are identified, they must be valued. The sum of all properties you own, after reduction for certain expenses and other allowable adjustments, will be the base for calculating your estate's tax.

Generally, your gross estate comprises all property, whether real estate (land and buildings), personal property (furniture, jewelry, etc.), or intangible property (copyright, license, etc.), to the extent the estate tax rules require including such property. Any interests in property at the time of your death that are listed in your probate estate (the assets that must go through the court system for distribution to your heirs) are included. For example, a bonus you were entitled to at the time of your death is considered to be part of your gross estate. If you own insurance on the life of another person, such as under a buyout agreement from your business, the value of this policy belongs in your gross estate. Business and partnership interests are included. Even property you gave away during your life can be required to be counted in your gross estate. For example, if you transferred property but retained the right to the income, or even the right to designate who will obtain the income, these assets can be brought back into your gross estate. Where you transferred property to another person who could only obtain the right to use and enjoy that property after your death, the entire value of this property is included in your estate. If you transferred property but reserved the right to change who will have the right to enjoy that property, this will also be included in your estate. Insurance proceeds receivable by the executor of your estate, or by any other beneficiary if you retained incidents of ownership in the policy (such as the right to change the beneficiary) will also be taxed. The list goes on.

The value of the assets at the date of your death is generally the amount to be included in your gross estate. The value to be used is called the fair market value. This is the price at which the property would change hands between a willing buyer and a willing seller, neither being under any compulsion to buy or to sell, and both having reasonable knowledge of the relevant facts. Where a stock traded on a public exchange is included in your estate, the value is easily found in any major newspaper. For assets such as real estate and closely held business interests, valuation can be a substantial point of contention between your estate and the IRS. A special valuation rule is provided for farms, ranches, and certain property used in a closely held business.

The assets in your gross estate receive a tax basis equal to the fair market value at death permitting your heirs to avoid any income tax gain inherent in the assets you own should they later sell that asset.

EXAMPLE: You own a building with an adjusted tax basis (investment, less depreciation, plus improvements) of $20,000 and a fair market value on the date of your death of $100,000. Had you sold the building, you would have realized a taxable gain of $80,000 ($100,000 − $20,000) and paid tax of about $22,400. However, since you died holding the building, your heirs will inherit it with a new tax basis of $100,000. The tax basis is stepped up to the fair value at death. If your heirs sell the building the next day, they will have no taxable gain.

> **TRAP:** Many wealthy taxpayers have discussed and tried to plan for the possibility of the Congress reducing the $600,000 lifetime exemption (unified credit) against the estate and gift tax. Reducing the unified credit would be difficult and in many ways counterproductive since it would subject a large percentage of taxpayers to another complex tax that most Americans have not had to address. If the Clinton Tax Act does not meet revenue expectations, another approach to raise additional revenues might be to eliminate this step-up in basis of assets owned at death. If such a change were to be made, it would have complex and costly tax consequences for every taxpayer and his or her heirs.

Your estate is allowed deductions for funeral expenses, estate administrative expenses, claims against your estate, debts relating to any property included in your gross estate, charitable bequests, and qualifying bequests to your surviving spouse. Where expenses could qualify to be deducted on either your estate tax return, or for income tax purposes, you must select one place to claim the deduction since a double benefit is not permitted. Losses, such as a casualty loss, are also deductible. When these items are deducted from your gross estate, as determined in the preceding section, the result is your taxable estate.

The tax rate used for calculating the tax was 50 percent; however, the Clinton Tax Act increased the maximum rate to 55 percent. The increase is effective retroactively to January 1, 1993. This federal estate tax is then determined as follows: A tentative tax is calculated on the sum of your taxable estate, increased by your adjusted taxable gifts made after 1976. These are gifts made in most prior years on which you incurred a gift tax. The idea is that since a single tax structure is used for estate and gift tax purposes, all taxable transfers, whether made during your life or after your death, should be added and subjected to the same graduated tax rate schedule. However, a credit for gift tax on those amounts prevents double taxation of the gifts. This tentative tax amount is then reduced by the gift taxes that would be payable on your gifts made after 1976. A number of other credits may also be applied to reduce your estate tax, including a credit for prior transfers, for death taxes paid to your state, and so forth.

GIFT TAX

The gift tax is a tax on the right to give away property during your lifetime. The tax is calculated by multiplying the value of the property given away by the same tax rate schedule used for the estate tax. The actual calculation is somewhat more complicated because it is not an annual tax like the income tax. Rather, it is a lifetime tax. If you earn more income in a given tax year, it is added onto your other income for that year so that you get pushed into a higher tax bracket. The gift tax is similar but is calculated over your lifetime instead of annually. Therefore, to move your gifts up the graduated tax rates, all gifts made by you during your lifetime are added together and multiplied by the gift tax rates. You then subtract the amount of gift tax paid in prior years.

There is an annual exclusion of $10,000 per year per recipient. This means you can give away up to $10,000 to as many different people as you wish in any one year without incurring any gift tax. This is an annual exclusion so you can give away $10,000 every year to the same person (or other people). It is available for gifts of a *present interest,* an important technical term that creates complications where you wish to make a gift to a trust. If you're married, you and your spouse together can give away $20,000 per year to as many people as you wish. This important technique in estate planning is called gift splitting. This enables either you or your spouse to actually make the gift and have the other nondonor spouse join in the gift. Where the other requirements for the annual exclusion are met, gift splitting enables one of you to make a transfer of up to $20,000 per recipient (donee) with the gift being deemed to be made one-half by each spouse. Each spouse's $10,000 annual exclusion is applied to eliminate any taxable gift. To qualify for this valuable benefit, you must meet these requirements: You're married; both you and your spouse are citizens or residents of the United States; the spouse making the gift does not remarry during the remainder of the year; you both agree (consent) to this tax treatment for the particular gift, and for all gifts made by either of you while married during the calendar year. This is done by singing and filing the annual gift tax return, Form 709.

There is also a once-per-lifetime exclusion of $600,000, called the unified credit, which can be applied against either or both the gift tax and estate tax until it is used.

EXAMPLE: You make a gift of $50,000 in cash to your son during the year. The first $10,000 is not taxable since it qualifies for the annual gift tax exclusion. Assuming you have never made taxable gifts before, the remaining $40,000 will not trigger a current tax either. Instead, it will offset part of your $600,000 exclusion. If in the next year you make a gift of a business worth $750,000 to your daughter, there will be a tax due. The first $10,000 of the gift will be tax free as a result of the annual gift tax exclusion. The next $560,000 will not trigger a current tax since it will be offset by the remainder of your lifetime unified credit ($600,000 total − $40,000 used against the prior year's gift to your son). The balance of $180,000 will trigger a current gift tax cost since it cannot be offset by either the annual exclusion or the unified credit. In the third year, you give your son and daughter each $10,000 in cash. No tax is due since you again have a $10,000-per-person annual gift tax exclusion in that year to offset the gifts.

GENERATION SKIPPING TRANSFER TAX

The generation skipping transfer (GST) tax is exceptionally complicated and can be confiscatory in some situations. The purpose of the GST tax is to equalize intergenerational property transfer taxes. The result is actually imprecise because the GST tax and the gift or estate tax, which would have been incurred by the skip generation if you had not made a generation-skipping gift, are not necessarily equal.

The GST tax is charged on every generation-skipping transfer. The GST tax was to be 50 percent after 1992, but the Clinton Tax Act has increased the rate to 55 percent, retroactive to January 1, 1993. Therefore, the GST tax is calculated as a flat 55 percent tax rate on the taxable amount of a generation-skipping transfer.

EXAMPLE: You become a grandfather and wish to present a $1,000,000 gift to your grandchild (cash, an interest in a property, or another asset). The GST tax, assuming you have used up your $1 million lifetime exemption is at the maximum tax bracket, $550,000. Further, the GST tax paid by you is considered to be a gift to your grandchild as well. So the gift tax to be paid on the $1 million transfer is based on a total gift of $1,550,000 ($1 million actual gift + $550,000 GST tax, which is deemed to be a further gift). At the 55 percent maximum gift tax rate, you will owe a gift tax of $852,500. To make the $1 million gift, you will have had to pay taxes totaling $1,402,500 ($550,000 GST tax + $852,500 gift tax). Thus the total cost of making the $1 million gift is $2,402,500. If you have to earn the money to make this transfer, you will have to use after-tax dollars for the gift. This means you would have to earn, assuming a 44 percent combined federal and state tax rate, $4,290,179 ($2,402,500/(1 − 0.44)) in order to pay for the $2,402,500. Thus, to make a $1 million gift to your grandchild, you would need to earn 4.3 times that amount.

The GST tax can apply to a broad range of property transfers, including transfers of property in trust (e.g., a gift to a trust established for a grandchild), life estates (e.g., a child has the right to income from the property for life, and on the child's death a grandchild receives the property), remainder interests (e.g., a grandchild receives the property after the death of a child and the termination of the child's life estate), and so forth.

For the GST tax to apply, a taxable event—a generation-skipping transfer—must occur. The simplest example is a grandparent's gift of property to a grandchild. More technically, the GST tax applies where there is a transfer of property (or income from property) to a person who is considered to be a member of a generation at least two generations below the generation of the person making the gift (e.g., a grandchild or a trust for the benefit of the grandchild). A trust is also considered a skip person where no distributions can be made to nonskip persons. A nonskip person is a person who is less than two generations below the generation of the person making the gift (e.g., your child or sibling). Where your child has died and a grandchild survives, your child will not be considered a skip person so a transfer to your grandchild won't trigger the GST tax.

> **EXAMPLE:**   You're generation 1; your child is generation 2; your grandchild is generation 3. Therefore, if you make a gift to your grandchild, this would be a gift to a member of a generation at least two generations below your generation. A gift from you to your child would not be, so the GST tax would not apply.

Three events can trigger the GST tax:

1. *Taxable Distribution.* Where there is a distribution of property or money from a trust to a skip person, the GST tax may apply.

> **EXAMPLE:**   You establish a trust for the benefit of your child and grandchild. Any gift by the trustees to the grandchild would trigger the GST tax. The grandchild is a skip person since he or she is two generations below you, the donor.

The tax is based on the fair value of the property transferred, reduced by any expenses incurred in connection with determining the GST tax. If the GST tax is paid out of a trust, the amount of tax paid is treated as an additional distribution subject to the tax. The GST tax on a taxable distribution is charged against the property that was given, unless specific provisions are made for a different treatment. The transferee (your grandchild in the preceding examples), however, is liable to pay the GST tax.

2. *Taxable Termination.* In this event, the interests of a beneficiary of a trust (the person entitled to receive income from a trust, such as a child) terminate as a result of a death, lapse of time, or release of a power (right). This will be considered a taxable termination resulting in a GST tax unless: (1) Immediately after the termination a non-skip person has an interest in the property; or (2) no distribution can be made to a skip person. The GST Tax on a taxable termination is payable by the trustee of the trust. The amount of tax is calculated based on the value of all property to which the taxable termination occurred, reduced by expenses, debts, and taxes.

EXAMPLE: You establish a trust for the benefit of your child. On the child's death, the assets of the trust are held for the benefit of the grandchild. If at the death of the child, there is no beneficiary of the same generation as the child, the value of the trust will be considered to have been transferred in a transaction subject to the GST tax.

3. *Direct Skip.* This is a transfer of an interest in property, subject to the estate or gift tax, to a skip person. The GST tax for a direct skip is to be paid by the person making the transfer (probably you).

EXAMPLE: You transfer property worth $100,000 to an irrevocable (cannot be changed) trust for the benefit of your grandchild. Since the transfer is a gift for federal gift tax purposes, and a direct skip, it will trigger the GST tax.

Once it has been determined that a gift is subject to the GST, the GST tax must be calculated. For tax purposes, the property is generally valued at the time of the generation-skipping transfer. Where the transfer also triggers a gift tax, the amount of GST tax paid by the donor is treated as a further gift subject to the gift tax.

Once the tax has been calculated, a credit for taxes paid to your state may be available. This will occur where the GST tax transfer occurs by reason of a taxable distribution or a taxable termination at the time of your death. You're also entitled to a $1 million exemption. This exemption must be irrevocably allocated to any property transfers you make. This allocation is generally made on your gift tax return. However, the allocation method used cannot be changed.

To explain the use of the $1 million exemption, another bit of jargon must be introduced, the *inclusion ratio*. The GST tax exemption percentage (the inclusion ratio) is set when you make the gift and allocate your exemption. The inclusion ratio is: (1 − the applicable fraction). The applicable fraction, where you make the gift to a trust, is determined as follows:

$$\frac{\text{Amount of GST Exemption Allocated to Trust}}{\text{Value of Property Transferred to Trust}}$$

> **EXAMPLE:** You set up a $1 million trust fund for your children and great-grandchildren. You allocate your entire $1 million GST tax exemption to the trust. Its assets appreciate to $10 million before being distributed in a taxable distribution or termination. None of the transfers of trust property to your children and grandchildren is subject to the GST tax because the applicable fraction is 1, and the inclusion ratio, zero.

One approach to addressing this potential GST tax problem is to allocate some portion of the $1 million GST tax exemption to the trust. The decision as to how much of your exemption should be allocated is extremely complicated. If you allocate any portion of your GST tax exemption to a trust, that portion of the exemption is considered used, whether or not a GST tax is ever incurred. So, if you make the allocation, and no tax is incurred, you've wasted that portion of your exemption. If the trust in the preceding example declined to $600,000, rather than growing to $10 million, you would have wasted $400,000 of your exemption. What you really have to do is analyze all the relevant factors and estimate the likelihood of the trust incurring a GST tax. If taxation is probable, then you should wager some of your exemption on the trust. Where the chances of taxation appear small, you should preserve your GST tax exemption for other planning opportunities.

CHANGES AFFECTING ESTATE, GIFT, AND GENERATION SKIPPING TRANSFER TAXES

With the preceding overview of the three transfer taxes—estate, gift, and generation skipping transfer taxes—the Clinton Tax Act changes can be analyzed. The Clinton Tax Act made three relatively simple-sounding changes, each of which has a potentially substantial cost to the families of wealthy taxpayers:

1. The top tax rates for estate and gift tax purposes have been increased from the 50 percent level they were to have reached in 1993 to 55 percent. Since this change is retroactive to January 1, 1993, it can require estate tax returns filed prior to the passage of the act to amend those returns to pay an increased tax. (Bills have been introduced to repeal the retroactive tax increases and make them effective at a later date, such as August 10, 1993, when the Clinton Tax Act was passed.) Be sure to consult with the attorney handling the estate to see if an amended tax return will be necessary.

   Specifically, cumulative transfers (whether by gift while you are alive, or by will or revocable living trust following your death) will be taxed as shown in Table 5.1.

2. The phaseout of the graduated tax rates and the unified credit will occur on transfers from $10,000,000 to $21,040,000.

3. The generation skipping transfer tax rate is 55 percent.

The effect of these changes is simply to increase the tax cost for wealthier families. Although a stated purpose of the Clinton Tax Act is to foster growth of small businesses, many families will face increased difficulties in passing a family business and other assets on to their children or other heirs intact.

TABLE 5.1 Transfer Tax Rates

Taxable Transfers Over	Taxable Amount Not Over	Tax Amount in First Column	Rate of Tax on Excess over First Column (%)
0	$ 600,000	0*	0*
$ 600,000	750,000	$ 155,800	37
750,000	1,000,000	248,300	39
1,000,000	1,250,000	345,800	41
1,250,000	1,500,000	448,300	43
1,500,000	2,000,000	555,800	45
2,000,000	2,500,000	780,800	49
2,500,000	3,000,000	1,025,800	53
3,000,000	+	—	55

*To simplify the table, it is assumed that no tax is due on transfers of $600,000 or less.

ESTATE PLANNING FOLLOWING THE CLINTON TAX ACT

Tax planning following the Clinton Tax Act will include all the many strategies used prior to the act to avoid estate, gift, and generation skipping transfer taxes. Estate tax planning is now even more important than before. At the margin, the effects are substantial.

EXAMPLE: If you earn an additional $100.00, income tax at the marginal rate will take $39.60. Thus, $60.40 is left. If you wish to pass this to your children, the estate tax will take $33.20 (55% × 60.40). Your children may only receive $27.20. If state and local income, estate, and inheritance taxes are considered, the amount will be even less. Tax planning is essential.

The following sections summarize some of the techniques available. The best approach, however, is a comprehensive estate and financial plan targeted to address your particular assets, financial planning goals, and personal concerns.

The Irrevocable Life Insurance Trust

EXAMPLE: An investor's $4 million in assets are tied up in nonliquid start-up businesses. To pay the estate tax, he purchases $2 million in insurance (using a simple assumption of about a 50 percent tax rate). Unfortunately, the $2 million in insurance is included in the investor's estate and will itself generate an additional $1 million in estate tax. The net effect is that only $1 million in insurance is available, not the $2 million intended. The irrevocable life insurance trust is the best solution to this dilemma.

The use of a irrevocable life insurance trust can provide a number of important advantages. This is a trust that, once formed, you cannot change. The trust takes out insurance on your life (or the life of you and your spouse). When properly structured, this type of trust can remove the value of any insurance proceeds from your estate. The insurance trust can then use the tax-free proceeds to purchase assets from your estate so that your estate will have the funds necessary to pay any estate tax due. When these benefits are coupled with the tax free compounding of value inside the insurance policy, you have a true estate planning home run.

To effectively remove the proceeds of insurance policies you presently own (rather than new policies purchased by the trust), such policies and all incidence of ownership of those policies must be transferred to the trust more than three years prior to your death.

Annual per Donee Gift Tax Exclusion

Take maximum advantage of the annual gift tax exclusion. Over a number of years, an aggressive gift-giving program can remove substantial assets from your estate without triggering any gift or estate tax. Although the Kiddie Tax has eliminated the income tax benefits of making gifts to children under 14, the significant estate tax rates of up to 55 percent and the burdensome GST tax rates provide substantial estate-planning benefits from a gift program.

> **TIP:**   For a child over age 14 where the Kiddie Tax does not apply, the income tax benefits of a gift can be more substantial than under prior law as a result of the increase in the spread from the minimum 15 percent tax rate to the highest effective tax rate of perhaps 44+ percent (when the various phaseouts etc. are considered). The increased estate and GST tax rates make gifts more valuable from an estate planning perspective. Finally, there has been talk of Congress reducing this annual exclusion amount. If the Clinton Tax Act does not raise the revenues predicted, this restriction could be reconsidered in the future.

You can give up to $10,000 of assets ($20,000 if spouse joins in the gift) in any year to any recipient without triggering gift tax. Transfers that are exempt under this $10,000/$20,000 rule also avoid the GST tax so your heirs get a double tax benefit. Where a husband and wife elect to split their gift, the GST is deemed to have been made one-half by each. Over a number of years, this can result in a substantial transfer without incurring any GST tax.

Although the $10,000 annual exclusion is available for the GST tax, the requirements are different from those applicable for the gift tax. Thus, a transfer might qualify for the annual $10,000 gift tax exclusion, but not for the GST tax. The $10,000 annual exclusion is only available for GST tax purposes on a direct skip transfer. This is a gift directly to a grandchild (or later generation), or in some instances to a trust for a grandchild. It doesn't apply to a taxable termination or a taxable distribution.

Transfers for Educational and Medical Benefits

You can give away unlimited amounts of money to pay for a child or grandchild's education and medical benefits. Where a large estate is involved, and there are several children, grandchildren, and perhaps even great-grandchildren, this can present a tremendous planning opportunity. These gifts will avoid any gift, estate, or GST tax and will not use up any of your annual $10,000 gift tax exclusion or your once-in-a-lifetime $600,000 unified credit.

What Property Is Best to Give Away

One of the most critical decisions is what property to give away. Once your personal financial and business needs are adequately addressed, the following suggestions will be helpful:

- Give property that is most likely to appreciate in the future. This will remove the most assets from your estate for the least transfer tax cost.
- Insurance is an ideal asset to give away. Term insurance, for example, may have little if any current value; on your death, however, it will balloon to a substantial value. Removing it from your estate can be one of the most important aspects of your gift planning.
- Give away property that will help your estate qualify for the estate tax deferral and stock redemption provisions.

Million-Dollar GST Exemption

A once-in-a-lifetime exemption is allowed that would permit you to transfer up to $1 million of property to grandchildren without triggering a GST tax. This exemption can be allocated by you, or your executor. Plan for this exemption by setting up multiple trusts under your will and granting your executors the authority to make certain decisions necessary for GST planning. This provides the maximum amount of planning flexibility.

Charity Bailout of Closely Held Business Stock

If you own stock in a close corporation and wish to transfer control to a child without triggering gift tax or income tax on a redemption, a charity stock-bailout can offer significant tax benefits. You can make a gift of any portion of the stock to a charity. At some later date, the charity may, in its sole discretion, sell some of the stock that it then owns back to the corporation. This planning technique, if properly executed, can provide you with a charitable deduction for the stock donated. The charity can eventually receive a cash amount for the contribution. The charity, however, cannot be obligated to sell any portion of the stock back to the corporation. Where a prearranged plan for the resale of the stock exists, it can be difficult to draw the line as to whether or not the charity was so obligated.

Private Annuities

In a private annuity arrangement, you can sell property to your child or other heir in exchange for a promise from the child to pay you a fixed periodic amount for life (an annuity). The discounted present value of the annuity should be set close to the value of the property transferred to minimize any potential gift tax.

Personal Residence Trusts

A valuable planning opportunity for passing your personal residences to your children in trust is available. This technique can help you achieve substantial gift and estate tax savings. A qualified personal residence trust (QPRIT) can be created for a fixed term of years during which you retain the right to reside in the residence. The estate tax savings of using a personal residence trust will be achieved only if you survive the term of the trust.

> **EXAMPLES:** A taxpayer age 50 transfers his residence valued at $1 million to a 15-year personal residence trust. The trust is created as if the taxpayer made a gift of $296,000. Assuming the taxpayer survives the 15-year term of the trust, the differential of $704,000 ($1 million minus $296,000) plus any appreciation, will escape taxation. At the end of the fixed term of years, the residence will pass to the family members designated in the trust document. These family members can receive their remainder interests in the residence either outright or in further trust.
>
> Father sets up a QPRIT using his principal residence for a term of 10 years. His two teenage daughters are the beneficiaries. On the tenth anniversary of the QPRIT, title to the house passes outright to the two daughters who are now adults. If Father wishes to continue living in the house, he must rent it from his daughters since they are the owners. Father should sign a written lease agreement, pay rent, and act in the same manner as an unrelated tenant would.

The residence can be either your principal residence or one other residence, such as a vacation home. Other than the residence, only a limited amount of cash can be retained in the trust. This includes cash for the payment of home improvements to be paid within three months; for the payment of trust expenses within three months, such as mortgage payments; and when the trust is created, cash to purchase a residence where the trust has already entered into a contract to purchase a personal residence. You cannot hold term interests in more than two QPRITs at the same time.

The benefit of the $125,000 exclusion for taxpayers over age 55 from the income tax on the sale of a personal residence will also apply to the trust as if the residence was sold by the taxpayers directly.

Similar concepts can be used to pass securities or interests in closely held businesses to family members or other beneficiaries in a tax-advantageous manner.

The Transfer of Income-Producing Assets to Older Children or Other Potential Beneficiaries

The Clinton Tax Act has increased the progressive nature of the income tax rates, and the highest estate tax rates. The 24.6 percent spread between the lowest and highest income tax rates is a throwback to the tax structure that had existed prior to the Tax Reform Act of 1986, which compressed tax rates and minimized the benefits of planning to transfer income producing assets to taxpayers in lower tax brackets. The maximum estate tax rate is 55 percent. Each of these rates can be even higher where various phaseouts and other complications are considered. These changes increase significantly the tax advantages of transferring assets to children. Where an asset is given to the child over age 14, it may qualify to be taxed at the lowest tax rate and avoid the estate tax costs. To apply this type of planning, however, you must understand the Kiddie Tax.

A common family financial-planning technique, prior to the Tax Reform Act of 1986, had been to give assets to your children that earned interest, dividends, or similar passive income. Tax rates were progressive (lower percentages for lower income) so that a parent in a high tax bracket could benefit by transferring CDs, stock, and so forth to a child and having the income taxed at the child's low tax brackets. Congress became concerned that this was becoming abusive—a tax shelter for the wealthy. It responded with the Kiddie Tax.

Where a child who has not reached the age of 14 before year-end earns income, special tax rules, called the "Kiddie Tax," apply. The Kiddie Tax taxes the net unearned income of a child under 14 at the parents' tax rate. The unearned income of your child includes income earned on assets (stocks, bonds, etc.) in your child's name, income earned on certain bank accounts with the child's and your name, income on Uniform Gifts to Minors Act accounts, and income distributed from a trust. This will occur to the extent that the trust income is taxable to the child. The child's income is divided into two components: (1) earned income (e.g., wages from a paper route), and (2) unearned income. The unearned income is reduced by the portion of the standard deduction the child can claim, generally $600 (which is inflation adjusted). However, if the child has itemized deductions relating to unearned income (investment expenses) of more than $600, then they are applied to reduce the taxable unearned income. The result of this adjustment of unearned income is called net unearned income and is subject to the Kiddie Tax.

The child's earned income is taxed under the regular rules as follows: The unearned income of all your children is added to your income and your income tax is recalculated. The difference between the tax you would have to pay after the recalculation, and the tax due on your return, is the additional tax attributable to your children's unearned income. This additional tax is allocated among the children.

> **EXAMPLE:** Parents' tax return shows a tax due of $40,000. Parents have two children, Tom and Jane, who have unearned income of $3,000 and $2,000 respectively. Each child's income above $1,000 can be subject to the Kiddie Tax, or $2,000 for Tom and $1,000 for Jane. This additional $3,000 of income is added to Parents' tax return. Assume that the parents' tax would increase by $930 to $40,930 ($40,000 + $930). $620 of this additional tax is allocated to Tom and the balance to Jane ($2,000/($2,000 + $1,000) × 930).

The Kiddie Tax rules can be summarized as follows:

- Wages your child earns working are not subject to the Kiddie Tax. They are taxed at the child's own tax rate.
- The first $600 of your child's income is offset by the child's standard deduction. The child is not permitted a personal exemption if claimed as a dependent on the parent's tax return.
- The next $600 of income is taxed to the child at his or her tax rate of 15 percent.
- Unearned income above this first $1,200 is taxed at the top tax rate of the parents, which could be 39.6 percent or even higher.

Prior to the Clinton Tax Act, the highest rate for the Kiddie Tax applicable to the child's income was 31 percent.

The following examples illustrate how the Kiddie Tax works.

EXAMPLES: Father gives Child $10,000 of stock, which generates dividends of $975. The first $600 is offset by the Child's $600 personal exemption. The next $375 is taxed at Child's tax rate of 15 percent. Child's tax can be calculated on Form 1040A.

Mother also gives Child $10,000 of stock, which generates an additional $952 in dividends. Child's income now totals $1,927 ($975 + $952). Child must file Form 8615, "Computation of Tax for Children Under Age 14 Who Have Investment Income of More Than $1,200." The first $600 is not taxed as a result of Child's standard deduction. The next $600 is taxed at Child's tax rate, presumably 15 percent. The remaining income of $772 is taxed at the parents' tax rate.

Where any parent's estate planning involves gifts to their child under age 14, the careful selection of an appropriate investment strategy can minimize the burden of the Kiddie Tax. Any assets are appropriate until the $1,200 income level is reached. After that point, invest in assets that will appreciate rather than generate current income: growth stocks, raw land, Series EE United States bonds. After the child reaches age 14, when the Kiddie Tax will no longer apply, these assets can be traded for income-producing assets. Investments in tax-exempt bonds also avoid the Kiddie Tax. It may even be possible to employ the child in a family business since the child's standard deduction can be applied to offset earned income.

There is an election that can save some of the cost and paperwork of preparing a separate tax return for the child. A parent can, in certain circumstances, simply report the child's income on the parent's tax return. To qualify, the child's income must not be more than $5,000 and must consist only of interest and dividend income. Further, the child cannot have made estimated tax payments or be subject to the backup withholding rules. A special form must be filed by the parent, Form 8814, "Parent's Election to Report Child's Interest and Dividends." The parent must also pay the lesser of an additional $75 or 15 percent of the child's income in excess of $600, in tax to make this election. The election can, however, have some tax benefits in certain situations. For example, the parent may have incurred interest expense that is limited by the investment interest limitation (especially with the new restrictions on calculating investment income after the Clinton Tax Act). This rule limits a taxpayer's current deduction for interest incurred to buy or carry investments to income generated by investment type assets. If the child's interest and dividend income is added to the parent's, this additional deduction may be available to eliminate any tax on the income.

Although the Kiddie Tax can be a costly trap for children under age 14, the expensive estate tax rates of up to 55 percent can make gifts to a child under 14 still advantageous if your net worth is large enough. When these gifts are made, the most common approach is to plan the gifts to comply with the requirements of the annual $10,000 exclusion from the gift tax, in order to avoid any gift tax implications.

> **EXAMPLE:** Shifting income-producing assets to your children will shelter most of the first $1,200 of income from the income tax. Assuming about a 5 percent yield on investments, this can translate into $24,000 of gifts per child. To avoid any gift tax implications, this would have to be given over a 3-year period (or less if each spouse gave part each year, or if gift splitting was used) using the $10,000 per person (donor) gift tax exclusion. This could save an estate tax of up to $13,200 ($24,000 × 55%).

Charitable Remainder Trust

A simple example can illustrate the use of a charitable remainder trust. You would donate appreciated property (real property, stock, etc.) to a charity and receive a charitable contribution tax deduction in the year of the donation. The charity will only receive the full benefit of the property at some future time. For example, you can reserve an income interest in the charitable remainder trust for your life and the life of your spouse as the income beneficiaries. If this is done, the income generated from the donated property will be paid to you for your life and thereafter to your spouse for her life. After the deaths of both you and your spouse, the charity will obtain full use and benefit of the donated property. Thus the amount of the charitable contribution deduction is equal to the fair market value of the property at the time of the donation to the charitable remainder trust, less the present value of the income interest retained by you and your spouse.

In addition to the current income tax deduction for a charitable contribution, you will also receive a valuable estate tax benefit as well.

If you're one of the income beneficiaries of the charitable trust, the value of the trust will be included in your gross estate when you die. However, the interest will pass to the charity creating an offsetting estate tax charitable contribution deduction. Thus, the value of the property donated will be effectively removed from your estate. The savings in both federal estate tax, state inheritance tax, and probate and administrative costs can enable you to transfer substantial benefits to a deserving charity at a very favorable actual out-of-pocket cost.

The Clinton Tax Act makes this estate-planning technique even more valuable for several reasons. The maximum income tax and estate tax rates have been increased. This increases the value of your deductions for both income and estate tax purposes. Also, the repeal of the alternative minimum tax preference item for donations of appreciated property eliminates one of the thornier problems that this type of planning had created.

> **TIP:**   A problem with using a charitable remainder trust is that the assets will no longer be available for your children to inherit. One technique to address this problem is to use some of the income tax savings from the charitable contribution deduction to fund the purchase of life insurance in an irrevocable insurance trust. The insurance can assure your heirs of a similar inheritance on your death. Although the Clinton Tax Act has made the taxation of trusts more burdensome (see the next section), an insurance trust holding as its primary asset an insurance policy should not generate enough income to pay tax at anything but the lowest tax rate. This is because the growth of the value inside the insurance policy is not subject to an income tax. In the appropriate circumstances the combination of a charitable remainder trust and an irrevocable life insurance trust can provide tremendous tax and investment benefits.

CHANGES AFFECTING HOW TRUSTS AND ESTATES ARE TAXED FOR INCOME TAX PURPOSES

The Clinton Tax Act made several changes that affect the taxation of trusts and estates. First, the terms *estate* and *trust* will be explained, and then the new rules will be discussed.

When a taxpayer dies, assets and liabilities are transferred to his or her estate. The estate is a separate taxpayer from decedent, with its own tax identification number, its own tax year, and so forth. The taxpayer's personal representative (also called executor) is then responsible for paying bills (including taxes), investing the estate's assets, and then distributing the assets to the taxpayer's heirs, typically as provided for under the taxpayer's will (although a living trust, or other document may govern). During the period of time the personal administrator manages the assets, an income tax return must be filed by the estate.

Trusts (except for certain revocable living trusts) are generally separate tax-paying entities from the person who formed the trust (the grantor). The person responsible for managing and investing trust assets, paying expenses (including taxes), and distributing the assets as required in the trust agreement (the legal document used to form the trust) is called a trustee. The person who receives the benefits of the trust, such as distributions of trust income, is called the beneficiary.

Estates and trusts are subject to the same increased tax rates that affect wealthy individuals. Thus the new maximum tax rate is 39.6 percent (see Chapter 2). However, the tax rate brackets for trusts and estates are even more compressed than those for individuals so that the higher tax rates take effect at lower income levels. The tax rates applicable to trusts are so high at such low levels that they represent a serious threat to investors trying to save money for their children's education and other worthy purposes. The new rates, shown in Table 5.2, must be carefully considered when evaluating various financial and estate planning options.

Prior law rates reached a maximum 31 percent rate at $11,250 of taxable income. The Clinton Tax Act reaches the 31 percent rate at $3,500 of taxable income.

TIP: The special rule described in Chapter 7, permitting individuals to pay the 1993 tax increase in three annual installments in 1994, 1995 and 1996, is not available to trusts and estates. Consult with your tax adviser to determine what additional payments must be made to avoid penalties.

The new 36 percent maximum tax rate will be indexed for inflation for tax years beginning after 1994. The 39.6 percent rate is calculated

TABLE 5.2   Tax Rate for Trusts

Trust/Estate Taxable Income ($)	Tax Rate New (%)
-0- to $1,500	15
$1,500 to $3,500	28
$3,500 to $5,500	31
$5,500 to $7,500	36
$7,500+	39.6

by applying a 10 percent surtax on trusts and estates with taxable income over $7,500. Capital gains income will not be subject to this surtax. Thus, as for individuals, the maximum tax rate on capital gains will remain 28 percent.

> **TIP:** An estate should consider electing a fiscal year to provide more time and flexibility in making distributions. Planning can often be difficult in these situations because of the time required to admit a will to probate and to obtain information on assets, income, and expenses.

Income in respect of a decedent (IRD) can also complicate planning to avoid the higher tax rates applicable to estates. This includes such items as individual retirement accounts (where the beneficiary is anyone other than a spouse who rolls over the proceeds into another IRA), deferred compensation payable after death, and other payments. If an IRD item is payable to the estate (for example, you name your estate the beneficiary under your IRA account), your estate will pay tax at the new higher rates. If the IRD items are payable directly to the beneficiary, the beneficiary will pay tax on the IRD. If you include contributions in your will, consider giving IRD items to the charities since they will not have to pay tax on the income.

The Clinton Tax Act has also made several changes to the taxation of trusts and estates subject to the alternative minimum tax (AMT; see Chapter 4). The AMT rate brackets have been increased in the same manner as for individuals. The AMT exception amount has been increased to $22,500 for trusts and estates for tax years after 1993.

What do these changes mean to investors evaluating the use of trusts? Certainly, the income tax costs can be greater than before. But that does not mean that trusts should not be used. Trusts usually have nontax or estate tax purposes that are far more important than income tax motives. A review of several common trusts will demonstrate this:

- *Education Trust.* Another common trust is an education trust for a child or grandchild. Although the higher tax rates are more likely to affect this type of trust than an insurance trust, the alternatives are not great. If a trust is not used, the assets could be left in the parents' (or grandparents') names. This exposes the assets to the risks of the parents' creditors and higher estate taxes. It does not provide for management of the assets following the parents' disability or death (unless a trust is set up under the parents' will, which then has the same tax result). If the funds are placed in the child's name, or in a uniform gift (or transfers) to Minors Act account (a custodial account formed under the laws of your state), two serious drawbacks are involved. First, if the child is under age 14, the Kiddie Tax applies so that the child's income will be taxed at your tax rates in any event. Second, there is no insulation from the child's creditors. Finally, what child has the maturity to handle large sums of money properly at a young age? If the assets are in the child's name, there is no protection. If the assets are in a custodial account, the child will have unrestricted access to the funds at the age of majority, 18 in most states. The assets could also be subjected to claims by the child's spouse in the event of a divorce. If the amount is not significant and the potentially substantial risks previously noted do not concern you, the use of a uniform gift to minors act account for a child over 14 can have tax advantages over the use of a trust. However, despite higher tax rates, most parents will continue to use trusts as an essential financial- and estate-planning tool for protection of their children's future.

- *Insurance Trust.* An irrevocable (it cannot be changed after it is established) life insurance trust is used primarily to keep life insurance proceeds out of your (and perhaps your spouse's) taxable estate. With even higher estate tax rates, this is even more important than before the Clinton Tax Act. Also, most insurance trusts are not funded with significant investment assets other than those necessary to pay the current insurance premiums. Therefore, even with higher rates, the income tax increases may not be significant to this type of trust. The insurance trust can also protect insurance proceeds invested after your death from spendthrift children beneficiaries, claims of a beneficiaries ex-spouse and creditors.

- *Living Trust.* Revocable living trusts are often used to provide for the management of assets during disability and to minimize or avoid probate costs and delays. These trusts are not affected by the Clinton Tax Act since they are pure tax conduits. All income and deductions are reported on your tax return; nothing is taxed to the trust.

The Clinton Tax Act changes will affect the administration of estates. Prior to the increased Clinton tax rates, income was sometimes accumulated in an estate until it was eventually distributed to the beneficiaries. Now, personal representatives managing an estate will have a greater incentive to make distributions of income and even distributions of principal in certain instances, in order to reduce the estates taxable income. Certain principal distribution will result in passing some of the estate's taxable income to beneficiaries, who may be in lower tax brackets. For example, distribution of a fixed dollar bequest (a pecuniary formula amount) will accomplish this. Unfortunately, local law and customs, as well as possible delays in the probate process, may make it difficult for the personal representative to accomplish this.

Tax-Planning Considerations for Trusts after the Clinton Tax Act

Planning is still important to consider. Where a trust will be taxable at a higher rate than the beneficiary, consider distributions to the beneficiary. Where the beneficiaries are children subject to the Kiddie Tax, this will be less likely. In other situations there can be substantial tax advantage to making distributions.

Generally, when a trust is a separate tax entity, it will be taxed in a manner that is somewhat similar to the way in which an individual taxpayer, like yourself, is taxed. The starting point for beginning the calculations of a trust's tax liability is income calculated like that for an individual. Then several modifications (discussed later in this chapter) are made. One of the most important concepts of trust taxation is that the trust will generally only pay tax on income that it accumulates. Where the trust distributes its income to its beneficiaries, the trust will be treated as a conduit for tax purposes. The income and deductions will be taxed to the beneficiaries to the extent the income is passed out of the trust to them. A trust, however, is not a perfect conduit since several items are affected by special trust tax rules. For example, losses do not generally pass through the trust to the beneficiaries until the year in which the trust terminates. This is because capital losses are generally excluded from the calculation of a trust's distributable net income (DNI). Thus, where a trust has a capital loss (e.g., from selling stock) and no capital gain, the loss is not passed to the beneficiaries. Capital losses, however, can be offset against capital gains of the trust.

Where the income of the trust is reported in part by the trust, and in part by the beneficiary, there may be some benefit gained from taking advantage of the lower tax bracket of each. In the past, this had been an important consideration in establishing a trust. However, changes in the tax law have limited, but not eliminated, this benefit. For 1994, for example, the first $1,500 of trust taxable income is taxed at the lowest 15 percent income tax rates. Thus, if the beneficiary were in a

39.6 percent tax bracket, there could be a tax savings by the trust accumulating, and not distributing, $1,500 of income. Prior to the Clinton Tax Act, $3,750 of income could have been accumulated at this lower tax rate. The accumulation of income, however, can later trigger a complex tax on accumulated distributions. How and when the tax is paid on income accumulated by the trustee in one year and distributed in a later year is quite complicated. The answers are found in a confusing set of rules that apply when income accumulated by the trustee in one year is distributed to a beneficiary in a later year (in tax jargon, an "accumulation distribution"). The tax rules that apply to accumulation distributions are called "throwback" rules. The idea is to tax the trust's income as if it had been paid to the beneficiary in the year it was earned, rather than being held by the trust. This result is estimated by "throwing-back" the income to the beneficiary's tax return for the year the income was earned by the trust and could have been distributed. The tax laws contain several modifications and assumptions that distort this process to make the required calculations.

> **TIP:** For a trust to accumulate income to be taxed at a lower bracket, or alternatively for the trust to distribute income to the beneficiaries to be taxed at their lower tax brackets will depend on the trustee's authority under the trust agreement. When you are having a lawyer prepare a new trust, weigh the pros and cons of leaving the trustee substantial flexibility to distribute or accumulate funds. This can provide the opportunity to plan for maximum tax benefit under the Clinton Tax Act rules, and for future changes. A sprinkle power can give the trustee the right to distribute income or principal to any one or more of several named beneficiaries based on need or other criteria. Providing the trustee the flexibility of a sprinkle power may also enable the trustee to distribute income to the beneficiaries in the lowest tax brackets. With the progressive nature of the income tax rates increased by the Clinton Tax Act, this type of planning can be even more beneficial.

Another planning consideration for trusts where income cannot be distributed to a lower taxed beneficiary is to restructure the investment portfolio of the trust to favor tax-exempt securities, growth stocks, and other investments that do not produce ordinary income taxed currently at the highest tax rates.

> **TIP:** Trustees must be careful in pursuing these types of strategies. First, be certain that the trust agreement authorizes the trading necessary and permits the types of investment that will achieve the intended tax results. Consider the different tax and economic consequences to the beneficiaries.

The results may not be obvious. For example, many trust agreements provide how income, dividends, gain, loss, and so forth should be divided between income and principal. If the trust agreement is silent, you will have to consult local law. For many trusts, the income beneficiary may differ from the beneficiary who ultimately will receive the trust property (the remainder beneficiary). A substantial change in investment posture to reduce income could favor a remainder beneficiary at the expense of the current income beneficiary and expose the trustee to claims. Consider your liability as a trustee in light of both local state law and the provisions of the trust agreement. Could you be challenged legally for violating your fiduciary responsibility as trustee to invest trust assets prudently if you invest all the trust's assets in municipal bonds?

A trustee who wishes to distribute income to avoid the high trust income tax rates may be concerned about the beneficiary having access to cash. An alternative, if the trust agreement permits, is to consider distributing property. In some instances, a property distribution can carry out to the beneficiary some of the taxable income that would have otherwise been taxed at a high rate to the trust. Also, if the type of property is carefully selected, it may be possible to distribute property that is not as liquid as cash so as to discourage a beneficiary from making undesired expenditures.

EXAMPLE: A beneficiary receives a distribution of stock in a closely held business which can not be sold from a trust worth $35,400. The trust's tax basis in the stock was $23,000. Assuming that the trustee does not make a special election to recognize gain or loss on the distribution, the beneficiary's tax basis in the stock will also be $23,000. The distribution will be considered to carry out to the beneficiary, income (DNI) to the extent of the lesser of the adjusted basis in the property or the fair value of the property. In this case, $23,000 would be considered to be distributed.

CONCLUSION

The changes the Clinton Tax Act made to the entire estate-planning area are costly and render it far more difficult to pass on your hard-earned assets to your heirs or other beneficiaries. Careful planning is now more important than ever before. The costly changes to the income taxation of trusts and estates only further complicate this planning.

6 Charitable Giving
It's Harder To Be Nice!

The Clinton Tax Act made several changes that affect charitable giving: The rules for gifts of appreciated property have become more lenient and the rules for documenting and reporting contributions are now much stricter. As with so many of the new rules, the changes affect small components of larger tax rules. Thus, an overview of some of the general rules affecting charitable giving is necessary to understand the effects of the new changes.

GENERAL RULES FOR CHARITABLE DEDUCTIONS

Contributions are gifts to, or for the use of, a qualified charitable organization. Charitable contributions are deducted as an itemized deduction on your personal tax return, Form 1040, Schedule A. The Clinton Tax Act has increased the tax benefits of charitable giving. The income tax benefits of charitable giving before and after the Clinton Tax Act can be illustrated with a simplistic example:

> **EXAMPLE:** A taxpayer donates $1,000 to a qualified charity. The taxpayer's marginal federal income tax bracket before the Clinton Tax Act was 33 percent and marginal state tax bracket was 3.5 percent. The effective tax benefit is as follows: (state tax benefit $35) + (federal tax benefit $330 − ($35 times 33%)) = $353.45. Thus, the actual out-of-pocket cost of the donation is $646.55. ($1,000 − $353.45). Following the Clinton Tax Act, the taxpayer's marginal federal income tax bracket is 39.6 percent and marginal state tax bracket is still 3.5 percent. The effective tax benefit is as follows: (state tax benefit $35) + (federal tax benefit $396 − ($35 times 39.6%)) = $382.14. Thus, the actual out-of-pocket cost of the donation is $617.86 ($1,000 − $382.14).

The higher marginal tax bracket after the Clinton Tax Act increases the tax benefits of charitable giving. This is similar to the benefit of any deductions following the Clinton Tax Act. Higher marginal tax rates make any deduction more valuable. The search for tax deductions will intensify in direct conflict with all the stated goals of the Tax Reform Act of 1986.

The estate-planning benefits of charitable giving have similarly increased. Properly structured charitable gifts made under your will (or a living trust) can significantly reduce potential estate taxes. Taking this action can help address potential estate liquidity problems, thus increasing flexibility to retain relatively nonliquid business or real estate interests.

DETERMINING THE INCOME TAX DEDUCTION FOR YOUR CONTRIBUTION

Where a cash contribution is made to a qualified charitable organization, the amount of the cash at the time of the contribution, subject to certain percentage limitations, is deductible. Where a contribution of property is made to, or for the use of, a qualified charitable contribution, a deduction equal to the fair market value of the property (subject to the percentage limitations described in this section) is deductible. Donations of property that has declined in value are generally inadvisable since no loss deduction will be available for the difference between the fair market value of the property and the adjusted basis of the property. Instead, sell the property and donate the net proceeds. That approach enables you to deduct the loss and then claim a charitable deduction for the cash donated. Where the value of the donated property exceeds your adjusted tax basis in the property (cost plus improvements, less depreciation), additional limitations and adjustments may apply. The limitations and rules that must be applied depend on whether the property is real or personal property, tangible or intangible property.

Generally, if you donate appreciated capital gains property, you will be entitled to deduct the full fair market value of the donated property. Capital gains property is property that—had it been sold instead of being donated to the charity—would have generated capital gains. However, where you deduct the entire fair market value of the property (thus avoiding tax on the appreciation), the amount of the charitable deduction is limited to 30 percent of your adjusted gross income. To avoid the application of this 30 percent limitation, you can make a special election. If you make this election, the fair market value of the donated property will have to be reduced by the appreciation. When this is done, however, you may claim a deduction of up to 50 percent of your adjusted gross income.

If you donate property that would have generated ordinary income or short-term capital gains if it had been sold, the charitable contribution deduction is limited to the fair market value of the property reduced by the ordinary income or short-term capital gain portion.

EXAMPLE: A taxpayer who is a dealer in real estate purchased a lot five months earlier for $250,000 and has held it for sale in the ordinary course of her business. If she sold the lot, she, as a dealer, would realize ordinary income. She donates the lot, which is presently valued at $320,000, to a school to use for overflow parking. Her charitable contribution deduction is limited to her $250,000 adjusted tax basis.

ALTERNATIVE MINIMUM TAX CONSIDERATIONS

Under prior law, if you were subject to the alternative minimum tax (AMT) (see Chapter 4), the appreciation in the gift could have been included in the AMT base as a tax preference item. If you were subject to the AMT, the tax benefits, for example, of donating a painting that had appreciated significantly since you acquired it would have been reduced dramatically. Congress was pressured by charitable organizations not to maintain this rule. As a result, interim relief was enacted so that the appreciation component of tangible personal property was not subject to the AMT. The Clinton Tax Act changed these unfavorable restrictions on contributions. Now, property contributed after June 30, 1992, will not trigger a tax preference item for AMT purposes. For capital gains property, other than tangible personal property (such as a painting), these rules will be effective beginning in 1993.

TIP: If you donated property in 1992 that was subject to this tax preference item in calculating your alternative minimum tax, you may be entitled to a refund. File an amended tax return for 1992 on Form 1040-X. You can obtain copies of this form by calling 800-TAX-FORM.

TIP: The tax laws include several limitations on deducting contributions in excess of certain percentages of your income. If you made contributions in prior years where some portion of your contribution was subject to limitations on deductibility for regular tax purposes (such as the limitation that contributions cannot exceed 50 percent of your adjusted gross income), then these contributions may be deducted in later years. This deduction of a contribution in a later year is called a carryover or carryforward. Where a carryover contribution deduction is claimed, it may carry with it the alternative minimum tax taint of prior law.

Corporations also benefit from more favorable rules governing their charitable contribution deductions. No adjustment will be made to the earnings and profits of a charitable contribution deduction in calculating the corporation's adjusted current earnings (ACE). This relates to a special adjustment that corporations must make in calculating the income subject to the AMT (see Chapters 4 and 17).

HOW CHARITABLE CONTRIBUTIONS MUST BE REPORTED TO THE IRS

To claim a charitable contribution deduction, you have to comply with various requirements for documenting the donation and reporting it to the Internal Revenue Service (IRS). The Clinton Tax Act just made these requirements much more onerous for donors and charities. To understand the changes, the general reporting requirements must be reviewed.

The reporting requirements for property contributions under prior law could be divided into three categories:

1. For deductions not exceeding $500, the requirements are a reliable written record and a receipt from the charity setting forth the name of the organization, the date and location of the contribution, and a description of the property.
2. Where the deduction exceeds $500, but does not exceed $5,000, Form 8283, "Noncash Charitable Contributions" must be filed.
3. When the value of the property contributed is greater than $5,000, the IRS requires that you obtain a qualified appraisal of the property. Where donations of two or more similar properties are made in the same tax year, they must be combined to determine if they meet the $5,000 threshold. If the property is securities that are publicly traded, no appraisal is required.

Where the securities are not publicly traded, an appraisal is required only where the claimed market value of the contribution is greater than $10,000.

TIP: Make sure the appraiser is familiar with the special requirements of making an appraisal for tax purposes and provides you all the information you will need to claim the deduction on your tax return. The appraiser's compensation cannot be set as a percentage of the appraised value. The appraisal may not be provided by the charity organization or the person who sold the property to you.

The following information must be reported: A detailed description of the property; the approximate date the property was acquired (if you constructed the property, the date the property was substantially completed); how the property was acquired (gift, purchase, exchange, etc.); the fair market value of the property on the date of the donation; and a description of the method used to determine the fair market value of the property.

Penalties can be assessed where the value of donated property is overstated. This penalty will be applied at a flat 30 percent rate where the amount claimed on your tax return as a deduction is more than 150 percent of the correct amount. An exception prevents the assessment of this penalty where the tax underpayment is less than $1,000.

The charity that accepts your contribution also has reporting requirements. It must report to the IRS on Form 8282, "Donee Information Return," its dispositions of certain charitable property (donations) within 2 years of the date of the donation. For donations over $5,000, the charity must complete Section B, Part I of Form 8283, acknowledging the donation. You then file this form with your tax return.

STRICT REQUIREMENTS FOR DOCUMENTING CONTRIBUTIONS

Under prior law, you could merely show an IRS agent a canceled check as proof of a charitable contribution. If the organization was a valid charity, the deduction was allowed. Unfortunately, beginning in 1994, any contribution in excess of $250 or more will require additional support to qualify as a charitable contribution deduction. These requirements significantly exceed the reporting requirements under prior law. The charity now will have to verify and report your contribution to the IRS. Each charity will have to give a receipt to each donor for every contribution. The charity can avoid this reporting requirement only by electing to file with the IRS a report of the contributions it receives.

A charity receiving a contribution in 1994 or later, in excess of $75, where part of the payment is a contribution and part is for goods or services, must provide a written statement containing a good faith estimate of the deductible portion to the donor.

EXAMPLE: You attend a charity ball at a cost of $100 per ticket. The actual value of the dinner served is $54. The charity must give you written notice that only $46 is deductible.

TIP: While the IRS should not combine separate contributions made at different times to meet the $250 threshold, you're best off to request a receipt in any situation that could appear to be an attempt to avoid this new reporting requirement.

These reporting requirements are horrendous and will burden charities that are already under considerable financial stress as a result of the slow economy. The complexity and difficulty of implementing these new rules is significant. If your child attends a private school and you are required to pay a $500 fee for an annual concert the school cannot give you a receipt since the $500, however labeled, is probably a non-deductible tuition payment. What if your child's grandmother or aunt donate $500 to the school? It is not a tuition payment for them, its really a contribution. However, if grandma's "contribution" was really made in lieu of your $500 non-deductible tuition payment, is it really deductible? Can or should the school give grandma the required receipt? What are the charities obligations to investigate the source and motive behind a donation? Unfortunately, there are no detailed rules yet.

VALUATIONS REPORT BY IRS

Congress directed the IRS to prepare a report about the possible use of advance valuation procedures. In this system, the IRS would agree to the valuation of tangible personal property (such as artwork) before the gift is made.

CONCLUSION

The increase in tax rates and elimination of the costly alternative minimum tax preference item for donations can make the tax savings from being charitable more rewarding after the Clinton Tax Act. Charitable tax-planning techniques, such as a charitable remainder trust (see Chapter 5), offer significant planning opportunities. Unfortunately, for small donations, the record keeping has become extremely burdensome for both the donor and the charity.

7 Miscellaneous Changes Affecting Investors

The Clinton Tax Act includes changes in a wide spectrum of tax rules affecting many individual taxpayers. This chapter discusses several important changes that were not addressed in prior chapters. These diverse changes demonstrate the broad and complex scope of the Clinton Tax Act.

INVESTMENT INTEREST LIMITATION

The Clinton Tax Act further tightens a special limitation on deductible interest expense. This limitation, known as the investment interest limitation, limits the deductions you can claim for interest expense on debt used to buy and carry investment property to the amount of net investment income you realize in a particular tax year. Net investment income was defined as investment income less certain permitted expenses. Under prior law, investment income included dividends, interest on bonds, net gains from selling investment property (now eliminated), less expenses incurred to generate that income (to the extent these expenses exceed 2 percent of your adjusted gross income). The most common interest expense subject to this limitation is interest expense on a margin account used to buy stocks and bonds. By preventing the inclusion of gains on the sale of investment assets in the calculation, the tax laws seek to prevent you from claiming an ordinary deduction (maximum tax rate 39.6 percent) for interest used to carry an investment that itself is taxed at a favorable 28 percent capital gains rate.

> **TIP:** The investment interest rules are not limited to interest deductions for debts used only to carry stock and bond investments. They apply to other investment assets as well, such as raw land, artwork, and bullion.

Understanding the effect of the changes to the investment interest rules requires first learning how the limitation works.

Overview of the Investment Interest Limitation

For many years, the tax laws contained a limitation on the ability to deduct interest expenses incurred to own investments (e.g., interest paid on a mortgage taken to buy raw land). The basic calculation of the investment interest limitation is relatively simple and will demonstrate how the limitation works. It will also provide a good framework within which to explain the new change. The basic rule is that interest paid to carry investments is deductible up to the amount of net investment income:

$$\text{Investment Income} - \text{Investment Expenses}$$
$$\text{(excluding investment interest expense)}$$
$$= \text{Net Investment Income}$$

With this overview, each component of the calculation can be discussed.

Which Interest Expense Is Subject to the Limitation?

The first step in determining the amount of investment interest expense that can be deducted is to determine your investment interest expense for the year. This task is complicated by the many restrictions that the tax laws place on deducting various types of interest expense. Investment interest expense includes any interest paid or accrued on debt incurred or continued to purchase or hold property for investment. Examples include interest paid on a mortgage to buy raw land and interest expense allocable to portfolio income (interest on certificates of deposit, dividends, etc.). Interest expense excluded from the investment interest rules can include interest expense incurred on a passive activity subject to the limitations under the passive loss rules (see Chapter 12) instead of the investment interest limitation. This could include interest on a rental property subject to the passive loss limitation rules if you do not qualify for either the $25,000 exception for active involvement or for the exception provided under the Clinton Tax Act for an active real estate professional. Because of the applications of the various rules involved, interest expense on a particular investment could be subject to the passive loss limitations in one year and the investment interest limitations in another year.

This rule treating some interest as subject to the investment interest limitations and some to the passive loss limitations makes planning and bookkeeping extremely difficult. These fluctuations will depend on the time you participate in a particular activity, the income earned on investments, and other factors. Be cautious when projecting interest deductions since these complications could result in a costly oversight.

Many interest payments are not subject to the investment interest limitation. Interest expense incurred on a passive activity, as previously noted, will not be subject to the investment interest limitation. Interest expense subject to one of the many other Internal Revenue Code limitations will also be excluded. This is important since each type of interest must be planned for separately. This includes interest incurred during the construction of a building, which must generally be added to your investment in the building and depreciated over the life of the building. Interest expense incurred on a personal residence (qualified residential interest) is subject to its own special rules (Chapter 8). Personal interest expense, such as on automobile loans, is excluded from the investment interest limitations and is not deductible. Interest incurred to carry tax-exempt bonds is generally not deductible (under the theory that, if the interest earned isn't taxable, the interest paid to borrow money to buy the bonds shouldn't be deductible). Once you have segregated your investment interest expense from other types of interest expense, the limitation to which it can be subjected should be calculated.

Investment Income under the New Clinton Rules

The next step in calculating the limitation on investment interest expense is to determine your total investment income. Investment income includes interest, dividends, royalties, and—prior to the Clinton Tax Act—gains (in excess of losses) on sales of investment property. The latter change is discussed in this chapter. If any of this income is from an active trade or business (such as real estate mortgage lending), it is generally not included. Another complicated category of income is income from a trade or business. This could include dividends by an S corporation, involved in an active business, that are paid to a shareholder. These rules are beyond the scope of this book. Consult your accountant.

The Clinton Tax Act placed an additional restriction on these complex investment interest limitation rules. Beginning in 1993, net capital gain income will not be considered investment income and thus will not be included in calculating the amount of deductible interest.

> **TIP:** This new restriction will have the most impact on aggressive investors who have highly leveraged portfolios. Investors whose goals favor growth stocks over an income–producing portfolio will be more negatively affected because growth–oriented investors are attempting to earn capital gains that may not be offset by investment interest expense. Income–oriented investors earn dividends and interest that will still be able to offset interest expense incurred to carry investments.

An exception will permit you to include net capital gains in investment income (thereby increasing the amount of interest expense that is deductible) where you agree to tax your capital gains income at your highest ordinary income tax rates instead of the maximum 28 percent rate. The rationale for this new election is simple. As noted earlier, the new law seeks to prevent an unfair advantage that taxpayers could realize by deducting interest expense used to carry an investment at 39.6 percent ordinary income rates while receiving favorable 28 percent capital gains rates on the gain on the same investments. This special election equalizes the tax treatment for your deductions attributable to, and your gains generated by, the same investment. Where your income is taxed at less than the 28 percent rate, this election may prevent unintended tax costs from being incurred.

> **TIP:** If you are in the highest federal income tax brackets, you may be better off making the election if you have both excess investment interest expense and net capital gains. The answer, unfortunately, may not always be so simple. Instead of making this election, you could simply carry over investment interest expense that is not deducted to the next and future years where you may have an opportunity to deduct it against increased interest, dividend, and other investment income. The carryover rules are illustrated in an example later in this chapter.

> **EXAMPLE:** You are an investor in the maximum 39.6 percent tax bracket with $100,000 of capital gains and $100,000 of investment interest expense. Assume that you do not have any other investment income in 1996. However, you expect $100,000 of investment income from dividends and interest (not capital gains) in 1997. Ignore the complexity of due dates and estimated taxes to simplify the calculations.

Scenario 1. No election: If you do not make the election to tax capital gains at the maximum 39.6 percent tax rate in 1996 you will have no investment interest deduction since you do not have any investment income (capital gains is not included). Your capital gains will be taxed at 28 percent, for a tax cost of $28,000 in 1996. In 1997, the investment income will be offset by the investment expense carried forward from 1996 (where it couldn't be used because there was no investment income) to 1997.

Scenario 2. Election made: If the election is made, the investment interest expense would be deductible in 1996, and the capital gains would be taxed at a 39.6 percent rate. Thus, for 1996 if the election is made, the transaction is a wash. In 1997, however, the $100,000 of dividend and interest income is subject to the maximum 39.6 percent tax rate, resulting in a tax cost of $36,900. On a present value basis, assuming an 8 percent discount rate, this tax cost is equivalent to $34,166 in 1996.

In this example, it is better not to make the election than not to make it. However, the result will depend on your marginal tax bracket, interest rate assumptions, and so forth.

Investment Expense

In calculating net investment income, which will be the ceiling on the investment interest you can deduct, the next step is to reduce investment income by certain expenses. Investment expenses are all the expenses directly connected with the production of the investment income including legal, accounting, and financial planning fees. The tax laws only permit a deduction for many of these expenses (miscellaneous itemized deductions on your Form 1040, Schedule A) to the extent they exceed 2 percent of your income. Therefore, you need only reduce your investment income for purposes of the investment interest limitation calculation by the amount of expenses allowed (i.e., those in excess of the 2 percent floor). Interest expense is specifically excluded from investment expenses for this calculation.

Net Investment Income—The Limitation

Net investment income is your investment income less any investment expenses. This amount will, be the limit on the amount of investment interest expense you can deduct in any tax year. Investment interest expense that cannot be deducted in the current year due to this limitation is carried forward to the extent of any investment income in those years.

EXAMPLE: An investor pays $45,000 in investment interest in 1994. His net investment income, however, is only $26,000. He can only deduct $26,000 of his investment interest expense. The remainder, $19,000, is carried forward to the next year. In 1995, the investor pays $32,000 in investment interest expense but has no investment income. He can't deduct any investment interest expense in 1995. His carryover to 1996 is now $51,000 ($19,000 carryover from 1994 + $32,000 carryover from 1995). In 1996, he doesn't pay any investment interest expense. His investment income was a significant $124,000 due to the capital gains realized on the sale of appreciated bonds. Under the law prior to the Clinton Tax Act, he could have deducted the entire $51,000 of investment interest expense carryover amounts in 1996. Following the Clinton Tax Act, no deduction will be permitted in 1996 since capital gains are not included in investment income. On the other hand, had the $124,000 been due solely to investment income such as bond interest and not capital gain, it would have permitted the deduction of the full $51,000 of investment interest expense under the tax laws before or after the Clinton Tax Act.

TIPS: The same planning strategies applicable to investors subject to the investment interest limitation under prior law continue to apply. For example, it may be possible to plan initially (or restructure existing) loan transactions so that interest expense will properly be characterized as a type of deductible interest expense, instead of as investment interest. If you borrow funds personally and loan the funds to an S corporation in which you have an investment, the interest expense could be characterized as investment interest expense incurred to carry your investment in the stock of the S corporation. Instead, plan the transaction so that the interest expense qualifies as a trade or business interest expense that can be deducted. Consider having an S corporation, in which you are an investor, borrow funds. Under appropriate circumstances, this could convert interest expense into trade or business interest expense, not subject to this rule. You may be able to use your home equity line to finance certain investments and deduct the interest as qualified home mortgage interest without regard to the investment interest limitation (see Chapter 8).

For a few taxpayers, a surprising strategy may prove advantageous if the numbers work out. While most investors are scrambling for tax-exempt bonds to shelter income from the new higher tax rates, investing in taxable bonds generating current income could be advantageous if you're subject to the investment interest limitation. The investment income generated could then increase the deduction you could claim for investment interest expense. The decision will depend on your personal tax and investment situation, taxable versus tax-exempt bond yields, and other factors.

PERMANENT PHASEOUT OF ITEMIZED DEDUCTIONS

Itemized deductions must be reduced at the rate of three cents for every dollar of adjusted gross income above a threshold amount ($108,450 for 1993). This amount is estimated at $111,800 for 1994. The threshold amount is increased for inflation. The maximum that your expenses can be reduced is 80 percent. Certain expenses, such as medical expenses, casualty losses, and investment interest expenses are not subject to this limitation. This reduction is applied only after taking into account another required reduction of your miscellaneous itemized deductions by 2 percent of your adjusted gross income. The 3 percent limitation is broader in the sense that it applies to all itemized deductions whereas the 2 percent limitation only applies to the miscellaneous itemized miscellaneous category.

EXAMPLE: Taxpayers are married and file a joint tax return reporting adjusted gross income (AGI) of $245,350. Their itemized deductions (assume all are subject to the 3 percent limitation) total $32,000. Itemized deductions are reduced by the following formula: $133,550 ($245,350 AGI − $111,800 threshold amount estimated for 1994) × 3% = $4,006. Total itemized deductions cannot be reduced to less than 80 percent (80% × $32,000 = $25,600). Since this cap is not applicable, the full $4,006 reduction applies.

TIP: The 3 percent reduction of itemized deductions is worse than it sounds. This reduction is applied after all the other deductions that can limit your itemized deductions. These include the 10 percent of adjusted gross income reduction of casualty losses, the 7.5 percent of adjusted gross income reduction in medical expenses, and the 2 percent of adjusted gross income reduction of miscellaneous itemized deductions.

The reductions (which effectively are tax increases above the stated 39.6 percent maximum rate) were scheduled to end after 1995. The Clinton Tax Act made the reductions permanent. This has always been a favorite approach of Congress to make the budget numbers work: Find an existing tax provision that is scheduled to expire and either extend it or make it permanent. It is hard for taxpayers to complain about the extension since they were already subject to the unfavorable tax rule. Yet, the claim can then be made that new revenues have been raised.

The change will simply assure that the calculation of tax liability and the determination of your marginal tax rate (which can be important for investment decisions such as determining the taxable equivalent of municipal bond investments) will remain complicated. If you have a large number of exemptions (see the following section) and itemized deductions subject to limitation, your actual marginal tax rate could be closer to 45 percent than the 39.6 percent publicized rate.

PERMANENT PHASEOUT OF PERSONAL EXEMPTIONS

You are generally entitled to claim a personal exemption for yourself, your spouse, and certain dependents, such as your children. In 1993, the personal exemption amount is $2,350. This should increase to approximately $2,450 for 1994. Prior to the Clinton Tax Act, high-income taxpayers were required to phase out a portion of their personal exemptions reduced by 2 percent for each $2,500 of adjusted gross income above a threshold amount (which is increased for inflation). The threshold amount for 1993 is $162,700. For 1994, this amount may increase to $167,700. This limitation was to end after 1996. The Clinton Tax Act has made it permanent. The threshold amounts for triggering this reduction will be indexed for inflation.

> **EXAMPLE:**   A couple has adjusted gross income of $221,550 and four personal exemptions (two for them and one for each child). Their AGI exceeds the threshold amount by $53,850 ($221,550 − $167,700). Therefore, their personal exemptions are each reduced by 2 percent: for (2% × ($53,850/$2,500 = 22) = .44) × $2,450 exemption = $1,078. For the four exemptions, the total reduction is $4,312 ($1,078 × 4). Thus, only $1,372 is permitted for each exemption ($2,450 − $1,078).

ESTIMATED TAX FILING

Where withholding taxes (such as those your employer withholds from your paycheck) do not pay a sufficient portion of your taxes during the year, you may be required to file estimated taxes. The Clinton

Tax Act modified one of the more burdensome aspects of this requirement. First, a brief review of the rules for paying estimated taxes is necessary to understand the change.

The general requirements for the payment of estimated taxes by individuals are as follows. If your tax liability for the year is $500 or more, you could be subject to penalties if you fail to pay estimated taxes. If you pay to the IRS, in estimated taxes (paid quarterly with Form 1040-ES) and through withholding on your wages, 90 percent of the total of your tax liability for the current year, no penalty will be assessed. Estimated taxes are required to be paid in four installments, by April 15, June 15, and September 15 of the current tax year, and January 15 of the following tax year. Where estimated taxes are underpaid, a penalty is assessed based on the interest that would have been charged on the underpayment of tax for the time that the tax remained unpaid. The calculations are made on Form 2210. To avoid the penalty on underpayment of estimated tax, you must pay in 90 percent of the current year's tax liability.

Several years ago, there was an additional safe harbor; to avoid underpayment of estimated tax penalties, the taxpayer could simply pay in 100 percent of the prior year's tax. Congress prevented certain taxpayers from using this safe harbor where their modified adjusted gross income exceeded $75,000 and exceeded the adjusted gross income of the prior year by more than $40,000. The result was a horribly burdensome record-keeping and tax-accounting nightmare for any higher income taxpayer experiencing fluctuations in income from year to year. Many business owners and investors were subjected to these impossible requirements.

The Clinton Tax Act offers some relief. You will still be able to avoid any penalty for underpayment of estimated tax by paying in 90 percent of the current year's tax liability. Also, taxpayers will generally be able to pay in 100 percent of the prior year's tax liability to avoid underpayment of estimated tax penalties in the current year. However if your adjusted gross income is more than $150,000 in the prior tax year ($75,000 if you're married but file separate tax returns), you will be able to pay in 110 percent of the prior year's tax liability to avoid any underpayment of estimated tax penalty. While this may sound expensive, it can be cheaper and certainly far simpler than the requirements that had existed to base estimates on the current year's tax.

TIP: This rule does not apply to corporations. Special rules applying to certain estimated tax payments that S corporations or partnerships may be required to make are discussed in Chapter 14.

INSTALLMENT PAYMENT RULES AFFECTING WHEN YOU PAY YOUR TAXES

The explanation of the estimated tax rules creates a unique problem because of the retroactive nature of the Clinton Tax Act. The increased tax rates are effective retroactively to January 1, 1993. Many taxpayers, including investors and others who pay quarterly estimated taxes, may find themselves underpaid on their estimated taxes. Since penalties and interest charges can be assessed on underpayment of tax liability, you could, theoretically, face a big cost (in addition to the increase in tax). Congress was considerate enough to provide some relief. Their generosity is insulting at best since it was the unfair retroactive tax increase that caused the problem in the first place.

> **TIP:** This deferral provision does not extend to Social Security taxes or Alternative Minimum Taxes (AMT).

The Clinton Tax Act permits individual taxpayers to elect to pay the portion of the increase in 1993 taxes in three yearly installments: April 15, 1994, April 17, 1995 (April 15, 1995, is not a business day), and April 15, 1996. Where this is done, the general rules governing penalties on underpayment of estimated tax described earlier will be waived. The amount of tax you can defer is based on the increased 1993 tax you have to pay as a result of the higher tax brackets. You calculate the tax you would have owed under the old rates and the tax you actually owe. The difference is the amount you can defer. If you are late on any payment or the IRS is concerned about collecting this tax increase, the remaining payments can be required to be paid immediately.

If you are subject to the alternative minimum tax (AMT), you will not qualify for this benefit. When calculating the amount of your tax subject to this relief provision, you may have to calculate the AMT for 1993 even if you were not subject to the AMT.

> **TIP:** This election is made on your tax return for the tax year beginning in 1993. For most individuals, this is the return you will file by April 15, 1994. The exact manner of making this election is made by filing Form 8841, "Deferral of Additional 1993 Taxes." Be certain to consult with your accountant to properly make the election if appropriate. Where the amount of tax increase, however, is not that large, the cheaper route may be simply to pay the tax without the extra election since the

accounting fees and administrative burden of calculating this "break" and remembering to make the next two installments could outweigh the modest benefit of deferring the additional tax. Also, review your state tax filing requirements. Most state tax systems are based on modified versions of the federal tax system. The effects on state taxes will depend on your state tax system, what modifications if any your state will make in response to the Clinton Tax Act, as well as decisions made by you and your tax adviser.

PENALTY FOR SUBSTANTIAL UNDERSTATEMENT OF TAXES

If you substantially understate your tax liability, the IRS can assess a 20 percent penalty. A substantial understatement of taxes occurs where your understatement of the tax due on your tax return is more than the greater of 10 percent of the tax that should have been reported, or $5,000. Under prior law, if you could prove to the IRS that you acted in good faith, that the tax position you claimed was based on substantial authority, or that you adequately disclosed the facts in question by filing a Form 8275 with your return, you were sometimes able to avoid this penalty.

The Clinton Tax Act has modified the preceding rules so that, after 1993, you must have a reasonable basis to avoid the substantial understatement penalty. This means a standard which is substantially greater than "not patently improper." The intent of Congress is that this will be a rather high standard to meet. Unfortunately, the terminology is still vague, so court cases, IRS Rulings, and Regulations will all have to be considered in trying to understand the implications of this change.

INTEREST ON TAX REFUNDS

The Clinton Tax Act has given the IRS a 45-day grace period in making refund payments to taxpayers to minimize the cost to the government. Where the IRS makes a refund due you within 45 days of the due date of the tax return claiming the refund, or the date the tax return was filed, if later, no interest will be paid. The 45-day grace period will apply to amended tax returns and IRS initiated adjustments as well.

REFUNDS RESULTING FROM
RETROACTIVE CHANGES

Many of the changes made by the Clinton Tax Act were retroactive. If any of the following changes affect you, call your accountant and discuss whether you may be entitled to a refund (or unfortunately, have to pay more tax). You will generally have to file an amended personal income tax return, Form 1040-X:

- Self-employed taxpayers, such as consultants, who incurred health insurance costs, on themselves, their spouses, or their dependents after July 1, 1992, and filed their tax return without claiming the 25 percent deduction that was retroactively reinstated to July 1, 1992, may qualify for a refund. To qualify, you could not have been covered by a health plan of either your employer or your spouse. For you to have an employer would mean that, in addition to having your own consulting practice or other business, you would also work for an employer.

- Estate or gift tax returns, for large estates, that were filed for gifts or deaths after 1992, but before the new higher rates were passed, may owe more tax.

- Employees who received certain employer-provided educational assistance between June 30, 1992, and December 31, 1992, which was included in income, may qualify for a refund. The exclusion for up to $5,250 of such benefits was retroactively reinstated. Request that your employer issue you a corrected Form W-2 (Form W-2C). This should be attached to your Form 1040-X.

- Researchers who incurred certain costs of testing drugs for rare diseases or conditions between June 30 and December 31, 1992, may qualify for the reinstated Orphan Drug Credit.

- Investors who donated appreciated tangible personal property to charity between June 30 and December 31, 1992, and treated the appreciation component as a tax preference item may be entitled to a refund since this preference item for alternative minimum tax purposes was retroactively repealed to June 30, 1992.

- Investors in low-income housing may qualify for additional low-income housing credits. The credit was retroactively reinstated to June 30, 1992, along with several modifications.

- Taxpayers who increased qualified research expenses or basic research payments to qualified organizations between June 30, 1992, and December 31, 1992, may qualify for an increased research credit, since the credit was retroactively reinstated to June 30, 1992.

- Employers who paid wages to employees who are members of certain disadvantaged groups between June 30, 1992, and December 31, 1992, may qualify for an increased targeted jobs credit (40 percent of wages up to $6,000 and $3,000 for summer youth employees) as a result of the retroactive reinstatement of the credit.

- Investors in qualified small issue bonds after June 30, 1992, may qualify for tax benefits.

- Homeowners and renters whose principal residence or personal belongings were damaged as a result of a casualty in presidential-declared disaster area on or after September 1, 1991, may qualify for additional tax benefits where insurance proceeds had created a taxable gain.

- Disabled taxpayers who paid the luxury excise tax on a part or accessory installed on a passenger vehicle to enable him or her to operate the vehicle or to enter or exit the vehicle where the parts or accessories were not commonly available can obtain a refund of the tax. This change is retroactive to December 31, 1990.

- Consumers who paid the 10 percent luxury tax on airplanes costing over $250,000, boats costing over $100,000, or jewelry or furs costing over $10,000 on or after January 1, 1993, are entitled to a refund. Contact the merchant who made the sale.

CONCLUSION

This chapter has summarized a host of miscellaneous rules that could affect a broad cross section of taxpayers. The lesson is clear. The Clinton Tax Act affects investments and tax planning in many ways that may not have been noticed by investors when the various tax proposals were being considered by Congress. It is therefore imperative for investors to review the potential tax consequences of the Clinton Tax Act with their tax adviser to avoid any unknown traps.

PART THREE

RESIDENTIAL REAL ESTATE INVESTMENTS

8 How Residential Real Estate Investments Are Affected

TAX RATES AND CAPITAL GAINS AFFECTING YOUR INVESTMENT

The Clinton Tax Act has numerous effects on the tax consequences of home ownership, including the following:

- The higher marginal tax rates that affect individuals increase the tax benefit of the deductions associated with home ownership. The 39.6 percent marginal rate, when coupled with state and local taxes, can result in an effective marginal tax rate of more than 45 percent. The value of property tax deductions has thus increased. More tax shelter has been restored to home ownership.

   This additional benefit is certainly not sufficient to change patterns of home ownership, but it does reinforce the common planning point made after the Tax Reform Act of 1986—home ownership is one of the last good tax shelters available to most taxpayers. This will continue to be true.

   A similar benefit may be available for your home mortgage interest deductions as explained in the following section.

- Where a home is sold, the proceeds can be reinvested in a more expensive home to defer tax. Taxpayers over age 55 are entitled to exclude up to $125,000 in gain. Any gain not protected by these benefits will be subject to tax at the maximum 28 percent capital gains rate. This differential in the capital gains rate and the maximum tax on ordinary income is more significant than under prior law. This is another increased advantage of an investment in residential real estate after tax reform.

TAX ADVANTAGES OF LARGER MORTGAGES

The higher marginal tax rates increase the tax benefits from your home mortgage interest deductions.

> **EXAMPLE:**   A high-tax-bracket homeowner has deductions of $9,000 for home mortgage interest and taxes. Under prior law, the maximum federal tax benefit was $2,790 (31% × $9,000). Under the higher tax rates now in effect, the federal tax benefit is $3,564 ($39.6% × $9,000), an increase of $774.

At the new 39.6 percent marginal rate, the net-of-tax cost of a 7 percent mortgage has declined from 4.83 percent (7% × (1 − 0.31% marginal tax rate)) to 4.23 percent (7% × (1 − 39.6% marginal tax rate)). This modest 0.6 percent spread can make it more advantageous to favor debt financing and may increase the likelihood of your being able to invest the freed-up funds in a manner that should exceed the cost of your mortgage funds. The value of home mortgage interest tax deductions has thus increased putting more tax shelter back into home ownership.

> **TIP:**   The rules for home mortgage interest deductions are complex and often surprising. If you cannot deduct some portion of your mortgage interest, the increased tax benefit of a deduction at the new higher tax rates will not be realized. You must understand the basic rules for deducting a home mortgage and the traps that could affect you.

When you purchase a new home, you would generally assume that interest on your home mortgage will be deductible for tax purposes. This can be true, but there are important limitations. When buying a principal home or second (vacation) home, interest on up to $1 million of mortgage debt used to purchase or construct (or substantially improve) the house will be deductible. This interest is called acquisition indebtedness. Determining when a mortgage was incurred to purchase a home is not always so clear. What if you used bridge financing and four months later obtained a permanent mortgage on the property, only then paying off the bridge loan. Will the interest be deductible? If the bridge loan was not secured by the new home, the interest on it may not be deductible. The mortgage obtained later provides additional problems.

Interest on a mortgage will generally be deductible if the proceeds of the debt can be traced to the acquisition or construction of the home. Mortgage interest will also qualify if the payments to acquire the home were made within 90 days before or after you incur the debt. Dates are thus important to remember when the lender and you set the closing on your mortgage. You may, however, elect to treat the mortgage as incurred on the date a written loan application was made if the proceeds are disbursed within a reasonable time (30 days) after the application is approved.

For a mortgage to qualify, the lender must have a security interest in the home that is perfected under local law. As a result, informal loans from a relative or friend may also turn out not to be advantageous from a tax perspective. Make certain the loan is evidenced by a recorded mortgage on your home.

In addition to the acquisition indebtedness, you are allowed to take out an additional amount of debt up to $100,000 and deduct the interest on it. This debt must be secured by a lien on your residence. This debt is called home equity indebtedness. This home equity debt can be used for any purpose. To qualify, the residence must be used to secure the debt.

> **EXAMPLE:** A homeowner purchased a home for $100,000, taking out an $80,000 first mortgage. Two years later, when the house was worth $225,000, the homeowner built an additional bedroom at a cost of $15,000. He financed this with a home equity loan. The maximum amount of financing on which interest can be deducted as acquisition indebtedness is $95,000 ($80,000 first mortgage + $15,000 improvement). If the homeowner borrowed $120,000 on his home equity line, the interest on the additional $105,000 loan ($120,000 borrowed − $15,000 used for improvements) would have to be evaluated for deductibility as home equity indebtedness mortgage. This is only deductible on home equity financing up to the maximum $100,000 amount. The interest on the remaining $5,000 of the home equity loan will be treated as personal (consumer) interest, which is not deductible.

With the new higher tax rates, it may appear advantageous to refinance your home mortgage to increase the amount of deductible interest expense. Unfortunately, this will not generate the hoped-for increase in interest expense deduction. Interest on a home mortgage or home equity line will only be deductible if the loan is used to pay for acquiring, constructing, or substantially improving the residence (this is in addition to the interest on up to a $100,000 home equity line which is also deductible). If a home mortgage is refinanced, only an amount up to the remaining principal balance on the loan refinanced can qualify for tax deduction.

EXAMPLE: A homeowner purchased his home for $150,000. The home is now worth $320,000. His current mortgage balance is $120,000. He refinances this mortgage with a new mortgage for $155,000. Not all the interest paid on the $155,000 mortgage will qualify for a tax deduction. Only interest on $120,000 of the new mortgage will qualify for interest deductions, unless the additional $35,000 ($155,000 new loan − $120,000 original loan balance) is used to improve his home, or counts as part of his $100,000 home equity loan amount.

OTHER TAX CHANGES AFFECTING HOME OWNERSHIP

- The low-income housing credit has been reinstated and made permanent. The result may be that more housing will be available to lower income taxpayers (see Chapter 10).
- The increased earned-income tax credit should improve the ability of low-income taxpayers to pay for housing costs.
- Moving expense deductions have been modified. Some of the modifications will significantly reduce tax benefits of a business-related move; others will increase the tax benefits. Homeowners, real estate brokers, moving companies, relocation companies, corporate relocation departments, and others involved in the industry should all become familiar with the rules since they will significantly affect the costs of relocation. These rules are discussed in detail in the following section.
- The rules affecting casualty losses have been made more liberal. This should be of some modest benefit to those affected by major natural disasters (see Chapter 9).

MOVING EXPENSES RESTRICTED

Taxpayers have long deducted many of the costs associated with a move to a new residence. The value of these tax deductions has been an important benefit to employees and self-employed people forced to relocate. The requirements for the various deductions, and the categories of costs that can, or cannot, be deducted are complex. The Clinton Tax Act made several modifications to these rules. The result will be fewer deductions and some simplification. The bottom-line tax result will vary for different taxpayers depending on their circumstances. The tax benefits could increase, or decrease, compared with prior law. These changes will be explained in the context of the overall rules for deducting moving expenses.

The following deductions are permitted for moving expenses if you meet the requirements indicated:

Unlimited Deductibility of Direct Costs

Costs are deductible for moving household goods (furniture, clothing, dishes, and so forth) from your former home to your new home, including costs to pack, crate, insure, move, and store (up to 30 days) your household possessions. Other preparation costs, such as disconnecting appliances in preparation of the move, also can be deducted.

Traveling from your old home to your new home (including meals and hotels) for yourself and your family had been deductible in full under prior law. After 1993, only the costs of travel to the new location, including lodging but not meals, will remain deductible.

Indirect Cost Deductions Eliminated by New Law

Indirect costs (house-hunting, temporary living expenses, and expenses of selling, buying, and leasing a residence) were deductible under prior law up to $3,000 (the maximum for house-hunting and temporary living expenses was further limited to $1,500). After 1993, none of these expenses will be deductible. The types of expenses that had been deductible under prior law are as follows:

1. Premove house-hunting trips including traveling from your old home to the area of the new job (after being hired) to look for a new home had been deductible within limits (house-hunting trips and temporary living expenses could be deducted up to $1,500) under prior law.
2. Temporary living expenses including meals and lodging in the new job locale for a 30-day period after being hired and while living in temporary quarters were deductible under prior law subject to certain limits.
3. Certain expenses of selling your old home or terminating your old apartment lease, and buying a new home or acquiring a lease on a new apartment were deductible under prior law. This could have included legal fees, commissions, payments to your landlord to break a lease early, and so forth.

The following common moving expenses could not be deducted under prior law and still cannot be deducted:

1. Losses on terminating club memberships.
2. Mortgage penalties.
3. Forfeited tuition.
4. Costs to install a telephone.
5. Expenses to refit carpets and drapes, moving costs of a nurse or maid, and so forth.

Requirements for Deductions

The following requirements must be met to deduct the expenses incurred in moving to a different city because of a new job.

Distance Test.   Under prior law, the distance (measured by the most commonly traveled route, not as the crow flies) between the location of your new job and your old home had to be at least 35 miles more than the distance from the location of your old job and your old home. After 1993, the distance is increased to 50 miles. The idea is that you should be moving to get a better commute than you would have if you stayed in the same house and commuted to your new job.

In addition, if the distance between your new place of work and your new residence is greater than the distance between your old residence and your new place of work, the IRS will may disallow the deduction under the work connection test described later in this chapter.

Work Time Test.   During the 12-month period immediately after the move, you must work full time for at least 39 weeks. The 39 weeks of work do not have to be consecutive. You do not need to have the job lined up before you move. However, if you do not actually work, no deduction is allowed. If you become self-employed before meeting this test, you must meet the self-employed test.

If you're self-employed, you must also work full time for a minimum of 78 weeks in the 24-month period immediately after the move. A self-employed person is considered to have begun work when substantial arrangements to begin work have been made.

If either you or your spouse meet the appropriate test and you file a joint return, you qualify to deduct moving expenses. You can add together the time spent working on different jobs to meet these requirements.

Work Connection Test. The move must be connected with your starting work at the new location at a new principal place of work. The move must be reasonably proximate in both time and place to the commencement of your new job. A new principal place of work is defined for an employee as the plant, office, shop, store, or other property where services are performed. For a self-employed person, it is defined as the center of his business activities. The principal place of work of someone employed by a number of employers on a short-term basis through an employment agency is the employment agency. The moving expenses must be incurred within one year from the date you first start your new job, unless you can demonstrate extenuating circumstances.

Reasonableness Test. Only reasonable expenses may be deducted. For example, travel expenses should be reasonable if they are incurred along the shortest and most direct route from your old home to your new home. Costs to travel a longer but more scenic route or to permit a stopover are not allowed.

How to Claim Moving Expense Deductions

Under prior law, moving expenses could be deducted only when you itemized deductions. The 2 percent of adjusted gross income floor (the hurdle rate you must exceed to claim miscellaneous itemized deductions) did not, however, apply. Under the new law, after 1993, the moving expense deduction will be claimed as a deduction to arrive at adjusted gross income (AGI). This will have a substantial tax benefit for many taxpayers. For taxpayers who do not itemize deductions, this assures a deduction where there would have been none. For other taxpayers, there may be a benefit since reducing AGI minimizes other tax costs. For example, the increased tax on Social Security is based on a modified version of your adjusted gross income. Reducing adjusted gross income reduces the amount of Social Security taxed.

New Rules for Employer Reimbursement of Moving Expenses

Under prior law, if your employer reimbursed you for moving expenses, the reimbursements had to be included in income. Your employer would have notified you of the amount of the reimbursement on your Form W-2 and also would have given you Form 4782, "Employee Moving Expense Information." You had to report as gross income on your tax return all the amounts paid by your employer. You then claimed an itemized deduction for the deductible amounts on the same return. The Clinton Tax Act significantly simplifies these rules in a manner that could provide important tax benefits for many businesses. Employer reimbursement of moving expenses is now excluded from the employee's income.

CONCLUSION

Home ownership as a tax shelter, through increased value of tax deductions for taxes, interest, and possibly moving expenses, tax-free appreciation, and other changes will continue to be one of the best tax shelters for many investors.

9

Disaster Relief: Tax Help for Flood, Hurricane, and Other Damage

Where your home and your personal belongings are destroyed by a disaster in an area that is declared by the President to be a disaster area, special new tax breaks are provided. To understand the new changes, the general rules for casualty loss deductions must be reviewed.

OVERVIEW OF TAX RULES AFFECTING CASUALTY LOSSES

In the event of a casualty loss, you may qualify to take a tax deduction for a portion of your loss. Insurance proceeds may also be received in certain circumstances without a tax cost.

Casualty losses are deducted on your personal income tax return, Form 1040—Schedule A (for itemized deductions). In addition, you will generally have to fill out Form 4684, "Casualties and Thefts."

DEFINING A CASUALTY LOSS FOR TAX PURPOSES

A casualty loss is defined for tax purposes as a loss from a fire, storm, or other similar casualty caused by either natural or external forces (a thief) in a sudden, unexpected, or unusual event. The recent disastrous floods and hurricanes that ravaged large parts of the country are included (it was these major natural disasters that spurred Congress to make the changes to the tax rules affecting casualty losses discussed in this chapter). An unexpected and rapid destruction of trees due to southern pine beetles or wood borers has qualified for deduction. However, damage due either to termite infestation or Dutch elm disease, is not deductible since the damage occurs slowly over a long period. An accidental loss is deductible if it is caused by a sudden, unexpected, unusual, and identifiable event that damages property. A mere decline in value without physical damage is generally not deductible. If you must abandon your home as a result of a disaster, you can claim a casualty loss.

DETERMINING THE TAX YEAR IN WHICH TO TAKE YOUR DEDUCTION

The year in which you deduct a casualty loss can have a significant effect on the tax benefit you receive, as well as the timing of any tax refund. The cash flow provided by a tax refund can be a considerable help in financing needed repairs. The Clinton Tax Act has made favorable, but complex, changes to these rules.

Generally, you deduct your casualty loss in the year your property is damaged. But there are a number of important exceptions to this simple rule. If your house was damaged in December 1993 and you know that all but the first $200 (the amount of the deductible on your insurance policy) will be paid by your insurance company early in 1994, you cannot claim a deduction in 1993. If you anticipate an insurance recovery, you must reduce the amount of your casualty loss deduction by that amount. If you collect less from the insurance company than you expected, deduct the unrecovered loss in the later year after the settlement has been finalized.

If in the later year you collect more than you estimated from the insurance company, this extra amount will have to be reported as income if you claimed a tax deduction for it in the earlier year. If you deducted the amount in the earlier year but couldn't benefit from the entire deduction, because of either the 10 percent adjusted gross income limitation or the standard deduction amount, the amount for which you did not realize a benefit does not have to be treated as income.

A special rule applies if the President declares your area a disaster qualifying for special federal government assistance. An election will allow you to deduct your casualty loss resulting from the disaster according to the preceding general rules, or on your tax return for the year before the loss occurred. This is done by filing an amended income tax return on Form 1040.

The benefit of this election can be twofold. First, if your income was lower in the prior year, you will obtain a bigger deduction (this is because the reduction for 10 percent of adjusted gross income will not reduce your deduction by as much). Second, you may get your tax benefit much sooner. If there had been a major hurricane in January 1992 in your area and the President declared it a disaster area, you could have claimed the deduction on your 1991 tax return. If you did not make this special election, you would have had to wait to claim the deduction on your 1992 tax return, filed a year later in April 1993. If you've already filed your tax return, you can amend it by filing Form 1040-X to claim the casualty loss in the prior year. Thus, you can claim a 1993 flood disaster loss on your 1992 federal tax return by filing an amended tax return to get a tax refund. Or you can claim it on your 1993 tax return.

> **TIP:** Because unreimbursed casualty losses can only be deducted to the extent that they exceed 10 percent of your adjusted gross income, it can be beneficial to claim your loss in the year in which your income is lower. The decision must also consider the tax due in the year you wish to claim the loss. The safest strategy is to project the loss deduction for each year in which the deduction can be claimed and choose the best.

The decision as to which year to claim the loss is now more complicated because of the changes made by the Clinton Tax Act. The tax rates in 1993 could be higher for you than they were in 1992. However, if you claim the loss for the 1993 year, it may take longer to receive your refund. It really becomes a present value calculation to determine which option is better.

LIMITATIONS AND RESTRICTIONS ON DEDUCTING CASUALTY LOSSES

There are several important limitations on deducting a casualty loss. First, $100 for each casualty is not deductible. Next, when you add all your casualty losses (after deducting the $100 per casualty) the total is deductible only to the extent that it exceeds 10 percent of your adjusted gross income (AGI). AGI is all your earnings, less certain items such as alimony, but before itemized deductions. This deductible amount is added to all your other itemized deductions. The total of all your itemized deductions is only deductible to the extent that it exceeds the standard deduction. The phaseout of itemized deductions for high-income taxpayers may reduce your deduction further (Chapter 7).

EXAMPLE: A farmer and his spouse have gross income of $35,000. Their state income taxes are $3,000 and their property taxes are $1,000. They were fortunate in that they were on the fringes of a flood area and suffered only $11,300 in damage. They weren't insured for flood loss. Their casualty loss deduction is calculated as follows:

Casualty	$11,300
Less deductible	− 100
Subtotal	$11,200
Less 10% × AGI (10% × 35,000)	− 3,500
Deductible casualty loss	$ 7,700

Their total itemized deductions before casualty loss is $4,000 ($3,000 state income taxes + $1,000 property taxes). Assume that they are entitled to a $6,000 standard deduction. Only the first $2,000 of casualty loss will not provide them any additional tax benefit ($6,000 standard deduction − $4,000). Thus, their casualty loss will provide them an additional $5,700 tax deduction ($7,700 − $2,000 they would have had from the standard deduction anyway). If they are in a 15 percent tax bracket, this will give them a tax savings of $855—not a lot toward a $11,300 loss.

Where you have several items of property, such as a couch, a bookcase, and a carpet destroyed in a fire, you do not have to deduct $100 from each item when calculating your casualty loss deduction. You only have to deduct $100 per casualty. Since your couch, bookcase, and carpet were all destroyed in the same fire, you can add up your entire loss and subtract a single $100 exclusion. It is a $100 exclusion per event even though many items were destroyed. Closely related events can be considered a single event.

The Clinton Tax Act made a helpful change in this area. Where you have many items damaged or destroyed, the computation of any gain or loss may now be made on a pool of dollars so that you do not have to allocate insurance proceeds on an asset-by-asset basis. You compare the cost of replacing all assets (e.g., your house and your personal property—television, VCR, sofa, etc.). A mix of some losses and some gains can be offset without the requirement of calculating all gains and losses individually. This rule also gives you the flexibility to invest insurance proceeds in a ratio that differs from the ratio in which you were paid. If your insurance distribution was based on a ratio of 75 percent for the value of the real estate and 25 percent for the value of the personal property, you can now reinvest those distributions in any other ratio. A reinvestment of 60 percent in real estate and 40 percent for personal property could be made with no adverse tax consequence.

> **EXAMPLE:**   Assume your insurance policy paid you $95,000 for your home and $31,500 for personal property, for a total of $126,500. If you reinvest these insurance monies (according to the rules described in this chapter) fully in a replacement home, even in different proportions, there will be no taxable gain. Thus, if you spent $105,000 for your new home and only $21,500 (or more) for personal property, there would be no taxable gain.

If you refuse to file an insurance claim (e.g., you are afraid the rates will go up), you cannot deduct the casualty loss. If the property was insured, you must file a timely insurance claim to claim a tax deduction.

HOW THE TAXABLE LOSS IS CALCULATED

The calculation of your casualty loss can be quite complicated. It is the lower of the following two amounts: (1) the decrease in the value of your property as a result of the casualty; or (2) your adjusted basis in the property. The decrease in value is the fair market value of your property before the casualty loss minus the fair market value of your property after the casualty loss. Your adjusted basis in the property is the price you paid for your house less any depreciation you deducted on a home office or rental apartment that was part of your house. After you determine the amount of the loss, you must subtract $100 per casualty, 10 percent of your adjusted gross income from all your casualty losses, and expected insurance recoveries, and consider your standard deduction, as discussed earlier.

HOW TO PROVE YOUR LOSS TO THE IRS

There are several ways to prove the amount of your casualty loss. If the casualty was from a theft, car crashing into your property, or similar event, file a police report immediately. The best evidence you can have is an independent police report. This will probably also help you in recovering from your insurance company as well. Promptly advise your insurance agent of the damage, and shoot photographs of the damage to your property as soon as possible after the event. The comparison of these photos with the ones you took as part of your household inventory, before any damage was done will highlight your loss. At the first opportunity, confirm your initial phone call to your insurance agent in writing. Save copies of everything for your tax return.

Try to collect receipts, canceled checks, invoices, and so forth to prove the following information for your casualty loss: nature of the loss, evidence that the loss was the direct result of the casualty, cost of the property destroyed, any depreciation claimed on the property (for example if you had a home office), the value of the property before and after the casualty, any insurance recovery.

If your property was damaged by a tornado, save a copy of the next day's local newspaper discussing the damage to your area. This could be a great help if you are audited by the IRS and the agent questions your deductions. If the damage is extensive and your loss will be large, consider getting an appraisal of your property.

If you cannot prove the cost of the property destroyed and its fair market value, then the IRS will sometimes accept repair bills as an estimate of damage. Be prepared to show that the repairs were necessary to restore the property to its precasualty condition. This is where a picture can be worth a thousand words.

HOW TO AVOID TAX ON INSURANCE PROCEEDS RECEIVED AS A RESULT OF A DISASTER

Where property, such as your home, is destroyed and insurance proceeds are received, you may have to report a taxable gain as if you had sold the house, unless you reinvest the insurance proceeds in qualifying replacement property within the specified time period. The Clinton Tax Act made this tax-free reinvestment of insurance proceeds more lenient. The period for reinvestment is longer and the method of calculating gain is more lenient.

Under old law, gain on insurance proceeds received as a result of a disaster had to be reinvested within 2 years of the close of the tax year in which the gain was realized to avoid any tax cost. New law provides a 4-year period to reinvest insurance proceeds on gain from the sale of a principal residence without any tax consequences.

EXAMPLE: A rancher suffered a flood loss to his home in July 1993. The tax year ends December 31, 1993. Insurance proceeds are received in November 1993. The rancher has 4 years after December 1993 (until December 1997) to reinvest in a replacement property and avoid any tax cost.

A special rule permits renters to be treated as if they owned property for purposes of this reinvestment rule.

The effective date of the provision is September 1, 1991. This very favorable protaxpayer provision will help victims of the recent Midwest floods as well as of Hurricanes Bob and Andrew, Typhoon Omar, and other natural disasters.

> **TIP:**   If your principal residence was affected by a significant natural disaster and insurance proceeds created a taxable gain, review your recent tax filings to see if there is an opportunity to file a refund claim by using an amended tax return (Form 1040-X).

CONCLUSION

The Clinton Tax Act has made several helpful changes to the casualty loss rules. Unfortunately, the rules remain complex and the limitations severe. Where the amounts involved are large, it is advisable to consult with a tax professional. In all cases, however, the tax benefits, even though helpful, will fall far short of financing your recovery if you were not adequately insured.

10

Low-Income Housing Credit: Tax Benefit for Investing in Residential Real Estate

The Clinton Tax Act renewed, on a permanent basis, the low-income housing tax credit that had expired at the end of 1992. Congress also made numerous technical changes to the credit. It is designed to spur investment in low-income housing in line with the President's goals of helping the working poor and improving certain targeted areas.

> **TIP:** Low-income housing credit investment transactions should become more popular. Because the credit is now permanent, greater comfort is available to structure investment transactions that will qualify for the credit. This should increase the stock of housing available for those with lesser means. Unfortunately, as with many well-meaning, Clinton Tax Act changes, complexity and limitations make this tax benefit far less effective than necessary to achieve the important social goals desired.

This valuable tax-planning opportunity can present a true tax shelter for many taxpayers. The following overview will help you understand the changes in the credit.

> **TIP:** The low-income housing credit is extremely complex. The following discussion provides merely an overview. It does not address numerous important details. You should always obtain professional tax advice when evaluating a low-income housing tax credit project. Also, carefully evaluate the economic and other risks associated with the project, the long-term and nonliquid nature of the investments, and the typically limited cash flow from such investments.

SET-ASIDE REQUIREMENT

An investment must meet a number of requirements to qualify for the low-income housing credit. A minimum portion of the building must be set aside for low-income families. There are two alternative means

112

of meeting this test, and the owner must irrevocably choose which of them will apply.

The first test requires that 20 percent or more of the residential units in the project must be both rent restricted and occupied by individuals or families with incomes no greater than 50 percent of the median income level for the area. The second alternative requires that 40 percent or more of the rental units must be both rent restricted and occupied by individuals or families with incomes no more than 60 percent of the median income for the area. These tests help assure that the tax benefits are largely used to help low-income people and families.

The term *rent restricted* means that the gross rents paid by low-income families cannot exceed 30 percent of the qualifying income level (either 50 percent or 60 percent of the median income for the area) for that family. Certain federal payments and allowances are excluded from this calculation. The cost of utilities (except telephone) paid for by the tenant must be included in the rental figure for this test.

The income tests are redetermined on an annual basis, both as to the tenant's income level and the income level for the area. However, a tenant will not be disqualified solely for certain minimum changes in income. Also, if an even stricter set-aside requirement is met, greater increases in income levels will be tolerated without disqualifying a tenant. Low-income use based on the preceding tests must be met for a 15-year period.

MISCELLANEOUS REQUIREMENTS

The apartment units must be suitable for, and used for, occupancy on a nontransient basis. Various reporting requirements must be met. The taxpayer must certify to the IRS the project's continuous compliance with the credit requirements, the year in which the building was placed in service, the adjusted basis and the eligible basis of the building, which of the necessary elections are being made, and so forth.

DETERMINING THE ELIGIBLE BASIS IN A LOW-INCOME HOUSING PROJECT

To determine the credit that you may be entitled to, the first step is to determine the eligible basis by adding the amount of expenditures that qualify for the credit. The eligible basis consists of three components:

1. The cost of eligible new construction includes the cost of qualifying new low-income buildings.
2. The cost of rehabilitation expenditures includes rehabilitation expenditures that at least equal the greater of either $3,000 per low-income housing unit, or 10 percent of the adjusted basis of the building. Only rehabilitation expenditures incurred during a 24-month period from the date the rehabilitation is begun can be included.
3. The cost of acquiring an existing building and any rehabilitation expenditures incurred before the end of the first of the credit period may also be included. These rehabilitation expenditures do not need to meet the $3,000 minimum expenditure requirement previously described. For the costs of an existing building to be included in the eligible basis, the building had to be acquired by purchase and had to have been put into use more than 10 years before the current acquisition or the most recent nonqualified substantial improvement. The cost of the land is not included. The previous owner must not have placed the building in service, for example as a rental property, within 10 years prior to your purchase.

Several additional rules apply in determining the preceding amounts. The cost of amenities, including personal property (fixtures and furniture), can be included. The cost of tenant facilities, such as parking lots, swimming pools, or other recreational areas can also be included if the tenants are not charged a separate fee for using them, and the facilities are made available on a comparable basis to all tenants. The presence of commercial tenants or uses in a building will not disqualify it. However, the cost of these nonresidential facilities must be excluded from the calculation of the eligible basis. No portion of any federal grant can be included in the eligible basis.

If an addition is made to a low-income housing structure, a scaled-down credit, based on two-thirds of the regular amount will be allowed. These additional credits will be available annually for the remaining years in the 15-year testing period during which the project must continue to meet all the low-income housing credit requirements.

If the building is located in certain qualified areas, the eligible basis is increased to 130 percent of the eligible basis previously calculated to provide an additional incentive.

THE PORTION OF THE ELIGIBLE BASIS DETERMINING THE CREDIT

Once you have determined your eligible basis, you must determine what portion of the eligible basis qualifies for the credit. The portion of the eligible basis that is attributable to low-income housing units is called the qualifying basis. It is calculated based on the smaller of one of the following:

1. Unit fraction, which is determined by dividing the number of low-income housing units in the building by the total number of residential units in the building.
2. Floor-space fraction, which is determined by dividing the total floor space in the building that the low-income apartments occupy by the total floor space of the residential apartments in the building.

In calculating the two proportions, low-income apartments include those apartments actually occupied by low-income tenants. Also, a vacated low-income apartment is still considered a low-income apartment assuming reasonable efforts are made to rent it and no similar apartments are rented to non-low-income tenants. Total units, however, include all the apartments, whether or not they are occupied.

TWO-TIER CREDIT STRUCTURE

The new low-income housing credit is a two-tier credit:

1. *The 9 Percent Credit.* This is available for new construction and substantial rehabilitation costs of a qualifying building. A substantial rehabilitation generally requires that the costs exceed a specified average per apartment unit.
2. *The 4 Percent Credit.* This is available for the cost of acquiring an existing building, rehabilitation costs that are not substantial (less than the per unit amount required for the 9 percent credit), and for new or existing construction financed with federally subsidized tax-exempt financing.

Each credit is available at the rate indicated on an annual basis for 10 years. However, if the low-income housing units are occupied after the beginning of the year, the preceding credits are prorated for the first year. This will result in a small credit that will have to be claimed in the eleventh year.

The 9 percent and 4 percent rates of the credit are revised on a monthly basis by the IRS to reflect changes in market interest rates. The objective of the monthly rate revisions is to adjust the credits so that on a present value basis (in today's dollars) the credits available over the 10-year credit period are equal to 70 percent (in case of the 9 percent credit) or 30 percent (in case of the 4 percent credit) of the costs on which the credits are taken.

STATE LIMITATIONS AFFECTING THE CREDIT

Each state is responsible for allocating low-income housing credits on an annual basis. The maximum amount of low-income housing credits awardable in any state is based on a formula that includes the state's population. One exception, however, exists. Low-income housing projects financed with tax-exempt private activity bonds are not counted toward this limit since they are subject to their own stringent limitations. To qualify, a building must receive an allocation of credit authority for the first year in which the low-income housing credit is to be claimed. The credits cannot be claimed in excess of the amount of credit authority allocated, no matter how large a credit may otherwise have been available.

HOW TO DETERMINE THE CREDIT

Now that each of the components of the low-income housing credit has been analyzed, the credit can be calculated. Table 10.1 illustrates the schematic of the low-income housing credit.

When the tentative low-income housing credit is subjected to the passive loss limitations, the available low-income housing credit for the year can be determined.

LIMITATIONS AFFECTING THE CLAIMABLE CREDIT

You must also consider several limitations that can affect how much of the low-income housing credit you can use. While the passive loss

TABLE 10.1   Low-Income Housing Credit Calculation

Eligible basis (cost of construction or purchase of the project)

×

Proportion of the eligible basis attributable to low-income rental units

=

Qualified basis in the project

×

70% or 30% present value credit percentage (subject to state cap)

=

Tentative low-income housing credit

limitation rules limit the amount of any credit generated by a passive activity, an important exception is provided for the low-income housing credit. This exception can allow you to use up to a deduction equivalent of $25,000 of low-income housing credits to offset any income (passive or otherwise). At the new 39.6 percent marginal tax rate, this allowance can be worth $9,900 [$25,000 × 39.6%]. The phaseout of this benefit does not apply to low-income housing credits as it does to other credits or passive losses. Also, unlike the active real estate participation rule discussed in Chapter 12, claiming the credit does not require you to participate actively in the low-income housing credit transaction.

TIP: These special rules favoring low-income housing, as compared with other investment transactions, make low-income housing perhaps the only real tax shelter left. Increases in limited partnership offerings to take advantage of this opportunity should increase. These investments, unlike other breaks from the passive loss limitations, will be available to many high-income investors as well.

RECAPTURE OF THE CREDIT

The building must meet the various requirements to qualify for the low-income housing credit for a 15-year compliance period. If the requirements are not met during the compliance period, then a portion of the credit will be recaptured. This means you will have to report as income the portion of the low-income housing credit that you really were not entitled to. The requirements are not met if the qualified basis of the building at the end of the current tax year is less than the qualified basis of that building at the end of the prior tax year.

> **TIP:**   Special relief is granted where a credit would have to be recaptured as a result of a casualty loss, such as Hurricane Andrew. If any noncompliance with the low-income housing credit rules is, however, due to a casualty loss and the noncompliance is corrected within a reasonable period, the credit will not have to be recaptured.

When the credit must be recaptured, no credit can be claimed in that year on the same property. The accelerated portion of the credit must be added back to taxable income. Interest will also be charged on these amounts and will not be deductible. The accelerated portion of the credit is best understood by looking at the structure of the credit. As noted earlier, the credit is generally claimed ratably over the first 10 years after the building is built or purchased. The compliance (test) period for which the building must meet the low-income housing requirements is 15 years.. Thus, the excess of the credit actually claimed, over what the credit would have been had it been claimed over a 15-year period, is the accelerated portion that must be recaptured.

> **EXAMPLE:**   An investor incurs $100,000 of qualifying expenses, all of which is included in his eligible basis. He claimed a 9 percent credit for 5 years, or $9,000 per year for a total of $45,000. The building fails to meet the required tests at the end of year 5. Had the credit been claimed over the 15-year period, only $30,000 of the credits would have been allowed (($9\% \times \$100,000)/15$-year compliance period $\times$ 5 years actually qualifying). Thus, $15,000 of the credits must be recaptured ($45,000 claimed − $30,000 allowed). In addition, a nondeductible interest charge will be assessed.

CONCLUSION

The low-income housing credit can be a very valuable tax benefit. However, before investing on the basis of the credit, great care should be taken to ascertain that the credit will in fact be available (all the necessary requirements will be met) and that once the credit is obtained, the taxpayer will in fact be able to benefit from it (the many limitations and tax law changes will not prevent the credit from providing any meaningful benefit). By reinstating and making permanent the low-income housing credit, the Clinton Tax Act has provided a valuable tax-sheltered investment opportunity for many taxpayers.

PART FOUR

COMMERCIAL
REAL ESTATE
INVESTMENTS

11 How Commercial Real Estate Investments Are Affected

The Clinton Tax Act includes a number of changes that should help the real estate industry. Some real estate investors could benefit substantially. The changes include easing the application of the passive loss rules, more favorable rules for donating real estate to charity, and breaks for certain troubled real estate businesses. Unfortunately, not all the changes are favorable, such as the increase in the depreciation period for commercial real estate.

One of the best benefits Congress could bestow on the real estate industry would be to limit its constant tampering with real estate deductions. The uncertainty of constant change obscures the long-term investment horizon necessary for major real estate transactions. The massive tax deductions of the Economic Recovery Tax Act of 1981, which fostered the growth of the tax shelter industry, helped wreak havoc on active developers, with 15-year accelerated depreciation deductions and other overly generous tax benefits. The sudden and dramatic change in policy in the Tax Reform Act of 1986, with passive loss rules, capitalization of construction costs, and so forth, contributed to the decline in property values and the collateral value that real estate provided for lenders. The Clinton Tax Act has in some ways mitigated the 1986 restrictions with some leniency given to active developers concerning the passive loss rules. However, the new 39-year depreciation period is absurd when compared with the economic reality of the useful lives of a typical building's components.

The following sections analyze some of the more significant changes.

THE EFFECT OF LOWER TAX RATES AND CAPITAL GAINS ON REAL ESTATE INVESTMENTS

The new higher 39.6 percent marginal tax brackets, coupled with modest relief from the passive loss rules for active real estate investors/

developers, the low-income housing credit, and other changes, helps to put some shelter back into real estate. Tax deductions will have more value post-Clinton Tax Act than they did before the act. The increased spread between capital gains (39.6 percent) and ordinary income (28%) is 11.6 percent (greater if state and local taxes are considered). This compares favorably with the pre-Clinton Tax Act spread of 3 percent (31 percent − 28 percent) and will encourage real estate investments over other types of investments. Since real estate investments can appreciate tax deferred (there is no tax until the property is sold) and then ultimately generate favorably taxed capital gains, some of the benefits that real estate investments enjoyed prior to the Tax Reform Act of 1986 are back. The ability to defer even capital gains by reinvesting in like-kind property and to obtain funds (cash out the appreciation in a property) tax free through mortgage financing, will continue to make real estate a popular investment.

PAYMENTS TO PARTNERS THAT AFFECT REAL ESTATE PARTNERSHIPS

The Clinton Tax Act modified several rules applicable to distributions to retired or deceased partners. In general, the modifications eliminate deductions that partnerships had obtained for some of these payments. Since many real estate investments are structured as either general or limited partnerships, the changes could affect these partnerships (see Chapter 14).

AVOIDANCE OF DEBT DISCHARGE INCOME ON SOME REAL ESTATE DEBT

Introduction to the Tax Changes

Where a property declines in value, the mortgage may have to be restructured with the lender to avoid losing the property. In the past, this restructuring, or workout, often had to address the potential for a taxable gain for a borrower who was relieved from the liability to repay some portion of the debt. This potential tax cost made restructuring a difficult task in some cases. The Clinton Tax Act provides some relief in these situations. To better understand the nature of the changes, a review of prior law rules is helpful.

Review of Prior Law Rules

General Tax Consequences of Real Estate Mortgages.   The tax basis (your investment, which also helps determine the amount depreciated) of real estate includes the full consideration you paid to acquire the property—seller financing, third party or bank financing, and the cash invested. Mortgages must similarly be considered when determining the tax consequences on your disposition of real estate. The general tax rule is that the principal amount of the mortgage indebtedness is treated as an amount received on the transfer of the underlying property. This has also been held to include mortgage debt incurred after the initial purchase of the property, for example, on a refinancing. The amount of gain to be recognized on the disposition of mortgaged property includes any cash and other consideration as well as the amount by which the liabilities exceed the remaining basis of the property at the time of the sale. The only exception to this rule is for the discharge of indebtedness income covered by a special rule discussed in the following section.

Prior Law Rules Governing Income from Discharge of Debt.   Generally, a mortgagor whose debt is canceled will have to recognize as income from the discharge of indebtedness the amount of the debt canceled. There are a few exceptions to this income recognition requirement: (1) the mortgagor is insolvent; (2) the mortgagor is in Chapter 11 bankruptcy; (3) the mortgagor is solvent, the debt discharged is purchase money debt of the seller, and the debt discharge is treated as an adjustment to the purchase price; or (4) certain farm debt was involved.

Where an insolvent mortgagor avoids recognition of income, certain tax benefits (attributes) must be reduced. The reductions must be made in the following order unless the mortgagor elects to first reduce the adjusted basis of depreciable assets or inventory:

- Net operating losses and carryovers.
- General business credit (rehabilitation tax credits, etc.).
- Capital loss carryovers.
- Basis of depreciable and nondepreciable assets.
- Foreign tax credit carryovers.

The election to first reduce the basis of depreciable property cannot reduce the basis below zero. The election is limited to the aggregate adjusted basis of depreciable property held by the mortgagor at the beginning of the year following the year in which the discharge of debt occurred.

When debts of an insolvent taxpayer, who is not in bankruptcy, are discharged, the maximum amount of debt that can be discharged without creating income is limited to the amount of the taxpayer's insolvency. This is defined as the excess of the taxpayer's liabilities over the fair market value of the taxpayer's assets immediately prior to the discharge.

Where the taxpayer is insolvent before the cancellation of indebtedness and is solvent afterward, the rules applicable to insolvent taxpayers govern to the extent that the discharge does not make the taxpayer solvent. The rule applicable to solvent taxpayers governs for the excess. A taxpayer who is solvent both before and after the cancellation of indebtedness cannot avoid income recognition.

For many real estate investors, a key problem in applying these rules is the manner in which insolvency is tested where the property is owned by a partnership, one of the most common forms of real estate ownership. Where the debtor is a partnership, the insolvency and attribute reduction must occur at the individual partner level. Thus, even if your partnership is insolvent you will not qualify for this tax benefit unless you are personally insolvent.

For a C corporation or S corporation, insolvency is tested at the entity level.

A foreclosure of property because of the mortgagor's default may be accomplished by a voluntary conveyance of property to the mortgagee, an involuntary or voluntary sale to the mortgagee, or sale to a third party. The key tax consequences to be determined in a foreclosure situation are:

- Tax basis of property foreclosed upon.
- Amount and timing of any forgiveness of indebtedness income.
- Taxable gain.

A foreclosure by the mortgagee on secured property is treated as a taxable sale of the property to the mortgagee. It doesn't matter whether the mortgage is recourse or nonrecourse. A sale of mortgaged property to a third party at foreclosure is also treated as a sale or exchange. The rules for determining gain or loss in a foreclosure are similar to the rules for determining gain or loss when property is sold. The excess of the amount realized (gross proceeds less expenses of the foreclosure) over the adjusted tax basis in the property is generally the taxable gain. The amount realized in a foreclosure is generally the amount of debt canceled.

In a voluntary conveyance to the seller/mortgagee where the mortgagor is not personally liable on the debt, the mortgagor receives no consideration, and the mortgage balance exceeds the fair market value of the property, the transaction will still be considered a sale or exchange. Thus, the loss can be a capital loss. As a result of the $3,000 annual limitation on deducting capital losses against ordinary income, it is critical to plan the recognition of such a capital loss carefully to obtain the maximum current tax benefit (see Chapter 3).

Property used in the investor's trade or business may qualify as a Code Section 1231 asset (see Chapter 3) so that a gain on disposition could be taxed as a capital gain and a loss as an ordinary loss.

If the mortgagor's adjusted tax basis in the property foreclosed upon is less than the net amount realized (including the outstanding principal balance the mortgagor is relieved of) on the foreclosure, a phantom gain results for which no cash distribution will be available to the mortgagor.

Using the New Rule to Avoid Income from Discharge of Debt

An investor (either an individual, fiduciary, partnership, or S corporation) may elect to exclude income from the discharge of debt under the Clinton Tax Act even where the limited number of situations under which gain could have been avoided under prior law are not present.

> **EXAMPLE:**   You own a rental property that you purchased for $2 million. The adjusted tax basis in the property (cost less depreciation plus improvements) is now $1.7 million. The mortgage balance is $1.6 million. The value of the property, however, has declined to $1.4 million. You are not insolvent or bankrupt. To keep yourself and the property above water, you are able to negotiate with the lender a reduction in the mortgage from $1.6 million to $1.4 million. The $200,000 reduction is applied to reduce your adjusted tax basis in the building from $1.7 million to $1.5 million and avoid recognizing any taxable gain for the $200,000 of debt relief.

The new leniency, however, is not an across-the-board break. For example, if your property is foreclosed upon (or you deed it to the lender in lieu of a foreclosure), you will still have to recognize gain equal to the excess of the mortgage canceled over the adjusted tax basis in the property. Numerous requirements must be met to qualify for this additional exception from the general rule requiring the recognition of income. For a qualified real property business indebtedness cancellation to avoid taxation, it must meet the following requirements:

- This new exception is only available for transactions after 1992.
- The property involved must be trade or business property.
- The debt must be secured by the real estate.
- The debt must have been incurred or assumed in connection with real property used in your business.
- Any debt incurred after 1992 only qualifies if its purpose was to purchase, construct, or substantially improve real property used in your business, or to refinance the outstanding balance of other debt used for such purpose.
- For a partnership, the determination whether the debt meets the requirements is made at the partnership level. The election to exclude the gain from income, however, is made by each partner individually. This latter rule may permit partners to reduce their tax basis in depreciable real estate other than the partnership assets where the tax basis in partnership assets is insufficient.
- There are two limitations on the amount of debt relief that you can exclude under this new provision:
  1. The excludable amount of income is limited to the excess of the debt over the fair market value of the property reduced by other qualified real property business debt.
  2. The amount excluded cannot exceed your investment (tax basis) in the depreciable real estate.

If the amount of qualified real property business indebtedness exceeds these limitations, income must be recognized to the extent that you are solvent following the transaction. The amount of debt relief excluded from income recognition must be applied to reduce your tax basis in your depreciable real property using special tax rules. If the property is later sold, the basis reduction is characterized as depreciation so that it will be subject to recapture rules. Recapture rules can recharacterize what would have been capital gain as ordinary income.

EXPANSION OF REPORTING REQUIREMENTS FOR DISCHARGE OF DEBT

The Clinton Tax Act has expanded the reporting requirements where a debt is discharged by certain lenders. The new rules require that where any debt in excess of a mere $600 is discharged, the lender must report the transaction. Lenders affected by this rule include thrifts, banks, credit unions, and certain federal agencies.

REAL ESTATE INVESTMENTS BY TAX-EXEMPT ORGANIZATIONS

The Clinton Tax Act has made numerous changes that affect the tax consequences of tax-exempt investors (such as pension funds) in real estate. Many of these changes are favorable modifications to the rules concerning unrelated business taxable income (UBTI). Taxation of investments of tax-exempt entities in real estate investment trusts (REITs) has also been changed somewhat (see Chapter 21).

SPECIAL RULES AFFECTING REAL ESTATE RENTAL ACTIVITIES WITHIN EMPOWERMENT ZONES AND ENTERPRISE COMMUNITIES

Some, but not all, businesses conducted in designated empowerment zones and enterprise communities can qualify for valuable tax benefits enacted as part of the Clinton Tax Act (see Chapter 15). For example, a commercial rental real estate business will only qualify if at least half of its rental income comes from the rentals of property to enterprise zone businesses.

CONCLUSION

The Clinton Tax Act has made a number of significant changes that affect real estate, some favorable, some not. For the active real estate investor and professional, however, the changes are generally quite favorable. In addition to the changes discussed in this chapter, changes to passive loss rules and depreciation deductions are important and are analyzed in Chapters 12 and 13. The tax changes, which warrant consideration by every real estate investor, demonstrate that real estate investments continue to be a topic for legislators.

12

Passive Loss Rules—Easier for Some but Not All

The Clinton Tax Act made a long overdue change to the passive loss limitation rules that generally restrict your ability to offset losses from passive investments, limited partnership investments and rental real estate, against income from active sources, such as wages. For tax years beginning after 1993, certain active real estate investors will be relieved of many of these restrictions. Some knowledge of the passive loss rules is necessary to understand these changes, as well as how the passive loss rules will continue to affect investors hoping to utilize such tax benefits as the post-Clinton Tax Act tax credits. The following discussions are quite general. The passive loss rules are very complex and Congressional Committee Reports, lengthy Regulations, and IRS Rulings must all be analyzed in making any decision. This level of detail is well beyond the scope of this book.

OVERVIEW OF THE PASSIVE LOSS RULES

The passive loss rules arose out of concern that many wealthy taxpayers were sheltering too much of their income from taxation in real estate investments and other tax shelters. The general approach is to segregate the perceived culprits—tax shelter and rental real estate investments—and then to limit your use of the tax losses from such investments to offset the tax on your other income. The income or loss from these suspect investments is labeled passive. The other major categories are active (e.g., wages) and portfolio (e.g., dividends and interest). More specifically, passive investments (activities) (1) involve the active conduct of a trade or business in which you do not materially participate; or (2) are rental activities.

The possibility of rental real estate being a tax shelter has lessened dramatically as a result of the almost obscene increases in the depreciation periods that must now be used for commercial real estate. When

128

the Economic Recovery Tax Act of 1981 was passed, commercial real estate could be depreciated over 15 years. When the new Clinton Tax Act depreciation rules become applicable, commercial real estate will be depreciated over 39 years providing little opportunity for significant tax deductions. A new tax benefit in the post-Clinton Tax Act environment will be the potentially large amortization deductions large corporations may realize on the purchase of businesses with important brand names and trademarks. The passive loss rules, however, will not apply to most of those transactions.

Limited partnership interests are usually considered passive. Material participation requires you to be involved on a regular, continuous, and substantial basis in the particular activity. Some of the rules for determining whether you materially participate are based on the hours you work in a particular activity.

Losses from passive activities can generally only be used to offset income from passive activities. Unused losses currently are suspended until the earlier of: (1) your realizing passive income to offset such losses; or (2) your selling your entire interest in the activity. When you sell your entire interest, suspended losses from that activity can be used without limitation.

The passive loss rules, in very general terms, divide earned income into three broad categories, subject to several exceptions. These categories of income and losses, and some of the major exceptions are illustrated in Table 12.1.

The table shows a limited number of crossover points or "bridges" between the various categories of income. The following sections discuss these crossover points and define the types of income included in each category.

The key concept of the passive loss limitation rules is that losses from the passive category (including tax losses on net leased real estate when you are not an active real estate professional under the new Clinton Tax Act exception) cannot be used to offset income in the other two categories. The actual application of the rules is far more complex.

TREATMENT OF TAX LOSSES THAT CANNOT BE DEDUCTED CURRENTLY

If the passive loss limitation applies so you cannot deduct incurred tax losses, these losses are generally deferred until a later tax year when you can use them to offset passive income. If you have income or gains

TABLE 12.1   General Income Categories for Passive Loss Rules

Active Income		Passive Income		Portfolio Income
Primary trade or business	(Bridge 2) ←	Net leased realty Limited partnership interests	(Bridge 1) →	Interest Dividends Royalties
Employee's salary etc.	(Bridge 3) ←			
Active real estate professional's income	(Bridge 4) ←			

Bridge 1: Certain passive income (e.g., interest on working capital balances of a business) will have to be treated as portfolio income.

Bridge 2: Certain real estate activities in which the investor actively participates (not materially participates) will, depending on taxpayer's income level, be treated as losses from an active business. There is a $25,000 limitation on the amount that can qualify for this special treatment.

Bridge 3: The special tax credits available for low-income housing and for rehabilitating certain old buildings can be used to offset active business income up to $25,000. Active participation, however, is not necessary to claim this benefit. This $25,000 limitation is phased out when adjusted gross income reaches $200,000 and is eliminated at $250,000 of adjusted gross income.

Bridge 4: The Clinton Tax Act has added an exception to permit certain active real estate professionals to offset some specific losses from real estate rental activities against active income.

in the passive income category in the next tax year, for example, you can apply your unused passive loss carryforwards (or certain income tax credits earned) realized in the prior tax years against the current income to obtain a tax savings.

To the extent you have not been able to use up your passive loss carryforwards from prior years before you sell your investment, you can use these losses to offset the gain you would otherwise have to recognize on the sale. Congress believed it was generally appropriate to postpone the determination as to whether a passive investment generated an overall gain or loss until the nonparticipating investor disposed of his or her entire interest in the investment.

EXAMPLE: An investor owns a limited partnership interest. The investment was made in 1992. As a result of depreciation and other deductions exceeding income in the early years of the venture, the investor realizes losses each year of $25,000. Since this is the investor's only passive investment, the losses are suspended and remain unused since there is no other passive income to offset. By 1996, the investor has accumulated unused ("suspended") losses of $125,000 at the rate of $25,000 per year for 5 years. At the end of 1996, the investor sells his limited partnership interest for $200,000 profit. This profit is reduced by the $125,000 in losses not yet used. Thus, the taxable gain is only $75,000.

Several restrictions prevent you from taking advantage of your losses before you really dispose of your investment. Merely changing the form in which you own your investment will not be sufficient to trigger the losses.

EXAMPLE: An investor decides to transfer his limited partnership interest to a new corporation he formed (a Code Section 351 tax-free transfer to a controlled corporation). He hopes to trigger $125,000 in suspended losses since he has "disposed" of his investment. This type of transfer will not be sufficient to trigger the losses.

To take advantage of the losses, you must dispose of your entire interest in the investment. Since the investor in the example controls the corporation that now owns the limited partnership investment, he will not be treated as if he disposed of his entire interest. A similar situation exists if the investor transfers his investment or business real estate to another person in a tax-free exchange for his or her investment or business real estate (a Code Section 1031 "like-kind exchange"). If the investor gives the asset to his children, perhaps even as part of an overall estate planning strategy to avoid the now higher post-Clinton Tax Act estate taxes, the suspended passive loss will still not be triggered. Instead, the $125,000 in suspended passive losses in the above example will be added to the investor's children's tax basis in the investment (the amount on which future gains or losses is determined). Thus, only when the children sell the investment will their gain will be reduced by the amount of accumulated losses the investor had.

TYPES OF TAXPAYERS SUBJECT TO THE PASSIVE LOSS LIMITATION RULES

The passive loss rules apply to all individual taxpayers, estates, and trusts as well as to certain corporations. The objective of applying the limitations to so many types of taxpayers is to prevent you from avoiding the limitations by structuring your activities or investments in a different form (such as holding a passive real estate rental property that generates tax losses in a corporation) to circumvent the rules.

Generally, C corporations are not subject to the passive loss limitation rules. However, a special rule subjects certain closely held C corporations to the passive loss limitation rules. C corporations are regular corporations (not S corporations) and are subject to the corporate level tax. Closely held C corporations are those with five or fewer individual shareholders owning more than 50 percent of the corporation's stock. Losses from passive activities of these corporations cannot be used to offset portfolio income (dividends and interest). These corporations may, however, use losses from passive investments to offset income and gains from active business income.

Personal service corporations are subject to a somewhat more stringent version of the passive loss rules than are closely held C corporations. Personal service corporations are those whose principal activity is the performance of services by employee-owners. These same employee-owners must own more than 10 percent of the stock in the corporation. There is no requirement for a personal service corporation to be closely held as there is for a C corporation.

Partnerships and S corporations are flow-through or conduit entities. Most tax consequences—income, gain, loss, and deductions—flow through to the individual partners or shareholders and are reported on their tax returns. Thus, the passive loss rules are generally applied at the partner or shareholder level. Each partner or shareholder must evaluate his or her work efforts to determine whether or not they represent an active business endeavor.

WHAT IS AN ACTIVITY?

The overview of the passive loss rules shows that defining the term *activity* is critical to applying and planning for various aspects of the passive loss rules. The scope of an activity delineates an active business from rental activities.

EXAMPLE: Assume you own a building where you operate a travel agency and rent out one floor. Must you separate the rental and travel agency results to apply the passive loss rules? If you don't, the depreciation deductions (and hence tax losses) from renting one floor could be used to offset the earnings of your travel agency. If they are treated as separate activities, you may not be able to offset the two.

You can use suspended losses without limitation when you dispose of your entire interest in an activity to an unrelated person and recognize all the gain or loss from the disposition. The narrower the term activity is defined, the easier it will be to meet this test and use losses without limitation. For example, you invested in a partnership that owns two apartment buildings. If one is sold, can you use any of your suspended passive losses? The answer depends on whether they are part of the same activity.

For a business or investment endeavor to be considered nonpassive (the losses deductible without limitation), you must materially participate. The broader the term activity is defined, the easier it will be for you to meet one of the threshold tests for material participation.

The definition of activity is important to determine the type of accounting records you must keep.

A number of factors may be considered in determining whether various investment or business endeavors constitute one or more activities: (1) the economic interrelationship and interdependence of the various endeavors (similar customers, common employees, etc.); (2) the extent of common control; (3) the degree of organizational interrelationship between the various businesses; (4) physical location (separate locations are more likely to constitute separate activities); (5) similarities and differences in the activities being compared. The groupings used should reflect an appropriate and reasonable economic unit and should not be for the purpose of avoiding the passive loss rules. Generally a real estate rental activity cannot be grouped with a non-real-estate rental activity.

The groupings you use must be applied consistently. Where a partnership or S corporation conducts the economic activities, the grouping decision must be made largely at the entity level. A partner or shareholder may then further combine the activities of various partnerships and S corporations.

CATEGORIZING INCOME, LOSSES, AND BUSINESS ACTIVITIES

It is important for taxpayers subject to the passive loss limitation rules to define the different income types and the income, gain, loss, and deductions included in each category. The definitions are critical since a tax loss on a particular activity classified as passive may be subject to limitations on when it can be deducted. By planning your activities, you might be able to spend enough time with that particular business or investment to convert it into an active business so that the passive loss limitations will not restrict your deduction. Alternatively, if your real estate losses in particular could be sufficiently large, it may be worthwhile to spend sufficient time in managing and operating your real estate investments so that you (not the particular investment) can qualify as an active real estate professional and thus avoid the application of the passive loss limitation rules. To engage in this potentially valuable tax planning, you must understand the different types of investments and income.

> **TIP:**   The Clinton Tax Act has increased the benefits of properly planning to avoid the limitations of the passive activity losses. Under prior law, the maximum tax rate was 31 percent. Under the Clinton Tax Act, the maximum tax rate is 39.6 percent. Thus, the current tax deduction realized from proper planning is worth more post-Clinton Tax Act than it was worth before.

Passive Income and Loss

A business or investment activity will generate passive income if you do not materially participate in its operations or management. Material participation requires your involvement in the activity on a regular, continuous, and substantial basis throughout the year. The test as to whether you meet this standard is applied each year. Thus it will generally not suffice to work for a small portion of the year, or for one year but not in other years, to render a business an active endeavor when, in reality, your participation is negligible. Also, the material participation of your partner in a business venture does not mean that you automatically are a material participant. Your involvement is tested separately.

Owning an interest as a limited partner will generally not be treated as being a material participant. Partnership agreements for limited partnerships usually restrict the potential involvement of limited partners in the management of partnership matters. Most importantly, under the state laws that govern partnerships, limited partners are not allowed to participate actively in the partnership's management and operations. If they do so, they could risk losing their limited liability. Limited liability means that if the partnership defaults on a loan, for example, the limited partners will generally only be liable up to the amount of their capital contributions or investments. There is an exception: Where you are both a limited and a general partner, participate in the partnership's activities for more than 500 hours during the year, and have materially participated in the activity during any 5 of the preceding 10 years (or the activity is a personal service activity), you will be considered to materially participate.

Another approach to understanding the definition of a passive activity is to define what is not a passive activity. Active business endeavors and portfolio investments do not generate passive income. These two categories are described in detail in the following sections.

As initially enacted, interests in real estate rental activities were generally categorized as passive whether or not you materially participated. The Clinton Tax Act liberalized this rule through an important exception that permits active real estate professionals to offset passive income against active income in certain instances, as described later in this chapter. Several other exceptions to the general rule that a rental real estate activity produces only passive income or loss are listed in the following section.

Active Income and Loss

Working as a full-time employee or consultant providing personal services is deemed to be material participation. Income from personal services is specifically excluded from being treated as passive income.

A business or investment endeavor will be considered active where you materially participate by one of the mechanical tests provided by the Internal Revenue Service (IRS) including the following:

- You participate in the activity more than 500 hours per year.
- You materially participated in the activity for 5 of the 10 preceding years.
- You participated in the activity for more than 100 hours during the year and no other person participated for more hours than you.
- Your participation in the activity constituted substantially all the participation for the activity for the year by anyone.
- You participate for 100 hours or more in various activities, and in the aggregate, more than 500 hours for all those activities.

TIP: Watch the word "activity" in the listed definitions. The special exception in the Clinton Tax Act for real estate professionals uses a different term "real property trades or businesses." This may have important implications, as discussed in this chapter.

The following concepts may also be considered in the analysis. Your services to, and other involvement with, the activity should relate to the operations of the activity and should make a significant contribution to those operations. Merely approving a financing target or making general recommendations regarding, for example, the selection of employees or managers, or appointing others to perform all the significant active operational functions, will generally not be sufficient. When evaluating your involvement, management functions will generally not be treated any differently from performance of nonmanagement services (e.g., physical labor). Mere formal and nominal participation in an activity will not help meet the material participation standard. The genuine exercise of independent discretion will. Knowledge and experience in the industry will be important in demonstrating that you materially participate in an activity through involvement in management.

Portfolio Income and Loss

The third major activity category in the passive loss limitation rules is portfolio income, which generally includes income generated from stocks, bonds, and other similar investments. The portfolio income category, however, is broader: It includes interest, dividends, and royalties; gains or losses on the sale of investment property that does not qualify as a passive activity; gains or losses on the sale of property that normally produces interest, dividend, or royalty income; dividends on C corporation stock; dividends from real estate investment trusts (REITs), and dividends from regulated investment companies (RICs). Distributions from real estate investment trusts (REITs), real estate mortgage investment conduits (REMICs), and certain dividends on S corporation stock are also included.

Income earned in the ordinary course of a business is excluded from the portfolio income category. For example, interest on accounts receivable and interest earned by a lending business on loans it makes are not considered passive.

Income or loss from active or passive activities, such as income from general and limited partnership interests, S corporation stock, and real property leases (except for certain nominal rentals of raw land), are typically not treated as generating portfolio income.

Relief for Active Real Estate Professionals from the Passive Loss Rules

Losses on some real estate activities may be characterized as active income category for certain real estate professionals. This new exception was added by the Clinton Tax Act to mitigate the harsh results that occurred when an active real estate investor had to apply the passive loss rules to various real estate endeavors. The new exception applies for tax years after 1993. Where you meet the following requirements, your interests in rental real estate investments will not necessarily be characterized as passive for the particular tax year:

- You are a real estate professional and spend more than half your time involved in a real property trade or business. Real property trades or businesses include construction, development, reconstruction, leasing, brokerage, development, redevelopment, conversion, rental, operation, and management.
- You spend at least 750 hours performing such services. Your involvement in different business can be aggregated for determining both the 750-hour test and the "more than half your time test" described earlier.

TIP: The rules do not appear to exclude a real estate professional whose only real estate involvement is owning and renting real estate. In contrast to the Tax Reform Act of 1986, Congress seems finally to have acknowledged that being a landlord can involve more work than merely sitting in an armchair and counting rent checks. However, you should pay careful attention to any future IRS pronouncements interpreting this new provision.

- You are a material participant in the real estate rental trade or business investments being considered. The rules for determining whether you are a material participant are the same as those described in the preceding general discussion. Thus, where you invest as a limited partner in a limited partnership and are not involved in the operations of the partnership, income from the partnership cannot qualify for this special exception.

> **TIP:** These definitions appear to focus on the term "real property trade or business." This viewpoint differs from that of the general definitions described earlier for material participation. Those definitions were based on the term "activity," which in some instances could be broader than "real property trades or businesses" since a single activity could conceivably include several real property trades or businesses. How the IRS will interpret this terminology is unclear.

The intent of the new rule was to ease the burden of the passive loss rules for active real estate professionals. Many real estate investors had structured real estate investments in limited partnership format. This provided a measure of protection from limited liability, facilitated estate planning, and provided other benefits. It can be difficult or impossible as discussed earlier in this chapter, to qualify limited partnership interests for the material participation requirement.

> Where you spend more than 500 hours during the year working on an investment, you materially participate.

> **EXAMPLE:**   Assume that you are a real estate professional. You earn $75,000 in supervisory fees for construction work on which you spent 500 hours, and $195,000 in development fees on projects where you worked 650 hours. You also own residential apartment complexes that you rent and manage. You realized tax losses (largely as a result of depreciation deductions) of $80,000. You spent almost 620 hours in the apartment business during the year. You spent 150 hours working in a travel agency that your uncle owns and operates as a full-time endeavor.

The new Clinton Tax Act rules will permit you to use your $80,000 of tax losses on your rental properties to offset your fee income of $270,000 because you meet the requirements of this new relief provision:

1. Development, construction supervisory, and rental constitute real estate trades or business.
2. You materially participated in each of the three activities because you spent more than 500 hours in each.
3. You spent more than the required 750 hours of service during the tax year.
4. More than one-half of your personal services were performed in real estate trades or businesses (1,770/1,920 = 92%).

> The material participation test will be determined on an annual basis. In applying the test, each real estate interest that you own will generally be considered as a separate activity. Alternatively,

you may make an election to treat all your real estate investments as a single activity.

TIP: This election should not be made without careful analysis of the potential consequences. If all your real estate activities are treated as separate activities, any unused passive losses from prior years will be triggered as you sell each real estate interest. If you make the election, this will not occur.

- On a joint tax return, either you or your spouse must separately satisfy the requirements for material participation. You cannot jointly meet, for example, the 750-hour test by each spending 375 hours. However, when one spouse satisfies this requirement, the rental activity will qualify for this benefit.

EXAMPLE: An entrepreneur is involved full time with a corporation he formed to develop and install roofing systems in various commercial and public buildings. The business has been profitable, and over the years the profits have been invested in developing a rather sizable real estate empire. Because of depreciation deductions and leverage, the rental properties generate tax losses that have been suspended since 1986 as a result of the passive loss limitation rules. The entrepreneur spends considerable time on the real estate properties, but because of the substantial amount of time devoted to his primary business, he cannot meet the requirement under the Clinton Tax Act of spending more than half his time on real estate endeavors. Thus, the Clinton Tax Act will not provide any relief.

TIP: The entrepreneur's spouse works only part time. It may be possible for the entrepreneur to restructure the real estate holdings by transferring them to his spouse. If she devotes 750+ hours, representing at least half of her personal services, to the management and operation of the real estate properties, it is likely she could meet the exception provided under the Clinton Tax Act since the activities would constitute more than half her time. Thus planning between spouses can be more important for qualification for this provision than under prior law.

- If you perform services as an employee, these will only count toward the material participation test if you own 5 percent or more of the employer. When applying the requirement that you must own 5 percent or more of an employer, a partner is not considered an employee of a partnership.

- For a closely held C corporation, if 50 percent or more of the gross revenues are from real property trades or businesses, the material participation test can be met.

TIPS: Carefully coordinate your estate planning, and gift-giving in particular, with these new rules. You must now balance the desire to divest yourself of all interests in a particular entity against the reduction of your interests below 5 percent thus losing the potentially valuable benefits described for that particular entity.

Where a particular investment is no longer classified as passive under the new rules, evaluate your suspended passive losses (passive losses unused in prior tax years). Suspended losses from that no-longer-passive activity can be used to offset income from the activity in future years. Unfortunately, it does not appear that the law retroactively converts those suspended passive losses into nonpassive losses, which could be deducted without regard to the passive loss limitations.

These rules raise several issues, planning opportunities, and yet more tax traps. For the real estate industry, however (and probably the economy generally), they represent long overdue relief.

TIP: This new rule, while beneficial for the majority of real estate professionals, is not necessarily advantageous for everyone in all circumstances. If you're an active real estate professional owning properties that generate income, you may wish to continue characterizing the income as passive in order to use that income for offsetting passive losses from other activities. If you fall into this category, your planning would be the exact opposite of most other real estate professionals. You would try to restructure your operations and activities to avoid being characterized as a material participant.

Besides the exception provided by the Clinton Tax Act from the passive loss limitation rules, you need to understand several other important exceptions to properly plan your investments.

Other Exceptions to the General Categories

The following sections highlight some of the numerous special rules and exceptions for the general categories.

Treatment of Minimal Rental Activities as Portfolio Income. Where you have idle land, such as raw land being held on speculation, you may rent it for a nominal amount to defray part of the carrying costs. Such nominal rentals may not be considered a true rental activity. The gain on the eventual sale of the property, as well as the nominal income, may have to be treated as portfolio income instead of passive income generated by a rental activity. This rule will be applied where the property is being held primarily for appreciation and the rental revenues are less than 2 percent of your investment (unadjusted tax basis) in the property.

Characterizing Certain Income Earned on a Passive Activity as Portfolio Income. If you invested in a limited partnership, generally your share of income is characterized as passive income. However, where the partnership assets consist of portfolio assets, such as stocks and bonds, and the partnership is not engaged in the active business of trading and dealing in those passive assets, then the income you receive as a limited partner will be treated as portfolio income. The objective is to prevent the use of the limited partnership format to avoid the proper application of the passive loss rules. If the partnership were engaged in an active securities business, then your income would be characterized as passive where you do not materially participate in that activity, or where your interest is that of a limited partner.

If the income earned on, or the gain from the sale of, your partnership interest was due to portfolio assets (stocks, bonds, REITs, REMICs), then that portion of the income or gain may be treated as portfolio income rather than as income from a passive activity. Thus, the portfolio income of a passive activity is taken into account separately as portfolio, and not as passive, income.

> **EXAMPLE:** A passive investor is a 50 percent partner in a partnership that earns $10,000 in passive real estate income and $8,400 in interest on a stock mutual fund it has invested in. He will be treated as if he realized $5,000 in passive income (50% interest × $10,000) and $4,200 in portfolio income (50% interest × $8,400) for purposes of applying the passive loss limitation rules.

Treating Certain Portfolio Income as Active Income. Portfolio income (e.g., interest) will not be treated as portfolio income if it is earned in your ordinary business activities. For example, interest earned on a commodity trader's cash balances is arguably integrally related to his business, which requires the occasional maintenance of large cash balances.

Limited Use of Certain Losses from Active Real Estate Rentals.
Under the Clinton Act, earnings or losses on an interest in real estate
rental activities are not considered to be from an active business, except for certain active real estate professionals. This means that losses
from real estate investments will generally only be available to offset
income from other passive investments (for example, from limited
partnership interests). Real estate losses generally will not be available
to offset wage or active business income. An important exception to
this rule enables many investors to treat some real estate rental losses
as deductible, losses subject to certain limitations, by the passive activity rules. Thus, these losses can be used to offset income from wages
or active businesses in which you materially participate.

This exception is intended to enable moderate-income taxpayers
who hold real estate as a means of providing for their financial security (the investment serves significant nontax purposes), and for which
they have significant responsibility, to deduct losses against other income and receive the tax benefits.

To qualify for this real estate loss exception, you must meet both an
income and a participation test. Your modified adjusted gross income
must be less than $150,000. The modifications to your adjusted gross
income include adjustments for individual retirement account contributions, alimony payments, and taxable Social Security benefits (see
Chapter 18). The Clinton Tax Act changes that increase the amount
of taxable Social Security could thus have the additional negative effect of reducing a senior citizen's tax benefit on rental real estate investments as well. The $25,000 allowance is allowed in full for
taxpayers with modified adjusted gross income up to $100,000. For
adjusted gross income above this amount, the $25,000 allowance is
phased out at the rate of 50 cents for each additional dollar of income.

> **EXAMPLE:** A stockbroker with adjusted gross income of $120,000
> has $32,000 of passive losses (in excess of any other passive income) that
> would qualify for the special allowance. How much can he use? First, the
> loss in excess of $25,000 is in excess of the allowance. Thus, $7,000
> ($32,000 − $25,000) can immediately be treated as a loss carryover
> ("suspended loss") to future years (see the earlier discussion). Next, a
> portion of his allowance will have to be reduced because his income ex-
> ceeds the $100,000 mark. The $20,000 excess will reduce his allowance
> at a rate of 50 cents for each dollar, or $10,000. Thus, he can use only
> $15,000 of his passive real estate losses currently to offset income from
> his wages as a stockbroker.

The second requirement to qualify for this allowance is that you must actively participate in the real estate rental activity. To actively participate, you must meet the following requirements:

- You must own at least 10 percent of the value of the activity (there cannot be more than 10 investors).
- The tax losses cannot be subject to any other limitations under different tax provisions.
- You must make management decisions or arrange for others to provide services (such as repairs) in a significant and bona fide sense. For example, you could approve new tenants, decide on rental terms, or approve repairs of large capital improvements. You do not have to do these directly. You can hire a rental agent and repairpersons. This standard is less than the material participation standard previously discussed. It is not necessary for you to be regularly, continuously, and substantially involved to meet this active participation test.
- The management decisions you make must not be contrived to meet this active participation test. For example, if the promoter of the investment really takes care of all the management decisions and sends you reports where you merely check off boxes to make decisions, this will not be enough.

Using Tax Credits to Offset Limited Amounts of Active Income. Income tax credits generated by a passive activity can generally be used only to reduce your regular income tax liability attributable to passive activities. They cannot be used to offset your alternative minimum tax liability (see Chapter 4). Tax credits can include, among others, the tax credits for investments in rehabilitation of old or historic buildings, research and development, and the jobs credit. This general rule has several exceptions.

A special rule applies to the limitation on tax credits earned on investments in rehabilitating old or historic buildings. The tax credits are converted to deduction equivalents to determine the amount of credits allowable under the $25,000 real estate active participation exception. With a 39.6 percent tax rate, the deduction equivalent of a $25,000 deduction is $9,900. This is higher than under prior law as a result of this increase in the marginal tax rate. The phaseout range of modified adjusted gross income for loss of this benefit is increased to begin at $200,000 and end at $250,000.

For purposes of the low-income housing credit, the active participation test is waived and the income phaseouts do not apply (see Chapter 10).

Where a credit cannot be used currently, it is suspended and carried forward to be used in future tax years subject to the same limitations.

CONCLUSION

The Clinton Tax Act has at least brought some reasonableness to the application of the passive loss rules by minimizing their impact on active real estate investors. However, the passive loss rules remain a confusing array of detailed traps for the unwary investor and must be considered in planning any investment and business transaction. The increased tax rates of the Clinton Tax Act make the cost of improper planning even more expensive than under prior law.

13 Depreciation Planning for Commercial Real Estate

The Clinton Tax Act made several important changes to the depreciation and related deduction rules affecting real estate. Some of the direct changes include increasing the amount of personal property that can be deducted in the year of purchase (elective expensing) and lengthening the depreciation period for commercial real estate to 39 years. Numerous indirect changes will have a significant effect on depreciation planning, however. This chapter will analyze these important ancillary changes and how they affect depreciation planning.

EXPENSING DEDUCTION

The Clinton Tax Act increases from $10,000 to $17,500 the amount of personal property (equipment, removable fixtures, etc.) that can be deducted immediately in the year acquired instead of being depreciated over the regular depreciation period (see the in-depth discussion of this change in Chapter 17). Special expensing rules with higher dollar limits are available for businesses located in empowerment zones ($37,500; see Chapter 15).

LONGER DEPRECIATION PERIOD FOR COMMERCIAL REAL ESTATE

New Depreciation Period

The Clinton Tax Act increased the depreciation period for commercial (nonresidential) real estate from 31.5 years to 39 years. This change is grossly unfair to the real estate industry because Congress ignored the entire conceptual framework for the Accelerated Cost Recovery System (ACRS and later MACRS). ACRS was first advocated for real estate for the same reasons the new 15-year amortization period was proposed for intangibles; namely, to simplify tax reporting and to minimize factual disputes with the IRS. Prior to 1981, real estate investors would use what was called component depreciation for their buildings. Electrical wiring would be depreciated over its useful life, say 8 years. The roof would be depreciated over its useful life, say 10 years. The building shell would be depreciated over its useful life, say 33 years, and so on. The result was in keeping with the economic concept of depreciation. However, complex and expensive disputes arose between the IRS and taxpayers over depreciation periods and cost allocations to the various components. So Congress simplified the matter by introducing a composite rate for the entire building of 15 years. This was raised in later years to 18 years, then 19 years, then 31.5 years, and now 39 years. The problem is most of the components of a building, even from the tough stance the IRS used to take on audits, have a lifetime nowhere near 39 years. The result is unreasonable.

What has occurred is the same unfair result that is plaguing small business, investors, and others in so many aspects of the tax law. Congress eliminated many deductions and tax benefits to simplify the tax laws. Then it raised the rates, depreciation periods, and other costs resulting in much more burdensome tax rates than in the past. This is why the new 39.6 percent rate may be more costly for many taxpayers than the 50 percent rates that existed in the early 1980s. The stated marginal tax rate is lower than the 50 percent rate, but with so many deductions limited, it may actually be more costly.

Effective Date of New Rule

The effective date of this new rule is generally for property that was placed in service after May 13, 1993, unless it was purchased or built under a written contract that was binding before May 13, 1993, and placed in service before 1994. "Placed in service" is defined as the date the property is in a condition or state of readiness for its assigned function. This does not necessarily mean that the equipment in a factory must be producing widgets for the building to be placed in service. But the building must be in a condition of readiness for the equipment to be installed.

TIP: Even if an entire building cannot be placed in service before the effective date of the new longer depreciation periods, perhaps a wing or other portion of the building can be completed and placed in service to qualify for the shorter depreciation periods. This may be accomplished by concentrating construction efforts on selected portions until completion.

LEASEHOLD IMPROVEMENTS ARE SUBJECT TO ABSURD DEPRECIATION RESULTS

Problems for Tenants Created by the Clinton Tax Act Depreciation Rules

The Clinton Tax Act further exacerbates a ridiculous depreciation result affecting depreciation deductions that a tenant can claim on leasehold improvements. Since the Tax Reform Act of 1986, leasehold improvements have been required to be depreciated over the applicable modified accelerated cost recovery system (MACRS) depreciation periods. For real property structural improvements, this is a 27.5-year period for residential real estate, 39-year period for nonresidential real estate after the Clinton Tax Act, or a 40-year period in certain specified instances such as for purposes of the alternative minimum tax. Both landlord and tenant must depreciate their improvements over these applicable MACRS periods. The only distinction between the depreciation rules applicable to landlords and tenants is that when a tenant vacates the leased premises and the lease terminates, the tenant will obtain a loss deduction for the remaining undepreciated costs of the leasehold improvements at that date. A landlord who owns the improvements at the termination of the tenant's lease may have to continue depreciating them over the remainder of the applicable MACRS recovery period. This result is generally required even after the tenant has vacated the premises. The economic results of this for a tenant can often be absurd, as illustrated in the following example.

> **EXAMPLE:**   A tenant opens a shoe store and installs $100,000 of real property leasehold improvements—walls, flooring, and so forth. The lease is for 5 years. The tenant may renew the lease but is certain that, even if he does, the decor of the store will have to be updated to remain competitive, which would mean replacing the $100,000 of improvements. The improvements, based on both the useful life and the lease term could logically be only 5 years. The tenant, however, must depreciate the $100,000 of improvements over the 39-year MACRS period. Depreciation deductions will be a mere $2,564 in each year, instead of the expected $20,000 ($100,000/5 years).

Although an important stated objective of the Clinton Tax Act was to help the economy by stimulating the growth of small businesses and jobs, especially in targeted development areas, this depreciation result will work against that goal by having a significant and adverse consequence to these very businesses.

> **TIP:** The depreciation tax benefits available to the tenant for leasehold improvements can still be greater, on a net present value basis, than the tax benefits available to the landlord from depreciating the real property leasehold improvements. This can occur because the tenant may deduct any undepreciated costs in the final lease year whereas the landlord may still be required to continue depreciating the same costs.

Calculation of Depreciation Benefits for Leasehold Improvements

Where the landlord is entitled to claim depreciation on the leasehold improvements, the applicable depreciation conventions are simply applied to the landlord's adjusted tax basis in the asset. For real property, recovery deductions are calculated on the straight-line method. The recovery period for nonresidential commercial property is 39 years. Depreciation is calculated using a midmonth convention. This means that any real property improvements placed in service during a month are treated as if they were placed in service at the midpoint of the month.

> **EXAMPLE:** Landlord installs $100,000 of real property leasehold improvements on January 1, 1995. This amount is depreciated over a 39-year period. Since the midmonth convention applies, only one-half month of depreciation is allowed for January 1995. Thus, the depreciation deduction in each year is:
>
> $$\frac{\$100,000 \text{ adjusted basis}}{39 \text{ years}} = \$2,564$$
>
> For 1995, only 11.5 month's depreciation is allowed, so the regular annual deduction must be prorated to reflect this:
>
> $$\$2,564 \text{ annual depreciation} \times (11\frac{1}{2} \text{ months}/12 \text{ months}) = \$2,457$$

Where the tenant is entitled to depreciate the improvements, the calculation is identical to that of the landlord in all but the last year of the lease. The tax law provides that in the case of any improvements made on leased property subject to the MACRS rules, the tenant must use the same depreciation method as the landlord. But in many situations, the lease will be shorter, often significantly, than the MACRS recovery period. In these cases, the actual tax benefits to the tenant will differ from those obtained by the landlord since the tenant will often be entitled to deduct any remaining undepreciated costs following the last year in the lease.

Where the lease term is less than the applicable MACRS recovery period, the tax benefit to be realized by the tenant will consist of two components: (1) the present value of the stream of annual tax benefits generated by the annual depreciation deductions, and (2) the present value of the tax benefit of the recovery (or loss) deduction in the final lease year of any remaining unrecovered leasehold improvement costs. A simple example will illustrate this calculation.

EXAMPLE: Assume the same facts as in the preceding example. The tenant will be entitled to the following tax benefits for each of the 5 years of its lease:

Annual deductions	$ 2,564
Tax rate	39.6%
Annual tax benefit	$ 1,015
Present value of tax benefit for 5 years @ 8 percent	$ 3,777 (A)

The second component of the tenant's tax benefit is its deduction at the termination of the lease of any remaining unrecovered cost of the $100,000 leasehold improvements. This is calculated as follows:

Original basis	$100,000
Less depreciation in years 1–5 (2,564 × 5)	12,820
Unrecovered basis	$ 87,180
Deduction in final year	$ 87,180
Tax rate	39.6%
Tax benefit	$ 34,523
Present value of tax benefit from 5 years @ 8% [$34,523 × .6806]	$ 23,496 (B)
Total present value of tax benefits (A) + (B)	$27,273

When a tenant installs and owns real property leasehold improvements, the tax treatment is a mandatory depreciation (recovery) over 39-year MACRS period. If the tenant is subject to the alternative minimum tax or other restrictions that make the alternative depreciation system (ADS) applicable, a 40-year recovery period is required. The only relief from this treatment is that a tenant is likely to qualify for an immediate deduction of any undepreciated value of structural improvements left by the tenant when the lease terminates. This loss deduction should only be available, however, where the tenant cannot salvage and remove the improvements from the leasehold premises. In many instances, a lease clause automatically vesting title in the improvements with the landlord on the termination of the lease will meet this prerequisite for the tenant's loss deduction.

An important ancillary issue where a tenant constructs leasehold improvements is whether the landlord will have any negative tax consequences as a result of such improvements. Generally, when the tenant makes improvements to property leased from the landlord, such as the build-out of a shell provided to a shopping center tenant, or the construction of a building on the land by a single user net lease tenant, the landlord will not have to recognize income equal to the value of such improvements.

Where the lease is structured so that the tenant owns the leasehold improvements, the lease will also provide, in many cases, that at the termination of the lease those improvements will inure to the landlord. While landlords may realize an economic benefit from receiving the tenant's improvements at the end of the lease term, the tax laws specifically exclude this value from taxation. This represents a potentially valuable tax benefit for landlords. This provision, however, also prevents the landlord from increasing the adjusted tax basis in the property by the value of leasehold improvements received. Since the landlord recognizes no income and has not paid for the property, he or she has no basis in such property. Thus, the landlord will not be allowed to depreciate leasehold improvements obtained in this manner.

> **EXAMPLE:** Landlord and tenant enter into a 5-year nonrenewable lease. Tenant constructs real property leasehold improvements worth $300,000, and depreciates the improvements over the 39-year depreciation period. In year 6, tenant vacates the leasehold, claiming a loss deduction for the undepreciated balance of the improvement costs. When tenant vacates the premises, the improvements, which then have a fair market value of $250,000, revert to landlord. Landlord recognizes no taxable income on this reversion. He cannot, however, increase his adjusted tax basis in the property to reflect the value of those improvements. Therefore, landlord obtains ownership of the improvements at no tax cost but cannot depreciate them.

This situation can provide favorable tax results for both the landlord and the tenant. The tenant was able to completely deduct (via recovery deductions in each year of the lease term, and a loss deduction at lease termination) the improvements by the end of a lease period.

Had the landlord made the improvements, he might have had to depreciate many of them over a 39- or 40-year period. Through arranging for the tenant to initially own the leasehold improvements, the landlord may obtain the use and benefit of the improvements for most of their useful life (i.e., from year 6 onward) at no tax cost, while still preserving a more rapid deduction and more substantial tax benefits (albeit by the tenant).

> **TIP:** To support this tax-free reversion, lease clauses should be carefully drafted to avoid any implication that either the initial construction of the improvement or its reversion to the landlord at the termination of the lease is intended as a rent substitute. Supportable arm's-length lease provisions must be used.

Landlords often provide tenants with cash allowances to be used in constructing leasehold improvements. The lease agreement and surrounding circumstances will determine the tax treatment of these payments. Tenant allowances were often structured so that the landlord would own the improvements. The problem with this approach is that the landlord will be required to depreciate (recover) the leasehold improvements over 39 or 40 years. In many instances, it is more favorable for the tenant to own and depreciate the improvements; at the end of a short lease term, the tenant will then be able to depreciate undepreciated costs on vacating the premises. To accomplish this, the lease could be structured so that the tenant rather than the landlord owns the improvements, as discussed earlier. For this approach to be viable, however, the improvements themselves cannot result in current rental income to the landlord. For example, if the landlord gives the tenant an allowance toward the construction of leasehold improvements by reducing the rent due, the landlord may be taxed on the full amount of rent. The landlord would then own the improvements made and could claim depreciation deductions on them.

ANCILLARY TAX CHANGES THAT AFFECT DEPRECIATION PLANNING

The complexities of the Clinton Tax Act assure that numerous ancillary changes will affect the planning for depreciation. Some of these include the following:

- The increase in the marginal tax rate from 31 percent to 39.6 percent makes depreciation deductions more valuable.
- The exemption of certain active real estate investors from the restrictions of the passive loss rules makes the benefits of depreciation planning useful for the first time since the 1986 Tax Reform Act.
- The Clinton Tax Act has made several changes to the alternative minimum tax (AMT) that affect real estate depreciation planning. For AMT purposes, depreciation is calculated applying the alternative depreciation system (ADS) rather than the regular modified accelerated cost recovery system (MACRS) provisions.

TIPS: When the new 39-year depreciation period is effective, there will only be a nominal difference between the 39-year regular tax depreciation deduction and the 40-year depreciation period required for purposes of the AMT. The election to use the 40-year depreciation period for regular tax purposes will be advantageous in many situations since it will eliminate the need to use two sets of books for regular tax and AMT depreciation deductions at what for many taxpayers will be a nominal additional tax cost.

The increase in the rates of the AMT makes planning for the depreciation implications of that tax a more important consideration for individual taxpayers.

- Corporations benefit from some simplification. The Clinton Tax Act eliminates, effective for assets placed in service after 1993, the requirement that a corporation calculate its depreciation deduction for purposes of the adjusted current earnings (ACE) preference (adjustment) item by using straight-line depreciation over the asset's class life (see Chapter 17).

PLANNING IDEAS TO MAXIMIZE DEPRECIATION TAX BENEFITS

The new post-Clinton Tax Act environment creates new incentives to use time-proven depreciation planning techniques to increase depreciation deductions to take advantage of the higher tax rates and the relief afforded professional real estate investors. Some of these include the following:

Squeeze Depreciation Deductions from Land

Every real estate investor knows you cannot depreciate land. While this is generally true, some land costs can qualify for depreciation. Careful planning can net you a much better depreciation deduction from your investment.

The concept underlying depreciation is that the expenditure you make for an asset, such as a building, will provide you benefit for a long time. Therefore, it does not make much sense to let you write off the cost of the asset or building in the year you pay for it. The building, however, will not last forever. At some future time, the building will be worn out by use and the effects of the elements. The costs you spent in acquiring the building should then be written off over this period of usefulness. Now take a look at land. Land, just like the building, will provide you with value for a long time. Therefore, just like the building, the amount you pay to acquire land shouldn't be deductible in the year you pay it. The costs associated with acquiring land are therefore added to your basis or investment in the land (they are capitalized). Land, unlike buildings, will theoretically be usable forever. It is not affected by use or the elements (in most cases anyhow). When your building is worn out and useless, you can tear it down and start again with a new building on the same land.

Based on the preceding generalizations, land is not considered to be a wasting asset for tax purposes and therefore generally cannot be depreciated. Some costs associated with land improvements can in certain instances, qualify for depreciation write-offs. The key planning idea is to identify and segregate these depreciable land improvement costs from other land costs.

Some land improvement costs are never depreciable. The costs associated with general clearing and grading of land are considered to be integrally related to the land itself and can never be deducted. These costs must be added to your investment in the land. Their only tax benefit will be to reduce the amount of any gain you may have to report when you ultimately sell the land.

The only land improvement costs that qualify for depreciation are the costs of improvements so closely associated with the development of a building that the improvements will have to be abandoned contemporaneously with the abandonment of the building. The theory is simple. These land costs are so integrally related to your building that they will become valueless when the building itself becomes worthless or is abandoned. These costs are then depreciated in the same manner

154 COMMERCIAL REAL ESTATE INVESTMENTS

as the construction costs for your building—27.5 years for residential construction and 39 years for commercial construction. Certain improvements may qualify for more rapid deductions.

This same theory supports the depreciation of certain landscaping located near, and integrally associated with, a building. Examples of qualifying land improvement costs include the construction of an artificial berm and moat surrounding a building. Berms designed to visually blend the building into the surrounding land should qualify since they can only have a use with the specific building they were designed for. The costs of digging foundations should qualify. Costs of backfilling and grading to lay sewer pipe may qualify. Access and utility roads and related improvement costs in certain industrial parks may qualify. Excavation and grading so closely associated with, and uniquely related to, the facility being constructed may qualify.

Identify the Maximum Amount of Personal, Rather than Real, Property

The more property you can treat as personal property (furniture, equipment, planters, certain plumbing hookups, etc.), rather than as real property (buildings and their structural components), the more rapid your depreciation deductions will be. Personal property can often be depreciated over a 5- or 7-year period using accelerated depreciation methods (calculations that push more of the depreciation deductions into earlier years). This contrasts favorably with commercial real property (buildings, improvements, etc.) that must be written off over 39 years.

> **TIP:** The Clinton Tax Act has made this type of depreciation planning (which was common prior to the Tax Reform Act of 1986) very desirable. The increase in marginal tax rates makes the rapid depreciation deductions available for personal property more valuable on a present value basis than before the changes. By increasing the depreciation period for commercial real estate from 31.5 to 39 years, the Clinton Tax Act has significantly increased the cost of not undertaking this planning. Finally, the increased amount of property that can be deducted currently under the elective expensing provision of Code Section 179 further enhances the benefits of this type of planning.

In general, for property to qualify as personal property (and thus be depreciable over a 5-, or perhaps 7-year period rather than the

39-year period applicable to real property), it must meet the following two tests:

1. It must be movable (e.g., a bookcase anchored with screws) rather than inherently permanent (e.g., built-in furniture that can't be removed without destroying it).

2. It must be more in the nature of an accessory to the conduct of your business (special plumbing hookups and additional exhaust fans in a restaurant) rather than a structural component of the building (a roof) that relates directly to the building's ability to serve as a building (it couldn't function as a building without the roof).

The following checklist will provide guidance to determine whether property can be considered movable:

- Is the property permanently attached to the building or can it readily be detached and moved? Removable hooks, adhesives, and screws will be more indicative of movability than cement and permanent adhesives.
- How difficult is it to move the property in question? Will it take a significant amount of time? Are special permits, personnel, or equipment necessary to move it, or can your regular maintenance people move it?
- How much damage will be done to the property being moved and to the building it is being moved from (e.g., built-in furniture)?
- Has the particular property or similar property been moved in the past?

When constructing a building or renovating an existing building, keep this planning idea in mind at the design and planning stage. In some situations, it may be possible to redesign certain property to make it qualify. For example, if the plans called for expensive imported tile cemented to the lobby floor of the building, consider whether a nonpermanent cement could be used and whether that would be sufficient to enable the property to qualify as personal property. Carpeting may be another viable option if it fits in with the design of the lobby. Rather than permanently gluing or nailing expensive paneling to the subwall consider fastening it with screws that can readily be removed. The additional labor costs to install with screws should be compared with the additional tax benefits you may obtain. Based on the earlier examples, it could be a very favorable payoff.

The following are examples of different types of property that may qualify for more favorable depreciation deductions:

- *Department Store.* Decorative lighting fixtures, display racks, carpeting, movable partitions, escalators, removable paneling, certain planters, curtains, hookups for computers in the credit collection department.

- *Supermarket, Restaurant.* Counters, display racks, waste compactors, signs, certain exhaust fans, certain plumbing and electrical hookups, kitchen equipment, refrigeration equipment (including pumps, condensers, and similar equipment), trash bins.

- *Office Building.* Furniture, equipment, removable files and bookshelves, removable paneling, carpeting, decorative light fixtures, certain hookups electrical connections, and possibly a special raised floor to accommodate computer equipment. If you're dealing with a "smart" office building, be alert for certain portions of security systems, special telephone and other equipment and their support systems, which may qualify. Your building may have a large portion of costs that qualify for this more favorable tax treatment. (In many cases, these components may be so integrated into the building that the IRS could argue they do not qualify. The best approach is to begin reviewing the matter with your tax adviser during the planning stage.)

CONCLUSION

The increase in tax rates and lengthening of depreciation periods for commercial real estate relative to depreciation periods for other types of assets create tremendous incentives for real estate investors to engage in the complex depreciation planning strategies that were common after the Economic Recovery Tax Act of 1981. Most importantly for active real estate investors, the easing of the passive loss rules will permit the tax benefits of this type of planning to be fully realized for the first time since the Tax Reform Act of 1986 introduced passive loss limitations.

PART FIVE

CLOSELY HELD
BUSINESS
INVESTMENTS

14 How the Clinton Tax Law Affects Business

The Clinton Tax Act had as stated goals improving the economy, creating new jobs, and helping certain targeted areas. The changes were complex, often having unexpected indirect effects on the structure and operations of business. In some instances, the changes will be quite costly. In other situations, they present new planning opportunities. However, whether the economic and social goals of some of the changes will be achieved will take years to determine. As an aid in understanding these changes, the following overview discusses how the most common types of business organizations are affected.

Many different types of entities can be used to conduct business: S corporations, C corporations, limited liability companies (LLCs), and partnerships are the most common. Nontax characteristics of the different types of entities are important to consider. Perhaps one of the most important nontax factors is the limitation of liability.

When starting a business, the investor must consider a number of tax issues. The first issue is, What form of organization should be used? The differences can be significant and can affect the tax consequences on forming the new business entity, transferring property to the entity, operating the entity, and making distributions to the investors.

Because each form of operation has its own tax, legal, and other implications, in many cases, the choice of entity can be very important. The Clinton Tax Act changes have affected the tax consequences of every type of business entity. The tax effects, particularly of the indirect changes that did not receive much media attention when the act was passed, are so substantial that they could cause you to change the form of your business. The following sections provide a general overview of the tax, legal, and economic characteristics of each entity, highlighting the consequences of the Clinton Tax Act.

C CORPORATIONS

What Is a Corporation?

Corporations are a legal entity organized under the laws of a specific state by filing articles of incorporation (a charter) that specify the corporate name, purpose, duration, and so forth. In addition, corporations must usually comply with ongoing requirements, which may include annual tax or information report filings, amendment of its charter if certain changes are made, and maintenance of directors. Corporations have at least three of the following four characteristics:

1. *Limited Liability.* The shareholders can generally only be held accountable up to their investment. For example, if a major lawsuit is settled, the shareholder's, personal assets unlike those of the partner in a general partnership, will not be at risk.
2. *Centralized Management.* A selected number of individuals will be delegated the authority to manage the daily affairs of the corporation.
3. *Continuity of Life.* The corporation, if state law and its charter permit, can be organized with a perpetual duration.
4. *Free transferability of interests.* This characteristic may enable a shareholder to more readily transfer interest in the entity to another than would be the case with an interest in a partnership. The ease of transferability, however, will depend on what restrictions may have been placed in shareholder agreements or other corporate documents.

How Is C Corporation Income Determined?

Profits are computed based on the various tax elections (depreciation method, etc.) and tax year determined at the corporate level (i.e., independent of the tax elections and tax year of its owners). When these net of tax profits are ultimately distributed to the corporation's shareholders as dividends, the shareholders must pay tax on the amounts received. This scenario results in two layers of taxation—double taxation. This can be rather unfavorable when compared with the result obtained with a partnership or S corporation (discussed later in this chapter). These latter two entities generally do not pay a tax at the entity level. Rather their earnings are distributed to their owners who pay any tax due.

Another result follows from this corporate tax scheme. If the corporation is subject to its own tax system, then if the corporation realizes losses, the shareholders cannot benefit from these losses. Again, this can compare rather unfavorably with the result available with a partnership, LLC, or S corporation. These latter entities can pass any tax losses they realize through to their owners.

Unlike a partnership, LLC, or an S corporation, the profits and losses are not passed through to the shareholders. As a result, where tax losses are anticipated during early start-up years, the C corporation may not be the best alternative. For example, a newly formed retail business could elect to be taxed as an S corporation, pass through losses in early years, and then terminate its S corporation election and be taxed as a regular, or C corporation in later profitable years. However, where a C corporation incurs losses, these losses can be carried back to the three preceding tax years, or carried forward to the next 15 successive tax years. The result is that the losses of a C corporation may not be wasted since they will offset future income. The Clinton Tax Act, however, has tipped the scales further against C corporations in this regard. Now that individual income tax rates can exceed corporate tax rates, the deduction of start-up (or other) losses on the individual tax returns of the shareholders will provide a more valuable tax break than the tax break the corporation could earn in later years by deducting a tax loss carryforward.

Corporations are taxed at rates from 15 percent to a 35 percent maximum rate following the Clinton Tax Act. The maximum rate had been 34 percent. Where a corporation distributes its earnings as dividends, the dividends are taxed again to the shareholders, resulting in a double taxation. This will occur so long as the corporation has earnings and profits from which the dividends are distributed. The earnings and profits tax law calculation is analogous to retained earnings on a financial statement.

Shareholder Compensation

For many closely held corporations, the shareholders are likely to be active principals in the business. Where this occurs, much of the income of the corporation will be distributed as salaries and bonuses. These are deductible by the corporation and taxable to the individual as income. This type of planning can minimize an important advantage often cited for flow-through entities. The Internal Revenue Service (IRS), however, can challenge these salaries under the doctrines of unreasonable compensation or assignment of income. Thus, even a regular corporation can avoid any corporate level tax. The desire to avoid corporate level tax, however, has lessened because the change in tax rate structure has resulted in higher individual than corporate rates.

Payment of Alternative Minimum Tax by C Corporations

Corporations can also be subject to an alternative minimum tax (AMT). The corporate minimum tax requires corporations to increase their taxable income by various tax preference items, make certain other adjustments, and multiply the result by a specified tax rate. A reduction is permitted for the AMT foreign tax credit. Corporations also receive an exemption similar in concept to the exemption given individual taxpayers subject to the AMT.

Double Taxation of C Corporation Earnings

The risk of double taxation on the sale of corporate assets can have a tremendous impact on the net economic earnings a shareholder can realize. Both the corporation and its shareholders can be subject to a tax where the corporation distributes its assets or liquidates. With limited exceptions, gain and loss must be recognized where the corporation distributes assets to its shareholders, as if the assets had been sold to those shareholders at their fair market value. Corporations also recognize gain on nonliquidating distributions of appreciated property.

Shareholders face two types of taxes on their stock in a C corporation: taxation on dividend distributions and the tax on the sale of the shares. In most instances, any sale will be controlled by the buyout provisions contained in the shareholders' agreement. The sale of stock should qualify as a capital gain. Similarly, capital gain may be realized where the corporation redeems a shareholder's stock.

Provision of Favorable Benefits on Investment Losses

Where a loss is realized on the sale of the stock, it may be subject to the limitations on deductions of capital losses. However, many close corporations will meet the requirements of special Code Section 1244, which can provide an ordinary, rather than capital, loss deduction on the sale of qualifying stock.

> **TIP:** Code Section 1244 become more valuable as a result of the increased tax rates under the Clinton Tax Act. An ordinary loss of $100,000 on an unsuccessful business venture would have generated only $31,000 tax savings prior to the Clinton Tax Act. Now it will provide as much as $39,600 tax savings, or even more in many instances.

To qualify for this benefit, the corporation in which you invest must be a qualifying small business. The following requirements must be met:

- The money and property contributed to form the corporation must not exceed $1 million. This requirement must also include all stock issued by the corporation.
- The stock must be issued in exchange for cash and property (not other stock or securities).
- The corporation must be an operating company. During the previous 5 years of operations, more than 50 percent of the gross revenue of the corporation must have come from sources other than royalties, dividends, interest, rent, annuities, and gains on the sale of securities.
- The stock does not have to be voting stock, but it must be stock. Bonds do not qualify. Preferred stock issued after July 18, 1984, may qualify.
- The corporation must be a U.S. (domestic) corporation.

If you meet the preceding requirements and realize a loss on your investment, you can deduct it as an ordinary loss. This is beneficial because stock is normally a capital asset for anyone other than a broker or dealer in stocks. If this rule were not available, your loss on such an investment could only be deducted against other capital losses, and only $3,000 could be deducted against ordinary income. The maximum amount that can qualify for this favorable treatment is $50,000, or $100,000 if you file a joint income tax return with your spouse.

> **TIP:** Code Section 1244 permits you to deduct as an ordinary loss against any of your income, the loss on the sale, exchange, or worthlessness of qualifying small business stock. Although this sounds almost the same as the new Clinton Tax Act rules excluding gain from the sale of qualifying small business stock under new Internal Revenue Code Section 1202, the rules, requirements, and results of these two provisions are different. The new Section 1202 provision permits you to exclude

gain on sales of qualifying stock. The old Section 1244 permits a loss deduction without limitations on qualifying stock. Unfortunately, in spite of the similar sounding names, the requirements for each are different. If you invest in a new business with the hope of making a large gain that will qualify for the new Code Section 1202 exclusion and the business venture is not successful, you may not necessarily qualify for the favorable deduction under Code Section 1244. You must therefore plan your investment to meet both Code Sections independently if you wish both benefits. The requirements for the new Code Section 1202 provision for excluding gain are explained later in Chapter 15.

Higher Corporate Tax Rates after the Clinton Tax Act

One of the more talked-about changes of the Clinton Tax Act was the increase in corporate tax rates. The rate increase was to have been a maximum 36 percent for corporations with revenues above $10 million. However, compromise negotiations in concluding the tax act resulted in an increase of only 1 percent to a top corporate tax rate of 35 percent on taxable income above $10 million. The new rate is retroactive in that it applies to tax years beginning after 1992. The 34 percent rate will continue to apply on corporate taxable income below this level. On taxable income under $75,000, lower rates will apply. The $100,000 tax benefit of the 34 percent lower tax rate that applies on income of up to $10 million, however, is recaptured via a surtax on taxable income between $15 million and $18,333,333. The surtax is assessed at a 38 percent tax rate. The highest marginal corporate tax rate can be 38 percent in this limited income range. Thus, on income above $18,333,333, corporations are subject to a flat tax of 35 percent on all income, including long-term capital gains. The result is a zig-zag of the marginal corporate tax rate that can make planning to avoid a higher rate bracket impossible. Table 14.1 shows the new rates.

When evaluating the actual corporate tax rates, keep in mind that most businesses are not corporations; they are run as sole proprietorships. Of those businesses that are corporations, a very large proportion, especially of closely held and start-up businesses (the ones the President continually noted are responsible for the most job creation) are organized as S corporations. S corporations generally pass their income and deductions through to their shareholders, who report their allocable share of income and deductions on their personal tax returns. The result is that the real tax on many businesses is not the 1 percent increase in the corporate rate. Rather, it is the increase of 39.6

TABLE 14.1   Corporate Tax Rates

Corporate Taxable Income—From Over	Corporate Taxable Income—Up To	New Effective Tax Rate (%)
0	$ 50,000	15
$ 50,000	75,000	25
75,000	100,000	34
100,000	335,000	39
335,000	10,000,000	34
10,000,000	15,000,000	35
15,000,000	18,333,333	38
18,333,333	+	35

percent marginal tax rate affecting individuals that most businesses will really pay.

Corporations often have fiscal tax years. These are 12-month periods other than January 1 to December 31. For these corporations, the changes in the corporate tax rate effective January 1, 1993, will result in a portion of their tax year being taxed at the old rates and a portion being taxed at the new higher, post-Clinton Tax Act rates. The result will be a dual calculation and blending of tax rates to achieve the proper allocation.

> **TIP:** Some corporations with fiscal tax years may have to file an amended tax return to reflect the tax due (at the higher rate) for a portion of 1993 included in their fiscal 1992 year tax return.

As with individuals, some leniency is provided where a corporation underpays its estimated tax for periods prior to March 16, 1994, as a result of the retroactive tax increase.

> **TIP:** Corporations can be affected by more than just the actual tax increase. Many corporations that prepare financial statements in accordance with generally accepted accounting procedures could face another adverse effect. Statement of Financial Accounting Standards Number 109 (FAS 109) "Accounting for Income Taxes" will cause many corporations to increase the reserve on their financial statements immediately to reflect the higher rate of tax that will be payable, in theory, on certain tax reserves. This is recorded as an income tax expense in the year of the change. Capital-intensive businesses are most likely to be affected by this reporting requirement. Investors analyzing earnings reported by publicly held corporations should factor this affect into their evaluation.

Corporate Tax-Planning Considerations after the Clinton Tax Act

The increase in corporate tax rates will increase slightly the incentive to benefit from traditional types of tax-planning strategies. The traditional tax-planning strategies for corporations will continue to be used, but the mere 1 percent increase will not likely affect tax planning significantly. The reward for successful planning will just be greater than under prior law for the most profitable companies which are subject to the new highest rate. More complex planning issues affect many closely held corporations, such as personal service corporations (discussed in the following section).

Tax traps that had haunted corporations before the Tax Reform Act of 1986 changed the historical relationship between individual and corporate tax rates (making corporate rates higher than individual rates) are again a concern; the Clinton Tax Act restored the historical relationship of individual tax rates exceeding corporate tax rates. One of these traps, the accumulated earnings tax, is explained later in this chapter.

The implications of the new tax rates on financial statement disclosures and reporting, especially relative to FAS 109, should also be considered.

Increased Tax Rate on Personal Service Corporations

The tax rate on personal service corporations is increased from 34 percent to 35 percent. A personal service corporation is a corporation whose principal activity is the performance of personal services that are substantially performed by owner-employees in the fields of health, law, engineering, architecture, accounting, actuarial science, performing arts, or consulting. Owner-employees are persons who own more than 10 percent of the stock of the corporation. Personal service corporations do not have the benefit of paying tax at the graduated corporate tax rates, which range from a low of 15 percent to the new high rate of 35 percent. All their income is taxed at a flat 35 percent rate.

Most personal service corporations avoid most or all of this high corporate tax by electing taxation as an S corporation so that all income is passed through to the owner-employees, or by paying all of the corporation's taxable income out as salaries to the owner-employees. The Clinton Tax Act, however, will affect this strategy.

TIP: One of the most important aspects of the tax rate affecting personal service corporations is the relationship of the highest corporate tax rate the personal service corporation will have to pay and the highest personal tax rate the owner-employees will have to pay. Since the personal tax rate can reach 39.6 percent, it is nearly 5 percent higher than the corporate rate. Where monies must be retained in the corporation to fund corporate operations, it may be cheaper to have the corporation pay the tax at a 35 percent rate, rather than distribute the monies to the owner-employees as compensation if it will be taxed at the 39.6 percent maximum rate. The Clinton Tax Act adds another twist to this analysis. The health care portion of the Social Security tax of 1.45 percent tax was assessed on wages up to $135,000. It will now be assessed without any cap on wages. Both the corporation and the owner-employee will bear this tax so that the total cost is really 2.9 percent. Thus, for highly compensated owner-employees, the incremental tax cost of paying out additional compensation to an owner-employee will be 42.5 percent (39.6% + 2.9%). Where funds are needed for corporate investment, the Clinton Tax Act may make the use of a C corporation, which retains income and pays the maximum corporate tax, a more favorable option than under prior law where the maximum corporate rate of 34 percent was higher than the maximum stated individual rate of 31 percent. Also, at the higher income levels above $135,000, no Social Security or medicare tax cost was incurred. Thus, under prior law, the tax cost would have been less to distribute the income (31 percent) and have the owner-employees loan or contribute the monies to the corporation rather than incur the corporate tax cost of 34 percent. Thus, in some situations, the Clinton Tax Act has changed the tax relationship from 3 percent in favor of paying compensation to 7.5 percent in favor of the corporation paying the tax.

This analysis suggests that businesses in a growth phase requiring the reinvestment of significant funds, and whose shareholders are high-income earners, may wish to terminate their S corporation status and become C corporations since the tax cost will be lower.

Conversion from an S corporation to a C corporation should not be made lightly. Consequences that could be more substantial than just the potential for annual tax differential include being taxed as a regular corporation with exposure to the corporate tax rates, the tough corporate alternative minimum tax, and the double tax on liquidation resulting from the repeal of the general utilities doctrine. This latter cost can be substantial. Penalties and additional corporate level taxes can also be assessed. The analysis is further complicated by yet other tax traps such as the personal holding company tax, or the disallowance of a deduction for unreasonable compensation.

A common method used by closely held C corporations to reduce or eliminate taxable income is to pay all income to the shareholder/ employees as salary. Salary is generally deductible as an ordinary and necessary business expense. Where the C corporation tries to reduce its earnings through payments of too large a salary to a shareholder/ employee, there could be yet another problem. If the compensation is deemed to be unreasonable, the IRS could challenge the corporation's tax deduction for the wages so paid.

Accumulated Earnings Tax Plagues Corporations Again

Where a C corporation retains income that is taxed at the now lower corporate tax rate, it could face a penalty tax on unreasonable accumulation of income. This tax, known as the accumulated earnings tax is assessed at the highest individual tax rate. The Clinton Tax Act, increased the maximum individual tax rate to 39.6 percent, and also increased the accumulated earnings tax rate to 39.6 percent, for years after 1992.

The accumulated earnings tax is a second tax that may have to be paid in addition to the regular corporate tax rate. The accumulated earnings tax is assessed where a corporation permits an unreasonable amount of earnings to accumulate in the corporation in order to avoid distributions to its shareholders where the income would be subject to a higher tax. After the Tax Reform Act of 1986, individual tax rates were lower than the top corporate tax rates so that there was an incentive to distribute earnings. However, the Clinton Tax Act restored the traditional relationship so that the highest individual tax rates again exceed the highest corporate tax rates.

Where an accumulated earnings tax is assessed, it is charged at a flat 39.6 percent rate on accumulated taxable income. For most corporations, this special term includes taxable income of the corporation subject to the following special adjustments:

- (−) Federal income taxes are deductible.
- (−) Charitable contributions are deductible to the extent they could not be deducted for purposes of the regular tax as a result of the limitation that contributions cannot exceed 10 percent of taxable income.
- (+) No deduction is allowed for dividends received. Most corporations can receive a deduction equal to a large portion of

dividends they receive from other corporations. This special deduction is added back.

- (+) Capital loss carryovers are not permitted. These are amounts that, while not deductible in certain years because of the limitation on capital losses, can be carried over to and perhaps deducted in other tax years.
- (−) An adjustment is permitted for net capital gains/losses (see Chapter 3). However, this amount must be adjusted by a special factor.
- (−) The accumulated earnings credit is the amount of income which the corporation can retain for the reasonable needs of its business. A minimum amount is permitted to most corporations (other than personal service corporations) of $250,000 (from the combination of both past and current earnings). The courts will often consider whether the liquid assets of the corporation are excessive when compared with its reasonable business needs. Reasonable business needs can include maintaining reasonable working capital, replacing plant and equipment, redeeming stock of a deceased shareholder, and paying down debt.

The accumulated earnings tax is again a concern that every closely held corporation in particular must pay attention to. The corporation should document, such as in board of director minutes, the commercial business reasons for retaining funds. These could include working capital needs, proposed expansion plans, contingent liabilities, and so forth.

Personal Holding Company Tax

Where a corporation is used as an incorporated pocketbook to receive and hold dividends, interest, and other passive investment income, or compensation income, it could be subjected to a special penalty tax called the personal holding company (PHC) tax. The motive for doing this is that where the corporate income tax rate is less than the maximum individual tax rate, it can be cheaper to leave passive investment income, or salaries, accumulated inside the corporation rather than distribute them to the higher taxed shareholders. Since the Tax Reform Act of 1986, this tax has perhaps fallen into obscurity because corporate tax rates were higher than individual tax rates. The Clinton

Tax Act, by restoring the historical relationship (other than the period between the Tax Reform Act of 1986 and the passage of the Clinton Tax Act) of having individual tax rates that exceed corporate tax rates, increases the risks of this potentially dangerous tax trap. In addition to making this penalty tax a more likely risk for corporations, the Clinton Tax Act has increased the penalty tax rate to 35 percent from 34 percent under prior law.

> **TIP:**   The higher PHC tax rate is effective retroactively to tax years beginning January 1, 1993, and later.

The PHC tax is assessed on undistributed PHC income of a PHC. This is PHC income reduced by dividends paid and federal income tax. A PHC is a corporation with at least 60 percent of its adjusted ordinary gross income for the year consisting of PHC income, and during the last six months of the tax year more than half the value of its stock is owned by five or fewer shareholders. PHC income consists of dividends, interest, royalties (excluding copyright and computer software royalties), annuities; rents (an exclusion is provided for real estate businesses where more than half the adjusted ordinary gross income is rents); mineral, oil, and gas royalties (an exclusion is provided where royalties are more than half the adjusted ordinary gross income); rents for film exhibition and distribution (an exclusion is provided where rents are more than half the adjusted ordinary gross income); amounts received under contracts for personal services; etc.

Corporate Estimated Tax Rules Modified

Where a corporation will have a tax liability of $500 or more, it must pay estimated income taxes in four quarterly installments to avoid any penalty for underpayment of estimated taxes. For a corporation using the January 31 to December 31 calendar year as its tax year, payments are generally due on April 15, June 15, September 15, and December 15.

The new rules for corporate estimated tax payments are more stringent, especially for larger corporations. Corporations with taxable income of more than $1 million in any of the three preceding tax years will have to pay in 100 percent of the current year tax liability, rather than the 97 percent required under current law. For the first quarter's payment, however, even large corporations can base their payment on the prior year's tax liability.

TABLE 14.2   Methods for Estimating Tax Payments

Estimated Tax Payment for Quarter	Months Included in Calculation	
	General Method	Clinton Method
1st Quarter	First 3 months	First 2 months
2nd Quarter	First 3 months	First 4 months
3rd Quarter	First 6 months	First 7 months
4th Quarter	First 9 months	First 10 months

Small corporations can generally base their estimated tax payments on 100 percent of the prior year's tax liability. However, where the prior year's tax return reflected a tax loss, this exception is not available and estimated taxes must be based on 100 percent of the current year tax liability.

A corporation has several options for estimating its tax liability based on annualized income. For example, a corporation may make a determination based on its annualized income for the corresponding portion of the tax year on an annualized basis. The Clinton Tax Act added an additional method for corporations to meet their estimated tax payments by basing payments on annualized income from certain months in the current tax year, as shown in Table 14.2.

TIP: Corporations should evaluate the timing benefits of the various payment options. Depending on a particular corporation's earnings pattern, different methods may prove advantageous for deferring tax payments. For small corporations, fluctuations between annual earnings can make the payment of estimated taxes based on the prior year's tax advantageous in some years and not others.

Stock for Debt Exception

The Clinton Tax Act repeals an exception that existed under prior law permitting certain corporations to transfer stock in satisfaction of debt while avoiding income taxation of the cancellation of debt income generated from transferring its debt for that stock. These corporations could also avoid having to reduce their tax attributes (tax credit, net operating loss carryovers, and other tax benefits) to obtain this favorable result. Although the avoidable income was limited to the amount of the taxpayer's insolvency, these rules had permitted a corporation to emerge from bankruptcy with tax advantages unavailable to new or solvent firms because it could use the tax attributes to shelter income earned after emerging from bankruptcy. This was an unfair advantage over competitors. The repeal of this favorable rule is generally effective for stock for debt transfers after December 31, 1994. However, the change will not apply to corporations involved in bankruptcy or insolvency proceedings that began in 1993. It does not appear that these rules will apply to entities other than corporations.

> **TIP:** Because the deadline is deferred until 1995, any corporation that faces a potential insolvency or bankruptcy should carefully evaluate the opportunities of this planning benefit before the window closes. Once this new rule takes effect, troubled companies may face a far more difficult task in trying to survive.

Discharge of Debt Rules Amended

Generally, where you owe a debt and are discharged from the obligation without paying the lender money (or property) worth the face amount of the debt, you will have to include the amount of debt discharged in your income. There are several important exceptions to this rule, which have been modified by the Clinton Tax Act.

If a taxpayer has a debt discharged while in a Title 11 bankruptcy or is insolvent (but not in bankruptcy), income may not have to be recognized on the discharge of debt. However, the excluded income must be applied to reduce other tax benefits (attributes) of the taxpayer. Foreign tax credits, research credits, and other business tax credits may be reduced.

Where you qualify to avoid recognizing income on a debt cancellation, you have to reduce certain tax attributes (benefits), including:

- Net operating loss carryovers.
- General business tax credit carryovers.
- The tax basis in assets.
- Carryovers to future years of any foreign tax credit.

The Clinton Tax Act extends this to include additional tax attributes that may have to be reduced. These rules are effective after 1993:

- *Suspended Passive Losses* (see Chapter 12). These are generally losses from passive activities, such as rental real estate where you do not qualify for the active participation or professional real estate investor exceptions. These losses may now have to be reduced and thus would not be available in future years to deduct against other passive income (or against any income in the year you sell your entire interest in the particular passive investment).

- *Certain Tax Credit Carryovers* (see Chapters 10 and 17). Tax credits are reduced at the rate of 33¹/₃ cents for each dollar of debt discharge.
- *Alternative Minimum Tax (AMT) Credits.* Where you pay the AMT, you are permitted a credit to apply against your regular tax liability in future years. This must now be reduced.

The new order for tax attributes you must reduce is as follows:

1. Net operating loss carryovers.
2. General business tax credit carryovers.
3. Alternative minimum tax (AMT) credit available as of the beginning of the tax year following the year in which the debt was discharged.
4. Net capital losses and carryovers to the year in which the debt was discharged.
5. The tax basis in certain assets.
6. Passive activity losses or credits carried over from the tax year in which the debt was discharged.
7. Carryovers to future years of any foreign tax credit.

If the amount of debt discharged exceeds all the tax attributes listed, no gain is recognized. By adding yet additional tax attributes to the list of possible reductions, the Clinton Tax Act assures that fewer taxpayers will avoid the cost of having their debt discharged.

S CORPORATIONS

What Is an S Corporation?

S corporations are generally not taxed; instead, they act as a conduit, and income and loss flow through and are taxed to the individual shareholders. A shareholder in an S corporation, like any corporate shareholder, can benefit from limited liability. Only the amount invested will be at risk. This is always touted as an important factor favoring an S corporation over a general partnership or a sole propri-etorship. However, for a start-up business, limited liability is rarely absolute since personal guarantees are often required for bank loans, leases, and other transactions. As a result of this favorable tax and le-gal status, S corporations became the popular choice for organizing numerous business activities following changes made in the Tax Re-form Act of 1986. The Clinton Tax Act may change this pattern for some investors.

What Changing Tax Rates Have Done to S Corporations

Prior to the Clinton Tax Act, individual tax rates were somewhat lower than corporate tax rates so that S corporations, unlike C corpo-rations, avoided the higher corporate tax rate and passed earnings to shareholders to be taxed at their lower rates. The Clinton Tax Act has changed this relationship, but the ability to pass earnings to share-holders without a corporate tax remains. For S corporations, there is generally only a single level of tax, at the shareholder level. Two excep-tions are the built-in gains tax and the tax on certain S corporations with subchapter C earnings and profits. The double tax that C corpo-rations face on sale or distribution of corporate assets is avoided by S corporations, which can liquidate with only one level of tax. However, compared with a partnership or LLC form of operation, an S corpora-tion has disadvantages since gain must be recognized on the distribu-tion of appreciated assets to the shareholders. The complex and costly corporate alternative minimum tax does not apply to S corporations.

The general rules affecting S corporations will be reviewed, and then the important indirect effects that the Clinton Tax Act will have on this popular entity will be analyzed.

Requirements to Qualify for S Corporation Treatment

Strict organizational and shareholder requirements must be met to obtain the tax benefits previously noted.

Organizational Requirements.   To qualify as an S corporation, the corporation must elect to be taxed as an S corporation by filing Form 2553 with the IRS within the first $2^1/_2$ months of the year. State corporation filing requirements and taxation should also be con-sidered since the rules may differ. The S corporation cannot be a member of an affiliated group of corporations. These are corporations connected by 80 percent or greater ownership. If these requirements are not met, then the S corporation election can only become effective on the first day of the following tax year.

Shareholder Requirements.   An S corporation cannot have more than 35 shareholders. Only individuals and certain estates and trusts can qualify as shareholders. This important limitation prevents joint venture arrangements, in which one of the joint venture partners is a corporation or other disqualified shareholder, from organizing as an S corporation.

> **TIP:** All shareholders should review their estate plans since the trusts often established as part of an estate plan (or in a will) are not qualified to be S corporation shareholders. The shareholders' agreement should have language restricting any transfer to a nonqualified shareholder.

Since S corporations are closely held businesses, estate planning for the shareholders is often an important consideration. As a result, many shareholders' agreements, even though they may severely restrict the transfer of stock, may permit the transfer of shares to a trust for the benefit of the shareholder's family. The only trust, however, that will qualify as a shareholder without terminating the S corporation status, is a qualified subchapter S trust (QSST). This planning is especially important in view of the Clinton Tax Act increases in both income and estate tax rates.

Class of Stock Requirement.   There can only be one class of stock. Therefore, when structuring loans to the corporation, all the formalities of a loan must be observed to prevent the IRS from challenging the purported loans as being an unpermitted second class of stock. Some differences are permitted in classes of stock so that some shares can be voting and others nonvoting. This can permit shares to be transferred to key employees or children without the principals losing voting control. The restriction to one class of stock can also present problems when attempting to allocate profits of the business to account for the differing contributions of the various shareholders. Although profits cannot be allocated as freely in an S corporation as in a partnership, consulting or employment agreements and bonus systems can sometimes be used to achieve the desired objectives.

The key point in adhering to the one class of stock requirement is assuring that distributions between the shareholders do not vary. Where the timing or the amount of distributions varies, the IRS may argue that a second, and disqualifying, class of stock has been created. This is a significant disadvantage compared with the partnership form of operation.

When issuing debt, shareholders must be careful to ascertain that the equity features of the debt do not taint it as a disqualifying second class of stock. Therefore, any debt should have fixed interest rates and payment dates, should not be convertible, and should be a written and unconditional obligation to repay.

What Happens When a C Corporation Becomes an S Corporation?

Where a regular C corporation elects to be taxed as an S corporation, two special tax traps must be considered. The first is the built-in gains tax. A tax will be imposed on the S corporation on any gain that arose prior to the corporation being converted from a regular corporation to an S corporation. This special tax applies during the 10-year period following the election to S corporation status and is assessed at the highest corporate tax rate. The maximum gain that can be subject to this special tax is limited to the net unrealized built-in gain that existed at the date the corporation became an S corporation.

> **EXAMPLE:** If a corporation owned a building with a depreciated book value of $1 million but was worth $2 million at the date the corporation was converted to an S corporation, the built-in gain would be $1 million. If the S corporation was sold or liquidated within 10 years, a corporate tax would have to be paid.

As a result, it is best to have the assets of any regular corporation valued in a written and independent appraisal as of the date an election is made for it to become an S corporation. One mitigating factor is that the corporation can use any operating loss carryovers to offset any built-in gains tax it incurs.

A second problem faced by a regular C corporation converting to an S corporation is a limitation on passive income. If the regular corporation has earnings and profits when it elects to be an S corporation, the S corporation could face a corporate level tax and possible loss of its S corporation status if excessive passive income is earned. The rule is that if more than 25 percent of the taxable income for a S corporation subject to these rules is passive, a tax will be charged on excess net passive income. If this 25 percent threshold is exceeded for 3 consecutive years, the S corporation status will be terminated.

S corporations are pass-through entities, so the passive loss limitation rules generally do not apply directly to them. Rather, the characterization of income or loss as passive, active, or portfolio will be made separately by each shareholder considering the shareholder's ownership interest, participation, and so forth. An S corporation shareholder can only deduct losses passed through up to the amount of his or her tax basis. Only the basis in the shareholder's stock, such as the price paid and amounts directly due to the shareholder from the corporation are included in the tax basis. The S corporation shareholder's basis cannot include a pro rata share of entity level debts (e.g., a nonrecourse mortgage on the property) as can a partner's basis. This dichotomy greatly favors the partnership form where real estate assets are owned.

How Distributions from S Corporations Are Taxed

To understand the implications of the post-Clinton Tax Act planning for S corporations, it is necessary to know the tax consequences of distributions from an S corporation. Where an S corporation has earnings and profits (analogous to financial statement retained earnings) from a tax year before it became an S corporation (when it was a C corporation), distributions are taxed based on the following priority of rules:

- A nontaxable return of investment up to the amount of the S corporation's accumulated adjustment account (AAA). The AAA is generally the sum of all income (excluding tax-exempt income) reduced by the following: nontaxable distributions, losses and deductions, and certain non-tax-deductible amounts. Special adjustments are made to AAA for oil and gas depletion.
- Dividends to the extent of accumulated earnings and profits.
- Nontaxable return of investment up to the amount of the shareholder's basis in the stock.
- Gain from the sale of stock. It would appear that this category should qualify for the exclusions under the new Clinton Tax Act rule for excluding gain on the sale of certain qualifying small business stock if all the necessary requirements are met (Chapter 15).

The shareholders can all make an election to have a distribution taxed as dividends rather than in accordance with the listed priorities.

Following the termination of the corporation's status as an S corporation (when it becomes a C corporation), distributions during a posttermination period will reduce the investors' basis in the stock up to the amount of the AAA.

Clinton Tax Act Changes That May Make You Change Your S Corporation to a C Corporation

The Clinton Tax Act can make it advantageous for some corporations to give up their S corporation status and become regular, or C, corporations because the act has restored the traditional relationship of corporate and individual tax rates: Individual tax rates again exceed corporate rates. Therefore, if a corporation is growing and reinvesting its profits in the business, which is common for start-up businesses, its overall current tax costs will be lower using a regular or C corporation than an S corporation. The corporate tax on profits in a C corporation will not exceed 35 percent (34 percent for all but the most profitable corporations). Thus 65 percent of profits could be invested on an after-tax basis back in the business. Where an S corporation is used, regardless of whether the profits are distributed or not, the shareholders will have to report their share of profits on their personal tax returns at rates of up to 39.6 percent (and higher when the phaseouts are considered).

> **TIP:** The conclusion that the corporate tax rates will be less than the individual tax rates is not quite as simple as comparing the various marginal tax rates. As with many Clinton Tax Act changes, seemingly minor changes that are easy to understand (like an increase in individual tax rates) have complex and profound tax-planning implications. Corporate tax rates, under the post-Clinton Tax Act rules increase to a 39 percent effective tax rate on corporate taxable income above $100,000 and not more than $335,000 (see Table 14.1). This is because of the phaseout of the benefits of lower tax brackets. Individual tax rates, as explained in Chapter 7, can be quite a bit higher than the stated 39.6 percent maximum rate as a result of the phase-out of personal exemptions, the limitations on itemized deductions, and other changes. Finally, the personal holding company tax and the accumulated earnings tax (both explained in this chapter) can affect the tax cost to a corporation attempting to accumulate profits for reinvestment.

If the decision to convert a S corporation to a C corporation is made, however, several tax issues must be carefully analyzed first. One of these is that if a decision is made in the future to again become an

S corporation, the built-in gains tax would apply. Depending on the nature of the business and assets, this could be a significant factor weighing against giving up S corporation status. For example, if your corporation has significant real estate holdings, and the real estate market in your area is at a relatively low point, future appreciation may be anticipated. If the C corporation owns appreciated real estate, it will face a double tax on liquidation and sale that the S corporation is not subject to. If you try to have the corporation elect S corporation status again, the built-in gains tax could be quite problematic.

If the S corporation status is terminated, the corporation must wait 5 years after the year of termination to reelect to be taxed as an S corporation. This makes it very important to consider whether the S election should in fact be terminated.

Where an S corporation terminates its special S election status, if there were any losses that the shareholders could not deduct because they exceeded their investment (basis) in the stock and debt, these losses may be deducted up to one year later if the shareholder's basis is restored during that time or before the due date for the last S corporation tax return.

If the S corporation has accumulated significant earnings and if these are paid out after the corporation terminates its S corporation status to become a C corporation, those earnings would have to be distributed as dividends, taxable to the shareholders but not deductible to the corporation.

LIMITED LIABILITY COMPANIES

Limited liability companies (LLCs) are a relatively new form of operating a business in many states. They are an unincorporated form of doing business. LLCs potentially offer important advantages over either partnerships or S corporations. LLCs can be taxed in the same manner as partnerships for federal income tax purposes, so LLCs have the flexibility of partnerships in allocating income and deductions. This can be quite important in a start-up business where different owners are contributing different skills, dollars, and assets. Importantly, an LLC can provide the limited liability protection that so often encourages investors to use the corporate form. This best of both worlds—partnership allocation flexibility and flow-through, and corporate limited liability—can make LLCs a potentially ideal investment vehicle.

Since LLCs will generally not be taxed, their shareholders will realize all income, expense, gain, or loss. Therefore, the rules applicable to individual taxpayers generally will govern the taxation of LLCs.

> **TIP:**   Since the Clinton Tax Act has resulted in individual tax rates that are now higher than corporate tax rates, there is no tax rate advantage to using an LLC. However, the tax advantage of an LLC is the ability to gain the liability protection of a corporation with the tax benefits of avoiding corporate taxation, such as the double taxation on dividends and when the corporation is liquidated. These are similar to the advantages discussed earlier for using an S corporation, but an LLC has much greater flexibility to make allocations to its owners than does an S corporation.

Although an LLC can offer these valuable advantages when compared with other forms of ownership, they are still relatively new. Many states have not yet adopted LLC laws, and many professional advisers are not that familiar with them. In time, however, much of this may change and the LLC form of business will probably become more popular.

PARTNERSHIPS

The partnership form business is a common approach. The partnership structure can have advantages over doing business as a corporation, S corporation, or sole proprietorship in appropriate circumstances. To understand the changes made by the Clinton Tax Act to the taxation of partners and partnerships, an overview of how partnerships are used and taxed is necessary.

What Is a Partnership

A partnership is a syndicate or group through which any business, financial operation, or venture is carried on. This can be contrasted with the mere coownership of rented or leased property, which does not constitute a partnership. Similarly, a joint undertaking merely to share expenses is not a partnership.

Advantages and Disadvantages of Using Partnerships

The most important facet of a partnership structure from a tax perspective is that a partnership is not taxed. Income and deductions all flow through to the individual partners and are taxed to them. This has been advantageous from two perspectives. First, there is no tax at the entity level. This compares favorably with a C corporation (S corporations generally pass their income through to their shareholders in a manner similar to that of a partnership), which is taxed at the corporate level. Distributions from a C corporation are then taxed again to the recipient shareholders. Partners and partnerships avoid this second layer of taxation. This conduit character has proven itself as the reason the partnership form of organization has been by far the preferred vehicle for structuring many business and real estate transactions. This conduit or flow-through feature enables individual partners to use the losses generated by the partnership on their own tax returns to offset other income, possibly subject to the passive loss and other restrictions.

General and Limited Partnerships

The simplest and most common type of partnership is a general partnership interest. A general partner is a partner who can be held personally liable on partnership debts (beyond the individual's initial capital contribution). A general partner is also allowed to participate actively in the management of the partnership's affairs. Thus, if the activities of the partnership constitute an active business, and the partner materially participates in those activities, then the general partner will receive active income or loss for purposes of the passive loss rules.

A limited partnership is more complex and costly to establish and maintain; however, it offers potentially valuable advantages over the general partnership form. A limited partnership has two types of partners. There must be at least one general partner, who is liable for partnership debts and is authorized to participate in management. There must also be at least one limited partner, who cannot participate in the active management of partnership activities according to state law. Further, a limited partner can generally only be held liable up to the amount invested. This limitation on liability is a major factor encouraging the use of limited partnerships. The passive loss rules generally treat any income or loss received by a limited partner as passive income or loss (see Chapter 12). Thus, if an investor has unusable passive losses and contemplates another income-producing real estate investment, a limited partnership interest that will produce passive losses to offset the investor's otherwise unusable passive losses would be preferable over a general partnership.

How a Partnership and Its Partners Are Generally Taxed

Partnerships are required to apply for and use a federal employer identification number. Tax returns (Form 1065) reporting all the gains, income, and losses of the partnership (deemed partnership) should have been filed. The partnership tax return would have contained a Schedule K-1 reflecting the income, losses, credits, and other items allocable to each investor and to be reported by each investor on his or her personal tax return. To report income, gain, loss, and so forth at the partnership level, any required tax elections would have had to be made by the partnership.

The taxable income of a partnership is generally determined in a manner similar to the taxable income of an individual. However, several specific deductions are not permitted to partnerships: personal exemption, charitable contribution, net operating loss, capital loss carryover, foreign taxes, itemized deductions, and so forth.

Since the partnership is in many respects independent of its partners, many tax decisions (called elections), including those concerning the research credit and depreciation, are made at the partnership level. Income or loss is determined at the partnership level. Thus, the partnership must choose a tax year, which is generally the same tax year as the majority of its partners. This will generally mean that partnerships will have a December 31, fiscal year-end.

Fixed or guaranteed payments to a partner for services the partner renders to the partnership, or for the use of capital, are often treated as if the payments were made to an independent person who isn't a partner.

> **EXAMPLE:** Smith is partner in the Smith and Jones partnership. Smith provides accounting services to the partnership and receives a regular monthly payment for these services. These payments are treated as if the Smith and Jones partnership had paid an independent accountant to do the work and are therefore deductible by the partnership. The partnership thus obtains the equivalent of a tax deduction for this guaranteed payment. The partner, Smith, would report the payment as ordinary income. This is accomplished by treating the guaranteed payment to Smith as part of Smith's share of the partnership's ordinary income.

Once a partnership's taxable income (or loss) is determined, it must be allocated to the partners so that each partner can report his or her share on a personal tax return. In addition, many specific types of partnership income and deductions must be reported separately to each partner. These include short-term capital gains and losses; long-term capital gains and losses; charitable contributions; alternative minimum tax preference items; medical expenses; and so forth. If you look at Form K-1 which you will receive from any partnership in which you invest, it will list all the items that must be separately reported. Each of these is then reported on a different line on your personal tax return.

Allocations of Partnership Income, Deductions, and Losses

Once the partnership's income is determined, it must be allocated to the individual partners. The simplest approach is to allocate income, deductions, credits, and so forth to each partner in the same proportion as that partner's interest in the partnership. For example, a 12 percent partner would be allocated 12 percent of all partnership items: 12 percent of cash flow; 12 percent of net income or loss; 12 percent of any tax credits (research, low-income housing, or rehabilitation tax credits), and so on.

Allocations, however, do not have to be made in the exact proportions as each partner's interest in the partnership if the partnership agreement calls for a different method. This is one of the principal advantages of the partnership form of organization. This flexibility sets the partnership form of organization apart from all the other forms of conducting business. For example, some partners may be given a priority distribution of cash flow (e.g., limited partners may receive the first cash flow until they have been paid a 8 percent preferred return on their investment). One partner may receive 80 percent of the gain ultimately realized on the sale of certain property (such as land and a building that the partner contributed to the partnership). The general partner may receive 25 percent of the remaining profits on the eventual sale and liquidation of the partnership, although he or she only had a 1 percent interest in the partnership's profits and capital (this could be offered as an incentive fee to the general partner to encourage performance). This freedom of allocation provides an opportunity to devise a distribution and compensation structure to best achieve the businesses goals. A partner's distributive shares of income, gain, loss, deductions, and credits are generally determined by the partnership agreement.

These special allocations cannot be made with total freedom. They must have what is called "substantial economic effect." Defining this term has proven to be one of the most complicated tasks faced by the

Treasury Department, the IRS, and the courts. In very simple terms, it means that the special allocations must be made for more than mere tax reasons. They should have some meaningful (substantial) economic and nontax impact on the partners making them.

The economic benefit or burden must be borne by the partner to whom the allocation is made. This requires:

1. Partners' capital accounts (ledgers reflecting all investments, income, and losses of each partner) must be maintained as required under the tax regulations. For example, partner capital accounts must be increased by certain items (money contributed to the partnership, tax-exempt income allocated to each partner, allocations of income and gain, etc.) and decreased by certain items (money distributed, loss, deductions, and certain expenditures, etc.).

2. On liquidation, distributions of partnership property must be made with consideration to each partner's capital account.

3. Following this final distribution, partners with negative capital accounts are required to restore (contribute) these amounts, or meet certain other complex requirements.

Limitations Affecting a Partner's Ability to Deduct Partnership Losses

There are a number of restrictions on a partner's ability to deduct his or her share of losses from a partnership. A partner, for example, cannot deduct a loss exceeding his or her tax basis (roughly investment, increased by income, reduced by distributions and losses) in the partnership interest.

The passive loss rules can limit a partner's ability to deduct certain partnership losses. The passive loss rules generally divide all activities (and the income or loss they generate) into three categories: (1) passive (activities in which the taxpayer doesn't materially participate, such as a passive tax shelter investment); (2) active (activities in which the taxpayer does materially participate, such as a full-time profession); (3) portfolio (interest, dividends, etc.). Passive losses cannot generally offset income in the other two categories. Unused passive losses are carried to future years until they offset other passive income or the taxpayer's entire interest in the activity is sold. The passive loss rules may be important in choosing between various types of partnerships since general partners can earn active income, whereas limited partners, who cannot participate in the management of the partnership, can only earn passive income.

Partners can also be subject to another set of limitations known as the at-risk rules. These rules can limit a partner's deductible losses to the amount the partner is considered to have risked in investing in the partnership. This can include cash and property invested in the partnership, and debt on which the partner is liable.

How Partnership Distributions and Liquidations Are Taxed

One of the first steps in determining the tax consequences of a partner's interest being sold or liquidated is to determine the tax basis in the partnership interest. The sale of a partnership interest is generally treated as the sale of a capital asset. The capital gain is the difference between the proceeds (called the amount realized) and the partner's adjusted tax basis in the partnership interest.

Usually, the first item included in the calculation of a partner's tax basis is the cash and tax basis of property the partner contributed to the partnership in exchange for receiving the partnership interest. No gain or loss is generally recognized on this type of transaction.

A partner's tax basis (investment) in the partnership is increased by the allocated share of partnership taxable income that he or she reports on a personal tax return. Basis is also increased by the partner's share of tax-exempt income. A distribution to a partner decreases the tax basis by the amount of the distribution.

Partnership debts may also be included in a partner's tax basis. If none of the partners has any personal liability for a nonrecourse partnership liability (a debt the lender cannot sue the partners individually to recover on), then the tax laws provide that all the partners (including limited partners) can include a portion of such liability in their tax basis (i.e., their investment in the partnership). The proportion that each partner would share in such liability is the ratio in which they share partnership profits.

The application of the partnership tax rules to distributions and liquidations can be very complex, as the following example illustrates.

EXAMPLE: A new partner pays $400,000 for a 20 percent interest in a partnership whose sole asset is a building that has appreciated substantially since the partnership bought it many years ago. The building is on the partnership's books at $500,000, so Sam's share (the inside basis) is $100,000. The partnership is depreciating the building over 39 years. The new partner has in effect paid $400,000 for a partial interest in the building but is only getting depreciation based on the partnership's original purchase price of the building, which is much lower. Also, if the building were sold for $2 million (the new partner's share being 20 percent, or the $400,000 he paid), the partnership would realize a $1.5 million gain ($2 million less $500,000 basis), the new partner's share being $300,000. This is not a reasonable result since the new partner's interest in the building only sold for the price he just paid for it. (If the partnership's only asset were sold, it would probably liquidate and the new partner would get an offsetting capital loss.) Unfortunately, many partnerships have multiple assets so liquidation isn't guaranteed. The capital loss limitations could also create problems.

If the partnership makes a special tax election, the new partner can get an adjustment to prevent being taxed on this $300,000 he really didn't earn from the sale of the building, and he can get a depreciation deduction that more closely reflects his actual investment in the building. The adjustment equals the difference between the $400,000 new partner paid and his $100,000 share of the partnership's basis in the building (the tax regulations use the selling partner's basis in his partnership interest as allocated to the building instead). Since we've assumed the only partnership asset is the building, new partner would then depreciate this amount over 39 years for an additional depreciation deduction on his personal tax return. This would be in addition to his share of the partnership's depreciation deduction (which is included in the calculation of the new partner's share of the partnership's income reported to him on Form K-1).

There is an important exception to the rule that the sale of a partnership interest is treated as the sale of a capital asset. Where a portion of the sale proceeds relate to two special types of assets, a partner may have to report part of his gain on the sale as ordinary income. These two special assets are unrealized receivables and substantially appreciated inventory. They are referred to as "hot assets." Unrealized receivables are the right to income that has not been reported under the method of accounting used by the partnership.

EXAMPLE: Medical Associates is a partnership of physicians. It reports income on a cash basis. This means income is only reported when patients pay their bills, not when the medical services are provided. If the partnership is sold, the accounts receivable due from patients who have received services but have not yet paid would be unrealized receivables.

Certain depreciation recapture and other technical adjustments are also unrealized receivables.

The second category of special assets, substantially appreciated inventory, is much more complicated to define. It includes inventory-type items (the term is much broader than what would generally be categorized as "inventory").

Where you sell or exchange an interest in a partnership after April 30, 1993, the Clinton Tax Act has made it more difficult to avoid ordinary income treatment on your proportionate share of the partnership's substantially appreciated inventory. Prior to this effective date, the partnership could take steps to help you avoid this adverse tax consequence by acquiring nonappreciated inventory so that the partnership would fail to meet the technical requirements of having substantially appreciated inventory. Now, any inventory acquired for this purpose is excluded from the calculations. There also had been an exception that made this rule inapplicable where the partnership's inventory did not exceed 10 percent of its assets (excluding cash). This exception has been repealed.

Tax Treatment of a Retiring Partner

Where a partner retires from a partnership, payments are often made to liquidate the retiring partner's interest in the partnership. These payments can be treated as distributions to the retiring partner. These distribution payments will be taxed to the retiring partner to the extent they are made in cash exceeding the retiring partner's adjusted basis for the partnership interest. Amounts above that are treated as capital gain, except to the extent of payments for unrealized receivables and substantially appreciated inventory, as described earlier.

Where payments are made to a retiring partner in exchange for the partner's interest in the goodwill of the partnership (the value of the name and reputation of the partnership) or for a partner's interest in unrealized receivables, they are not generally treated as a distribution in exchange for the partner's partnership interest. However, a special rule had permitted goodwill payments to be taxed as a distribution in exchange for the partner's interest where the partnership agreement (the legal document stating the rights and obligations of the partners) provided for a reasonable payment for goodwill.

Payments to a retiring partner not made in exchange for partnership interest are treated for tax purposes in one of two ways. They can be treated as the retiring partner's distributive share of partnership income. This means the amount would be treated as if it consisted of the partner's share of all the different types of partnership income, deductions, and losses reported to individual partners. To the extent that some of this payment would be treated as a share of partnership profits for the year, it would reduce the income taxable to the other partners for that year. The second possible treatment is as a guaranteed payment. This would provide the partnership a deduction for services rendered, as described earlier. Treatment as a guaranteed payment would also reduce the taxable income to be reported by the other partners.

The Clinton Tax Act changed the preceding rules effective January 5, 1993. With one exception, payments made to a retiring or deceased partner in liquidation of his partnership interest, for goodwill and unrealized receivables, cannot be treated as payments of a distributive share of partnership income or as a guaranteed payment. These payments must now be treated as if made in exchange for the partner's interest in the partnership. Such payments will be taxed as capital gains to the partner in most instances, but will not be deductible by the partnership. The one exception to this new rule is that payments to a general partner in a service partnership (medical, legal, architectural, or accounting) for past services will remain deductible as they were under prior law. These partnerships are excluded because capital is not a material income-producing factor (as in a real estate partnership).

> **TIPS:**   For service partnerships, the old planning opportunities not only remain, they have become more important after the Clinton Tax Act as a result of the increase in marginal tax rates and the increasingly progressive nature of the tax rate structure. Where the remaining partners are in the top tax bracket and the retiring partner is not, the transaction should be structured in favor of payments that are deductible to the partnership.
>
> Where a service partnership also owns significant assets, such as real estate, it may be advantageous to split the partnership into two separate partnerships: One partnership would primarily hold property and the second would be purely a service partnership.

MISCELLANEOUS CHANGES AFFECTING BUSINESS

Partnership and S Corporation Estimated Tax Rules Modified

Partnerships and S corporations are generally conduits for tax purposes. Their income, deductions, gains, and losses flow through to the partners and shareholders who report these tax consequences on their own tax returns. A few exceptions to this general rule can cause a partnership or S corporation to have to make estimated tax payments.

An S corporation, for example, can be required to pay estimated tax on the following special types of income:

- *Built-in Gains.* This can affect an existing corporation that elected to be taxed as an S corporation after 1986 and that had appreciated assets at the time of the election.

- *Capital Gains.* For S corporations in existence during 1986 and earlier, a tax on capital gains can be imposed in certain circumstances where net long-term capital gain is greater than $25,000 and more than one-half of taxable income.

- *LIFO Inventory Adjustment.* Where a regular C corporation uses the last-in, first-out (LIFO) method of accounting for inventory, it can be subject to a special tax on electing to be taxed as an S Corporation.

- *Net Passive Income.* An S corporation, which had been a regular C corporation before making the election to be taxed as an S corporation, can be subject to tax where it has earnings and profits (analogous to financial statement retained earnings) from those C corporation years and more than 25 percent of its revenues are passive investment income.

Another exception can apply to both S corporations and partnerships, and it also requires an estimated tax payment. Generally, a partnership must use the same tax year as its owners. The partnership's tax year is based on the tax year of the partners composing more than 50 percent of the interests in the partnership. This is referred to as a required tax year and is generally a 12-month period ending on December 31 of each year. An S corporation must generally use a tax year ending on December 31 unless it can demonstrate a business reason (something other than deferring its shareholders' tax payments) for using a different tax year. Certain partnerships and S corporations may elect to use a different tax year than that determined under these general rules (e.g., to facilitate bookkeeping matters). Using a tax year other than December 31 can result in deferring the tax payments owed by the individual shareholders and partners. Therefore, if this election is made, the partnership or S corporation may have to make estimated tax payments to the IRS to compensate for the deferral of tax. Following the Clinton Tax Act, the annual payment must be based on the highest individual tax rate of 39.6 percent plus 1 percent. Thus a payment based on a 40.6 percent tax rate is required.

Repeal of Luxury Tax Helpful to Some Businesses

Prior tax law had included a 10 percent luxury tax on certain expensive purchases. Airplanes costing over $250,000, boats costing over $100,000 and jewelry and furs costing over $10,000 were subject to this tax. The Clinton Tax Act eliminated the luxury tax on these items effective January 1, 1993. A major objective of the Clinton Tax Act was to balance the deficit at the expense of the wealthy. The repeal of the luxury tax seems to conflict directly with the primary goal the President stressed to the public.

> **TIP:**   If you purchased a luxury item and paid a luxury tax, contact the store and request a refund. If you are a merchant and a customer requests a refund, you are entitled to obtain a refund of the tax that you collected from the customer and paid to the IRS. File Form 843, "Claim for Refund and Request for Abatement." Only the person who paid the tax to the IRS, generally the retailer, can claim the refund from the IRS.

The luxury tax on automobiles remains in place, with certain modifications. Thus, if you purchase an automobile for more than $30,000, you will be subject to a luxury tax of 10 percent on the amount over $30,000.

> **TIP:**   There was some confusion about the indexing of the $30,000 amount for inflation. It appears that the 1993 adjustment was not made, so you may have overpaid your tax. Check with your tax adviser to determine whether a technical corrections bill or other IRS pronouncement addresses this matter. If it does, you may be entitled to a refund.

Automobile dealers will not have to pay a luxury tax on demonstration models. Costs to modify an automobile for the disabled are excluded from the tax.

Elimination of Lobbying Expenses Deduction

Expenditures to influence federal and state legislation through lobbying efforts will no longer be deductible beginning in 1994. This restriction is far broader than the limitations under prior law. Costs to research, plan, and coordinate lobbying efforts, as well as to communicate with senior executive branch officials to influence their actions are all nondeductible. Only a few minor exceptions are provided for. Expenditures of $2,000 a year or less are excluded from this rule. Costs of communication with government officials required by law or under compulsion of a subpoena remain deductible.

To assure the broadest reach of this new provision, the portion of dues paid to a union or trade association attributable to lobbying expenditures will not be deductible. Organizations are required to report the amount of nondeductible dues payments to their members. This rule is a planning nightmare and an unnecessary administrative expense for both trade organizations and their members. Organizations may not know the information they are required to report until their books are closed following year-end. The reports to members will then require members to modify their tax deductions.

> **TIP:** Trade organizations are given the option to pay a tax at the highest corporate tax level on lobbying costs in lieu of reporting to their members the portion of such expenses that are not deductible. While this is not a favorable solution, when administrative costs to the organization and its members as well as the reduced tax deduction to members are considered, it may possibly be advantageous. When evaluating the actual tax benefit to members, however, consideration must be given to the possible restrictions on members' deductions. Where members are employees, their deductions may only be available as miscellaneous itemized deductions. These are only deductible to the extent that they exceed 2 percent of adjusted gross income. Thus, for many members, there may be no deduction.

Lower Travel Deductions for Meals and Entertainment

The Clinton Tax Act significantly reduces the deductible costs for certain travel, meal, and entertainment expenses. The purpose of these changes was simply to raise revenues in a manner that few taxpayers would be able to complain about.

Prior to the Clinton Tax Act, 80 percent of the costs of business meals and entertainment were deductible. This has now been decreased so that only 50 percent of these costs will be deductible. This change is effective for tax years after 1993.

The change may not have as dramatic an effect on travel and entertainment expenses for some taxpayers as first expected:

- Where an employee who is required to account to his or her employer for expenses is reimbursed for travel and entertainment costs, the costs remain tax free to the employee. Thus, for employees with such plans, the tax effect is unchanged.

- Many employees who do not have accountable reimbursement programs provided from their employer were not able to claim any significant tax deduction for travel and entertainment expenses even prior to the Clinton Tax Act. This was a result of the rule that miscellaneous itemized deductions (which include travel and entertainment expenses) could only be deducted to the extent they exceed 2 percent of adjusted gross income. This restriction effectively prevented many employees from claiming any significant employee business expenses.

- The economic effect of the change may not be significant when compared with the importance of the business function.

EXAMPLE: An executive takes a client to lunch for a cost of $50. Prior to the Clinton Tax Act, the tax benefit of this deduction, with 80 percent deductible and a maximum 34 percent tax rate, was $13.60 ($50 × 80% × 34%). Following the Clinton Tax Act, the tax benefit of the deduction for the same lunch is reduced to $8.75 ($50 × 50% × 35%). The difference is $4.85 ($13.60 − $8.75), or 9.7 percent of the cost of the meal ($4.85/$50). For less than a 10 percent cost increase would the executive forgo the business benefits of the lunch? In many cases, probably not.

Other taxpayers may respond by noticeably reducing their travel and entertainment expenditures.

The Clinton Tax Act includes a credit to employers based on the Social Security tax they pay on employee tip income. This tax break may somewhat mitigate the potentially harsh economic consequences of the reduced travel and entertainment expense deductions.

Dues for clubs are no longer deductible for tax years after 1993, even if the club is used primarily for business entertainment. This restriction is broad and will include hotel, business, and travel clubs, as well as country, health, and other clubs. In view of the economic sluggishness that has hurt many clubs, the loss of any tax deduction, coupled with the restrictions on meal and entertainment expenses, may mean that some clubs will have considerable difficulties under the new rules. For others, however, the important business functions served could outweigh the negative tax consequences.

> **TIP:**   It may be possible for an employer to deduct amounts paid for club dues where the amounts are included in the employee's income as simply another form of compensation. Since individual tax rates are greater than corporate rates in many instances, this option is likely to be of limited use.

The Clinton Tax Act places tougher restrictions on claiming tax deductions when your family accompanies you on a business trip. Beginning in 1994, travel expenses for your spouse and children can only be deducted where the following stringent criteria are met:

- There is a business purpose for the family member's presence.
- The expense would be deductible under general rules.
- The family member is employed by the employer or other person who is paying the travel costs.

It is not clear whether the scope of the new law is such that it could jeopardize travel deductions for nonfamily members who are not employees. For example, consultants who travel with you could arguably be subjected to this rule. While this is unlikely to be the intent, clarification may be forthcoming from the IRS.

CONCLUSION

The Clinton Tax Act has changed scores of tax law provisions directly or indirectly affecting business and investments. Although many of the provisions are minor, for specific taxpayers and business entities, they may be significant. Therefore, the new rules should be reviewed prior to consummating any significant transaction.

15 Special Tax Benefits for Qualifying Businesses

Major goals of the Clinton Tax Act were to stimulate economic growth, job creation, and investment in depressed areas. Unfortunately, the complexity of the tax act, the higher taxes on upper income individuals, and other restrictions enacted could offset the special tax breaks designed to achieve these goals. Most businesses are operated as sole proprietorships (in the individual owner's name, not in a C corporation) or as either partnerships or S corporations (where all income flows through to the individual owners' tax returns). The increased taxes on individuals are thus the equivalent of increased taxes on the same small businesses the Clinton Tax Act was intended to help. The special tax breaks outlined in this chapter must be considered in this context. The country has many serious problems that the federal government should address. The tax laws are an excellent tool for accomplishing these goals. Unfortunately, the provisions described in the following sections, while undoubtedly well intended, are too little and too late.

INVESTMENTS IN QUALIFIED SPECIALIZED SMALL BUSINESS INVESTMENT COMPANIES (SSBICs)

If you sell publicly traded securities realizing capital gains (not ordinary income) and reinvest the gain in a specialized small business investment company (SSBIC), the taxable gain on the securities sold can be deferred. Any long-term or short-term capital gain may qualify. The reinvestment must be completed within 60 days. The types of businesses qualifying as SSBICs are those partnerships and corporations licensed by the Small Business Administration under Section 301(d) of the Small Business Investment Act of 1958. These are businesses that invest in small businesses owned by disadvantaged people.

The maximum amount you as an individual taxpayer can elect to roll over on a tax-deferred basis is $50,000 in any year. However, the maximum lifetime exclusion is $500,000. If you are married filing separate income tax returns, these limits are reduced to $25,000 and $250,000, respectively. C Corporations can elect to defer $250,000 in any tax year, up to a maximum exclusion of $1 million. Corporations that are part of a controlled group of companies are subject to a single limitation. Flow-through taxpayers (those for which income is taxed to the individual owner and not the entity), such as S corporations and partnerships, cannot qualify for this benefit. Similarly, trusts and estates do not qualify.

The income tax is merely deferred on such a transaction; it is not avoided.

> **EXAMPLE:** An investor sells publicly traded stock that she purchased several years earlier for $25,000 for cash of $40,000. The gain is $15,000 ($40,000 − $25,000). This gain is deferred if you invest the $40,000 in qualifying SSBICs. The deferral is accomplished by reducing your tax basis (investment) in the stock by the unrecognized gain of $15,000. Your tax basis is thus $25,000 ($40,000 − $15,000). When you eventually sell the SSBIC stock in a transaction for which the gain cannot be deferred, you will realize the entire gain, including the gain you had deferred earlier.

Where the SSBIC is a corporation, the basis in its common stock is not reduced to determine the gain eligible for the 50 percent exclusion for certain qualified small business stock. This other new Clinton Tax Act benefit is discussed in the following section.

CAPITAL GAINS EXCLUSIONS FOR QUALIFYING SMALL BUSINESS STOCK

The Clinton Tax Act includes an incentive for individuals (i.e., investors other than corporations) who have held qualifying stock in a qualifying small business (QSB) and sell it at a profit. This new benefit applies whether the stock you own is common stock or preferred stock. If you meet the various requirements, you can exclude up to 50 percent of the taxable gain when you sell, or otherwise dispose of, the stock. The half of the gain you don't exclude is taxed at favorable capital gains rates (28 percent compared with a rate of up to 39.6 percent) since under the Clinton Tax Act, the stated maximum tax on capital gains is 28 percent. Therefore, if you can exclude half of the gain, the effective tax rate on the entire sale is only 14 percent. Be careful in evaluating the benefits of this special tax incentive. If you are subject to the alternative minimum tax, the tax benefit could be less than expected.

> **TIP:** The income tax exclusion for gain realized on QSB stock can enhance any stock incentive program for a key employee. Stock (or options to purchase stock) in your corporation will encourage almost any employee to perform better. This new provision assures the employee that if successful, he or she and not the government will reap the lion's share of the rewards. Be very careful, however, in providing any stock in a closely held business to a key employee. As a minority (owning less than 50 percent of the stock) shareholder, a disgruntled employee can wreak havoc on your business. In many states, where a minority shareholder owns at least 20 percent of the stock, there are legal rights to force the corporation to fairly value his or her interest and buy out his or her stock, or face dissolution. However, an angry or revengeful employee with even a much smaller ownership interest can create substantial problems in some instances.

Several requirements must be met to qualify for this tax benefit:

- The investment must be held by you individually, or by you indirectly through a partnership, S corporation, common trust, or mutual fund.
- You must hold the stock more than 5 years. You cannot hold an offsetting short position in the stock.
- You must acquire the stock after 1993 as shares originally issued by the company, or as a gift or inheritance. (The corporation does not have to be newly formed, only the stock has to be newly issued.)
- You must pay for the stock with cash or property (but not stock). You may also earn the stock by providing services to the corporation (but not services as an underwriter).

> **EXAMPLE:** Tom, Jane, and Sam organize a new company. Tom contributes $25,000 of cash. Jane transfers three used trucks worth $22,000 and $3,000 of tools. Sam completes the legal and accounting work to form the new corporation, and negotiates contracts with customers and suppliers. These services are worth $10,000. Sam also contributes $10,000 in cash. Each of these three shareholders would meet this requirement.

- The stock must be stock of a C corporation. Stock in an S corporation whose income is taxed to the shareholders will not qualify. Neither will investments in domestic international sales corporations (DISCs), former DISCs, real estate mortgage investment conduits (REMICs) or regulated investment companies (RICs).
- The portion of your profit excludable from income cannot exceed $10 million or, if greater, 10 times what you paid for the stock. Up to 50 percent of the gain can be excluded.

TIP: For purposes of the alternative minimum tax, 50 percent of the excluded gain will be a tax reference item (see chapter 4). Thus, the real tax benefit of this provision will depend on your AMT position. This is unfortunate because the AMT could substantially eliminate the tax benefit (and investment incentive) created by this provision.

This effectively reduces the $10 million amount to $5 million. This test is applied on a shareholder-by-shareholder basis so that each shareholder could exclude up to a $5 million amount.

EXAMPLE: The limitation of 10 times what you paid for the stock can be more restrictive than expected, especially for smaller companies. For example, assume that a new business was formed with each shareholder contributing $25,000. Ten times this initial contribution to the corporation is $250,000. If half of this can be excluded, $125,000 escapes gain on the eventual sale of the company. This $125,000 gain would have been taxed as a capital gain at 28 percent, so the tax break is at most $35,000 (28% × 125,000). While $35,000 is a noticeable tax break, considering the risks of a start-up business and the risks of having to hold your investment for a minimum of 5 years, it is not that significant. In this example, the $35,000 savings is only $7,000 per year. Thus, in these situations the greater amount, $10 million per corporation would apply.

- The corporation must have less than $50 million in capital when the stock is issued to you. (This tax break was supposed to help small business. $50 million is hardly small. The investment opportunity is thus much broader than the name for this new rule implies.)
- The corporation must conduct an active business in something other than a service business (e.g., health, law, accounting, and so forth aren't included). If the corporation meets the requirements

of deducting start-up expenses for the investigation, creation, and formation of a new start-up corporation, it will qualify as a QSB. Engaging in research that qualifies for the special tax credit or deduction discussed in Chapter 17 will also qualify.

- The corporation cannot be involved in leasing, financing, hospitality (hotel or restaurant operations), farming, or mineral extraction.

TIP: If a specialized small business development company invests in qualifying other businesses owned by economically or socially disadvantaged persons, the active business requirement is avoided. This can present a valuable investment opportunity.

Where the corporation has not met the requirements of a specialized small business corporation (described in the preceding section) the tests can also require that only 10 percent or less of the corporation's assets may be real estate or passive investments in other corporations and that at least 80 percent of the value of the corporation's assets must be used in qualified businesses excluding those listed.

BUSINESS OWNERS IN TARGETED DEVELOPMENT AREAS: EMPOWERMENT ZONES AND ENTERPRISE COMMUNITIES

The Clinton Tax Act includes significant tax benefits for designated areas that the government has determined need specific assistance to spur economic growth. These measures represent only a token effort compared with the substantial problems and inequities they are designed to help. The hope is that these initial incentives will be sufficiently successful to encourage Congress to enact the broader legislation necessary to make material progress in addressing these problems.

Employers in any of 9 designated empowerment zones (6 urban and 3 rural) and 95 enterprise communities (65 urban and 30 rural), which will be designated by the Secretary of Housing and Urban Development (HUD) and the Secretary of Agriculture, will qualify for special federal incentives. To be included in the listing of qualified communities or zones, the areas must have a poverty rate of 20 percent or greater, plus meet specified population and size requirements. Different rules are provided for urban and rural areas. Areas will be nominated by state and local governments, which will have to specify a detailed development plan for each of the areas.

Business Owners in Targeted Development Areas: Enterprise Zones

Businesses in empowerment zones will be entitled to receive a tax credit of 20 percent on the first $15,000 of wages paid to qualified workers as well as costs incurred to train these workers. The credit cannot exceed $3,000 per year. The workers must be zone residents, providing services to an unrelated employer within the zone. The credit is scheduled to be phased out between the years 2002 and 2004. Employees in several types of businesses will not qualify. These include liquor stores, massage parlors, golf courses, country clubs, certain large farms, and gambling facilities.

For purposes of the alternative minimum tax (AMT), this credit cannot reduce more than 25 percent of the employer's AMT. Also, the credits cannot be carried back (assuming they are not fully usable in the year realized) to a tax year ending prior to 1994.

Employers may also qualify for another new special tax break—an increased expense allowance for writing off purchases of equipment and other qualifying Code Section 179 property (see Chapter 17). The maximum deduction will be the lesser of the cost of the qualifying property placed in service in the tax year, or $37,500. This is $20,000 more per year than allowed to taxpayers generally under the Clinton Tax Act. As with the general Code Section 179 election for deducting personal property, this benefit is reduced as the total qualifying investments exceed $200,000 per year. However, the reduction factor rate is only one-half that applicable to taxpayers generally.

This new benefit can help substantially reduce a start-up company's tax liability, thus helping to foster economic development in designated areas. To earn the benefit, however, the new business must have the financing to acquire the equipment. The tax-exempt financing benefit and the community development corporations (CDCs) described in the following sections may provide assistance in stimulating financing of these businesses. Further, the business must realize profits to enjoy a tax benefit. Many start-up companies realize little if any profits in early years.

To qualify for this benefit, the business must use substantially all its employee services and business assets in the zone, have a work force consisting of at least 35 percent zone residents, and derive at least 80 percent of its gross revenues from the conduct of an active business in the designated zone.

Not all businesses will qualify for these benefits. For example, a rental real estate business will only qualify if it rents commercial (not residential) properties. At least half of the real estate business's income must be from the rental of property to zone businesses. Where a business rents personal property, more than half of the gross rental revenues must be from zone residents or businesses in order to qualify.

> **TIP:**   State and local incentives may increase the federal tax incentives. Many state and local governments operate economic development units that can assist you. A local chamber of commerce can often help direct you to the right state agencies. Also, contact local utilities since many maintain incentive programs.

SPECIAL TAX-EXEMPT FINANCING FOR BUSINESSES IN QUALIFYING ZONES

The Clinton Tax Act also authorizes a new type of tax-exempt bond for purposes of financing business growth in qualified zones. These are subject to various limitations. For example, the state volume caps that apply to tax-exempt bond financing will also apply to these bonds (see Chapter 19). Borrowing with these special tax-exempt bonds by any business in a particular zone cannot exceed $3 million, or $20 million in aggregate of all zones where the business operates.

COMMUNITY DEVELOPMENT CORPORATIONS

The Clinton Tax Act authorizes special tax benefits for Community Development Corporations (CDCs). Up to 20 CDCs can be designated by the Department of Housing and Urban Development. These CDCs will be tax-exempt charitable corporations whose purpose will be to promote economic growth through increased employment and business opportunities in empowerment zones and enterprise communities. Contributions to CDCs will be deductible as charitable contributions. In addition, a tax credit equal to 50 percent of the contribution will be available, in increments over a 10-year period (5 percent per year for 10 years).

SPECIAL INCENTIVES TO PROMOTE INVESTMENT IN INDIAN RESERVATIONS

To encourage investment in physical plant and equipment on Indian reservations, the Clinton Tax Act includes more favorable depreciation deduction periods (see Table 15.1). Several restrictions apply to these benefits. They are available only for investments in property placed in service after 1993. Property used in gambling operations is not included. The property must be used in an active trade or business.

In addition, the Clinton Tax Act includes a special tax credit for wages paid on Indian reservations. The nonrefundable credit is 20 percent of wages and health insurance costs—up to $30,000—of tribe members who work on and live on or near the reservation. The credit is available only to the extent that the employer's payroll meeting the preceding criteria increases from 1993 levels. The credit cannot reduce the alternative minimum tax. If the employee is fired less than one year after hire, this special credit must be recaptured.

TABLE 15.1   Incentives for Investment in Indian Reservations

ACRS Recover Class	Special Indian Reservation Depreciation
3-year property	2 years
5-year property	3 years
7-year property	4 years
10-year property	6 years
15-year property	9 years
20-year property	12 years
39-year nonresidential real property	22 years

INVESTMENT TAX CREDIT

Permanent investment tax credits for firms with under $5 million in revenues were proposed but never enacted.

CONCLUSION

The Clinton Tax Act has added several new tax benefits for businesses meeting specific criteria. Where the various requirements can be met, these benefits can be substantial. Since these benefits were intended to serve as catalysts for specific types of investments, businesses that could possibly benefit from these new provisions should carefully evaluate their business plans to ascertain whether they will qualify, and if not, what steps can be taken to improve the likelihood of qualifying for these new tax benefits. These benefits may also stimulate new investment products to enable other investors to benefit from these opportunities.

16 Employees and Health Care Costs

A substantial number of provisions in the Clinton Tax Act will affect the cost of employing people in your business. The provisions cover a wide range of topics relating to your pension and health care deductions, fringe benefits for employees, and tax-reporting requirements, among others. This chapter will highlight many of these changes and some of the implications to your business planning.

SOCIAL SECURITY TAXES

The hospital insurance portion of the Social Security tax had been applied on income only up to a specified level. In 1993, the maximum wages (or earnings for self-employed taxpayers) subject to the 1.45 percent tax was $135,000 for employees and 2.9 percent for the self-employed. After 1993, this tax will be assessed without any limitation on wages or income. Shareholder/employees of S corporations should analyze with their accountants whether the approach they have been using for determining salary payments is still appropriate.

> **EXAMPLE:** A consulting firm has four employees, each earning $250,000 per year. Under prior law, the firm and each employee paid tax at a rate of 1.45 percent on the first $135,000 of wages. Now the entire amount is subject to tax. Thus, each employee will pay an additional $1,667.50 (1.45% × (250,000 − $135,000)). The firm will pay an additional $6,670 ($1,667.50 × 4 employees).

From the employees' perspective, deferring compensation, through qualified or nonqualified plans will be increasingly important because of the higher Clinton Tax Act rates. When compensation is deferred, the higher Social Security taxes will also be deferred. For example, incentive stock options (ISOs) will become a more favored form of compensation (see Chapter 3).

With the increased use of deferred compensation arrangements to avoid the current impact of the higher income and Social Security tax rates as well as the limitations on pension contributions, executives should investigate whether any insurance is available to secure these future payments. A key risk of nonqualified deferred compensation arrangements is that an employer having financial difficulty could default. Insuring against this risk unfortunately creates a tax risk for the employee. The Internal Revenue Service (IRS) can try to claim that the compensation is not really deferred since its ultimate payment is assured by the insurance. In appropriate circumstances, an employee may be successful in avoiding this tax problem. The employee and not the employer should arrange for the insurance and pay the premiums. Since the tax law is uncertain, be sure to consult your tax adviser before purchasing such a policy.

With these higher taxes, there will be an increased incentive to limit salaries distributed from S corporations and instead distribute cash in the form of dividends. Since S corporations pay no tax cost, this arrangement, if respected by the IRS, can minimize Social Security and other payroll taxes. This approach must be tempered by several factors. The IRS will not accept nominal wage payments from wholly owned businesses where substantial services are rendered. Also, some states tax the income of S corporations so that the purported savings in the hospital insurance portion of Social Security will have to be weighed against an increased state tax cost.

To determine your taxable income and self-employment income, 50 percent of the self-employment tax is deductible.

PENSION LIMITATIONS THAT MAKE RETIREMENT SAVING HARDER

As an employer, you have various options for providing retirement benefits for yourself and your employees. Where the retirement benefits are provided in the form of a qualified plan, the plan may qualify for tax exemption, you obtain a tax deduction for contributions to the plan, and the employees will not have to include the monies set aside in their income at that time.

Further, the contributions to the plans will grow for the employees' benefit on a tax-deferred basis. From the employees' perspective, qualified plans that defer tax on income which would be assessed at the new high 39.6 percent rates are more important than ever as a tax-planning tool. Taxes will be assessed at ordinary income rates on distributions made when the employee retires. However, many employees expect to be in lower income tax brackets when they retire, so the tax cost will be less than if they had taken the contributions as additional pay during higher-income working years. Distributions before age $59\frac{1}{2}$ can be subject to a 10 percent penalty tax. Some plans, called "401(k)" plans ("403(b)" in the case of tax-exempt organizations and certain other employers) give the employee the option to receive taxable compensation currently, or to have the employer contribute the amount to a retirement plan.

There are several types of pension plans. In a defined contribution plan, you, as employer, would make specified contributions each year. The ultimate benefit, however, would depend on the investment performance of plan assets and other factors. A defined benefit plan provides for a specified level of benefits on retirement. The amounts you put aside today are amounts actuarially calculated to arrive at a specific benefit level for employees' future retirements. In a profit-sharing plan, contributions are based on the firm's profits. Cash or deferred arrangements (401(k) plans) give the employee the option of taking cash or having the amount contributed to a plan.

The Clinton Tax Act limits the amount that can be considered in calculating the contributions to qualified pension plans. Under prior law, $235,840 could be used in the calculations for 1993 qualified plan contributions. The new law, which reduces to $150,000 the amount that can be considered, takes effect in 1994. This $150,000 will be indexed for inflation and increased in $10,000 increments after 1994. Employees participating in defined benefit plans may be affected even if their current salary is less than $150,000. For many small businesses and professionals, these changes may make it impractical to continue to maintain a plan to provide the benefits the principals desire.

TIPS: For smaller businesses and professional practices, pension plans can provide a substantial planning opportunity up to the new maximum contribution levels. Where proper planning is done, principals may be able to contribute the lion's share of pension contributions to their accounts rather than to the accounts of their employees. Thus, although the new limitations will restrict highly profitable businesses, other closely held businesses and professional practices may find the planning opportunities of a pension plan, even with the new limitations, too good to avoid now that the Clinton Tax Act has raised tax rates and restricted other planning options.

Discuss the new rules with your pension consultant. It may be possible to offset some of the effect of the new change with modifications to your plan.

Consider raising the percentage of compensation included in the calculation of benefits in order to make up for the difference of what is lost through the reduced level of compensation that can be taken into account. This could enable you to achieve the same level of contributions for yourself. The problem is that you must do this for all employees so the cost of maintaining the same contribution level as you had in prior years could be costly. Depending on the size of your payroll, it could be so expensive as to be prohibitive. Some small business owners may discontinue plans as a result of this.

Some employers will simply rely on nonqualified plans to assure the desired level of contributions for key employees. Nonqualified plans, however, have several drawbacks. The benefits involved could be taxable to the employee or could be subject to the risks of the employer's creditors and other claimants.

Special rules apply to participants in collectively bargained plans and retirement plans of state and local governments, which are beyond the scope of this book.

HEALTH INSURANCE DEDUCTIONS FOR THE SELF-EMPLOYED

Self-employed taxpayers, those reporting income on a Schedule C, and not on a corporate or partnership return or W-2, had been entitled to claim a deduction for 25 percent of the health insurance premiums that they paid for themselves, their spouse, and family. This deduction had expired. The Clinton Tax Act retroactively restores this deduction effective June 30, 1992. The deduction, however, expires again for tax years beginning after 1993. The deduction is claimed on the worksheet on page 21 of the 1992 Form 1040 tax return. You will have to use your full year tax payment rather than the 50 percent payment figure indicated in the instructions. If you were a partner in a partnership, or an employee of an S corporation in which you owned at least 2 percent of the stock, you may also qualify for this benefit.

TIP: If you filed your 1992 income tax return and did not claim the full deduction to which you were entitled, file an amended tax return on Form 1040-X to obtain it.

When you determine your earnings from self-employment to calculate your self-employment tax, the deduction for health insurance premiums is not applied.

Another restriction also is applied to this deduction. No deduction will be allowed for any month after 1992 where you or your spouse qualified to participate in another health plan.

> **TIP:** If you become eligible for an employer's health plan, you can still deduct the monthly payments up until the month in which you were not eligible for those benefits.

INCREASED WITHHOLDING ON BONUSES

Under prior law, where you paid an employee a bonus, commissions, or overtime pay, you could have elected to withhold federal income taxes at a flat 20 percent rate. This rate has now been increased to 28 percent for payments made after 1993. If you do not elect to use this 28 percent flat withholding, then the compensation must be combined with the regular payroll and taxes must be withheld according to the regular schedule for withholding taxes. In many situations, such as for all lower-earning employees, the use of regular withholding tables will often result in a lower tax than the new flat 28 percent rate.

> **TIP:** Under prior law, the flat 20 percent withholding rate added to the impact of paying a bonus by putting more cash into the employee's pocket. The new rule will take away some of the bang of giving a bonus.

SOCIAL SECURITY TAXES ON TIPS

Hotels, restaurants, and other food business will be entitled to a tax credit for their share of Social Security paid on reported tip income of their employees where the tips are not counted as wages for purposes of meeting the federal minimum wage requirement. This credit is available after 1993. The amount claimed for the credit cannot also be treated as a tax deduction by the employer. The purpose of this credit is to mitigate somewhat the harsh result these businesses may experience from the reduction in the business entertainment deduction.

TAX CREDITS TO HIRE NEW EMPLOYEES

The targeted jobs credit that existed under prior law and expired on June 30, 1992, has been retroactively reinstated.

> **TIP:** If you paid qualifying wages between July 1 and December 31, 1992, you should consider filing an amended tax return to claim additional tax credits to which you may be entitled. Retroactive credits may be difficult to qualify for because the necessary certifications of qualifying employees may not have been obtained since it was assumed that the credit had expired. Consult with your accountant and be alert for future IRS pronouncements providing guidance on this issue.

This reinstated credit will remain effective for an additional 3 years until June 30, 1995, for persons who begin work on or before December 31, 1994. This credit is at a rate of 40 percent of the first $6,000 of the first year's wages paid to certain disabled workers, or a worker from a disadvantaged group. The maximum credit is thus $2,400 (40% × $6,000). Since a credit is a dollar-for-dollar offset of tax liability (unlike a deduction, which offsets income and thus has a benefit equal to your tax rate multiplied by the deduction), the benefit of this credit will be equal for wealthy, and not so wealthy, employers.

Several requirements, under prior law, must be met to claim this credit. The deduction for the wages paid to targeted workers must be reduced by the amount of credit.

> **EXAMPLE:** You incur $10,000 in wages for a targeted employee. The maximum credit is $6,000 × 40%, or $2,400. The deduction claimed for these wages on your tax return is $7,600 ($10,000 − $2,400).

The following groups of employees may qualify for the credit: 18- to 22-year-old members of disadvantaged groups; qualified summer youth employees (but only $3,000 of wages for summer youth employees can be included); welfare recipients; general assistance recipients; handicapped persons involved in vocational rehabilitation programs; and so forth.

The employee must be employed for a minimum of 90 days, or 120 hours of service. Certification must be obtained that the individual qualifies as a member of an appropriate group.

Serious questions have been raised about the effectiveness of targeted jobs credits to improve and increase meaningful long-term job prospects for poor or disadvantaged workers. Often, larger or established businesses that would have hired the employees in any case reap the benefits. Unless the provisions in the Clinton Tax Act demonstrate a different result, this tax benefit could face restrictions or repeal in future tax bills seeking to raise revenues.

NEW RULES FOR EMPLOYER REIMBURSEMENT OF MOVING EXPENSES

Under prior law, if an employer reimbursed an employee for moving expenses, the reimbursements had to be included in the employee's income. The employee then claimed an itemized deduction for the deductible amounts on the same return. The result in most cases was that the employee had income in excess of the deductions, creating a tax cost. To make the employee whole for the cost of a job-required move, the employer also had to reimburse the employee for the additional tax cost. The tax cost reimbursement was itself taxable, leading to a complicated calculation called a "gross-up." This was necessary to determine the total amount that the employer had to pay the employee so he or she would not be out-of-pocket for any moving costs, or the associated income tax cost. The Clinton Tax Act significantly simplifies these rules in a manner that could provide an important tax benefit for many businesses with respect to deductible moving expenses under the new rules. Employer reimbursements of deductible moving expenses are now excluded from the employee's income. Not only should this simplify calculations, save accounting fees, and reduce administrative burdens, but the entire gross-up costs will be saved. This will provide a substantial cost reduction for large companies relocating employees.

This simplification and tax benefit applies only to moving expenses qualifying for deduction under the new Clinton Tax Act rules. Some employers, especially large corporations with formal relocation programs, often reimburse an employee for all moving-related costs, whether or not they are deductible. In these cases, the nondeductible costs will have to be included in the employee's income, and if corporate policy provides for it, gross-up calculations will still have to be made to reimburse the employee for Social Security (FICA) tax and income tax on those amounts.

LIMITATION ON DEDUCTING COMPENSATION OVER $1 MILLION

The Clinton Tax Act included a much talked-about change in the tax deduction for compensation of highly paid executives. After 1993, non-performance-based compensation for executives of publicly held corporations required to register their stock with the Securities Exchange Commission will not be deductible to the extent it exceeds $1 million. This restriction applies to the four highest paid officers of every corporation subject to these rules. An exception is provided, however, for compensation paid under a written contract that was binding on or before February 17, 1993.

> **TIP:** The Clinton Tax Act has left substantial openings in this restriction. Compensation deductions for a closely held business, or any non-public corporation, are not affected at all. Compensation based on individual performance and shareholder-approved performance-based compensation programs, for example, are not restricted. Thus, incentive stock option plans (ISOs), stock appreciation rights (SARs), and similar programs will not be restricted. Where the executive earns commissioned base compensation, the restriction will not apply. Nontaxable benefits may not be subject to this restriction.

Contributions to qualified retirement plans and salary reduction contributions are not included in the limitation. The exception for performance-based compensation may apply where the material terms of the compensation program, including the performance goals, are disclosed to shareholders and approved by a majority and the compensation goals are approved by the compensation committee of the board of directors, which must be composed of two or more outside directors. The goals should be preestablished objective performance standards that preclude discretion.

From the investor's perspective, this restriction is likely to create far more complex compensation programs for key executives, perhaps making analysis of this portion of an annual report even more difficult to understand. Consulting engagements to create qualifying terminology and plan descriptions to justify salary deductions will grow.

EDUCATIONAL ASSISTANCE FOR EMPLOYEES

Payments of up to $5,250 received by an employee for tuition, fees, books, supplies, and other educational expenses under a qualified employer education assistance program can be excluded from the employee's income. This has been an important benefit that businesses could provide their employees. The benefit, however, has been scheduled to end many times, only to be renewed at the last moment. The Clinton Tax Act has again renewed this valuable employee benefit retroactively to July 1, 1992. This tax break is now extended through the end of 1994.

> **TIP:** If you treated otherwise qualifying employee educational assistance payments as taxable in 1992 because it was not certain that this tax break would be renewed, you should ask your tax adviser how to correct this problem. The IRS should issue guidance in the future as to what steps to take.

To qualify for this benefit, the educational assistance program must meet several requirements. There must be a written plan that cannot unduly favor highly compensated employees. Records must be retained and a tax return filed. Reimbursements can cover undergraduate and graduate level class work, whether or not the employee is seeking a degree. However, graduate teaching or research assistance may not qualify. Tools or supplies the employee may use following the completion of the course work and the cost of meals, lodging, and transportation cannot be excluded from the employee's income. Courses involving sports, games, or hobbies may be excluded only if they relate to the employer's business.

In addition to having a qualified educational reimbursement program, an employer can exclude from income reimbursements or payments for substantiated job-related expenses of an employee. These could include educational programs required for the employee's job. However, to use this nonqualified exclusion (i.e., it is nonqualified since it is not under a written plan meeting the requirements described earlier), the additional requirements of a "working condition fringe benefit" must be met. This means that the employee would have had to qualify to deduct these expenses as a business expense if he or she had paid for them directly.

CONCLUSION

The Clinton Tax Act has complicated the corporate tax planning process. In most instances, the changes will result in increased tax costs, but planning opportunities remain for the diligent taxpayer.

17 Business Depreciation Deductions and Tax Credits

Depreciation, the deduction for the costs of assets that are useful for longer than the current tax year, has always been a favorite tinkering toy for Congress. The Clinton Tax Act is no exception. This chapter highlights many of the changes. The key change to stimulate growth, however, continues to elude the Congress: certainty. A real commitment to stop changing the ground rules so often would probably do more to stimulate investment in productive assets than many of the changes made in hopes of encouraging investment.

ELECTIVE EXPENSING INCREASED

The Clinton Tax Act provides that up to $17,500 of tangible personal property such as equipment, furniture, tools, computer, hardware, and similar property, can be written off in the year it is purchased for use in your trade or business. This elective expensing of personal property is often referred to as "Code Section 179 expensing," the number of the Internal Revenue Code Section stating this rule. This is an increase from the $10,000 amount permitted under prior law.

> **EXAMPLE:** An investor renovates his medical rental building. He spends $35,000 on carpentry work, carpeting, and so forth. Of the $35,000 spent, $17,500 is properly treated as personal property (removable fixtures, equipment, etc.). The investor could elect to expense the $17,500 personal property acquisition under this special rule instead of writing it off over the regular depreciation period.

This elective expensing is available for tax years beginning after 1992. If the purpose of this change is to stimulate investment, the reason for making the change retroactive (in that equipment purchased in 1993 prior to the passage of the Clinton Tax Act qualifies) is unclear. All that will result is a windfall tax break for some taxpayers, and a depletion of government coffers when the primary object of the Clinton Tax Act was to raise revenues.

What's the tax benefit to you of this immediate deduction? Assuming you are in the maximum 39.6 percent tax bracket, the maximum tax benefit would be $6,930 ($17,500 × 39.6%). Under prior law, the benefit was lower because the maximum deductible in one year was only $10,000, and the marginal tax rates were lower.

> **TIP:** Where the proper classification of improvements to real property is an issue, the tax benefit of this elective expensing is far more valuable. In the preceding example, if the carpentry costs had to be capitalized as part of the cost of the building, they would be depreciated over a 39-year period under the Clinton Tax Act rules. If, instead, the improvements were planned to qualify as personal property, then $17,500 could be deducted immediately. The difference in the tax benefit of an immediate deduction versus 39-year depreciation is tremendous (see Chapter 13).

This special allowance is phased out, on a dollar-for-dollar basis, when qualified investments in Code Section 179 property exceed $200,000.

> **TIP:** If you're buying assets that may reach the $200,000 phaseout, consider delaying some of your purchases to the early part of the next year, business requirements permitting. This could enable you to write off the costs immediately, rather than over a 5- or 7-year period under the Modified Accelerated Cost Recovery System (MACRS).

This special write-off provision is limited to the taxable income from the trade or business in which the asset is owned.

In some instances, this new larger elective expensing provision can affect your depreciation deductions. Non-real-estate assets purchased during the year are generally depreciated using a half-year convention. This means that the depreciation deductions assume you own the property for half of the year and you are entitled to a half year of depreciation deductions no matter when you purchased the property. Some taxpayers would acquire most assets near the end of the year and claim a half year of depreciation deductions. To prevent abuse of this rule, a midquarter convention must sometimes be used where substantial property is purchased near year-end. This rule assumes property was purchased in each quarter, so the deductions for the year will be lower where purchases are weighted toward year-end. Property expensed under the new increased elective expensing rule will not be subject to this midquarter convention. Further, in some circumstances, the proper selection of assets to deduct under the elective expensing rule can enable you to avoid application of the midquarter convention altogether in that tax year.

Any investor who can claim this extra benefit without much difficulty should claim it. For large investors, the value of the benefit is likely to be very small relative to the income or loss from your business or property, and relative to the size of the investment. The real issue is whether this incremental benefit as compared with prior law (the increase of the expensing allowance by $7,500) will really motivate businesses to increase purchases.

REAL ESTATE AFFECTED BY LONGER WRITE-OFFS

Many businesses own real estate. A detailed analysis of the depreciation rules and other rules affecting real estate is provided in Chapters 11, 12 and 13. The general change in real estate depreciation that will affect any business owning real estate is the increase in the period over which nonresidential real estate must be written off from 31.5 years to 39 years.

> **TIP:** As under prior law, the depreciation period for the alternative minimum tax (AMT) for real estate is generally 40 years (see Chapter 4). Under prior law, many taxpayers elected to use the 40-year period instead of the 31.5 period to simplify record keeping and to avoid the complicated calculations of real estate under the regular and AMT rules (if you use 40 years for regular tax depreciation, you need make no adjustments for AMT purposes). With a negligible 1-year difference under the Clinton Tax Act, it seems to be almost a foregone conclusion that electing to use the 40-year period in all instances makes sense.

NEW RULES FOR AMORTIZING (DEDUCTING) INTANGIBLES

Problems with Amortizing Intangible Assets

There has been substantial controversy for years between taxpayers and the Internal Revenue Service (IRS) concerning the deduction of the cost to purchase intangible assets when a business is acquired.

Typically, a group of different assets may be acquired together, including equipment, buildings, inventory, trade name, customer lists, and so forth. The intangible assets, unless the taxpayer could demonstrate a reasonably ascertainable useful life, could not be depreciated. The IRS would argue that the asset was really a component of goodwill and hence not deductible. The taxpayer would argue that it was an independent asset with an ascertainable useful life. The Clinton Tax Act attempts to end this particular controversy by providing that goodwill and related intangible assets can be amortized (deducted) ratably over a 15-year (180-month) period on a straight-line method (equal amounts each year).

> **TIP:**   The Clinton Tax Act actually goes farther than prior law in allowing amortization deductions for some intangible assets that would not have been deductible under prior law (e.g., goodwill and going concern value).

In addition to providing more favorable deductions in some situations and saving litigation costs with the IRS, the new rules could provide savings in appraisal and similar costs since, in many cases, the studies often conducted to justify and support amortization of intangibles under prior law will no longer be necessary. On the other hand, since some assets characterized as intangibles under the new law will have to be written-off over longer periods than prior law, appraisals, tax planning, and IRS disputes will continue in other situations.

Assets Qualifying for New Amortization Benefits

Goodwill and related intangibles subject to the new 15-year amortization include:

- Information and databases.
- Customer lists.
- Customer-based intangibles. This includes deposit bases of banks and other financial institutions. This asset had been subject to substantial litigation between taxpayers and the IRS over whether a deposit base had an ascertainable useful life (a prerequisite to claiming amortization deductions under prior law).
- Going concern value.
- Covenants not to compete. Covenants not to compete, regardless of the term, are included. This can be an onerous requirement in

many situations. Where a covenant not to compete only lasts for say 3 years, the costs allocable to it must still be amortized over a 15-year period when attributable to the acquisition of a business.

- Franchises.
- Trademarks.
- Trade names.
- Permits and licenses from government agencies.
- Supplier contracts and related rights.
- Patents and copyrights.
- Technical manuals.
- Employment contracts.

EXAMPLE: You purchase a business for $1 million and have the seller sign a covenant not to compete in a similar business within a 100-mile radius of the plant location for a period of 3 years. You consider this period essential to win over customers. Of the purchase price, $300,000 is allocated to the covenant. Based on industry standards, earning ability of the seller, and other facts, this amount is reasonable. Under prior law, you would have deducted $100,000 per year in each of the 3 years of the covenant not to compete. Under the new law, you must amortize the $300,000 ratably over a 15-year period regardless of the term of the covenant. Thus, you can deduct only $20,000 per year. Assume an 8 percent discount rate and a 39.6 percent tax bracket. Under prior law deduction rules, you would realize a tax benefit in each of three years of $39,600 ($100,000 × 39.6%). The present value of these three future tax benefits at 8 percent is $102,053 ($39,600 × 2.5771). Under the new 15-year amortization rule, you would realize a tax benefit in each of 15 years of $7,920 [$20,000 × 39.6%]. The present value of these three future tax benefits at 8 percent is $67,791 ($7,920 × 8.5595). The difference in value is $34,262 [102,053 − $67,791]. This is a reduction of more than one-third.

TIPS: The purpose of the new law was to simplify tax planning and allocations where a business is purchased. This provision, and the significant detrimental tax effect assures that this will be anything but the case. The Committee Reports to the new 15-year amortization rule appear to indicate that the payment of a fair wage to the seller of a business will not be treated as a covenant not to compete. Thus, reasonable compensation, rather than a covenant not to compete, will be deductible as compensation. This means that buyers and sellers will try to negotiate compensation agreements instead of covenants not to compete. The taxpayers and the IRS will then have to do battle over whether the salary was fair and whether services were provided. Sellers who are recipients of such compensation arrangements should be cautious of agreeing to perform services in a contract if they really do not intend to do so. The buyer may just require the performance of the services stated in the contract. If no services can be required, the IRS will not respect the contract and will instead treat the arrangement as simply a substitute for a covenant not to compete and require the appropriate 15-year amortization. Sellers should also factor in the cost of payroll taxes if they accept a consulting agreement arrangement. Finally, an employment contract must end on death of the substantial disability of the seller/employee. If the payment is really for something other than services, the seller will be leery of accepting such an arrangement in lieu of a payment which is more certain.

Most business acquisitions consist of a market basket of assets and rights. Buyers and sellers will simply take full advantage of the 15-year amortization period for goodwill and other intangibles, and then search for assets that can qualify for more rapid deductions than the 15-year period. For example, in a typical business acquisition, it is common to rent personal property such as equipment, purchase inventory, license the use of a name, retain key employees as consultants, negotiate employment contracts, purchase real estate, lease real estate, and so forth. The allocation of purchase price to some of these non-15-year amortization assets will become the new planning technique. To the extent that taxpayers are creative in their planning, disputes with the IRS will continue and the Clinton Tax Act will not achieve the anticipated simplification goals.

The new rules create a stream of future tax deductions (at the new higher Clinton Tax Act tax rates) and hence tax savings or cash flow. While these benefits will undoubtedly result in higher purchase prices for many assets sales, they generally will not be sufficient to push forward a deal that would not have happened for business reasons alone. This is in part because the amortization deductions available for assets that had not been deducted in the past will be offset in part by the longer amortization period required. Prior to this new rule, many purchased intangibles were amortized over periods much shorter than the 15-year period provided by the new law.

Assets That Do Not Qualify for New Amortization Benefits

Some assets do not qualify for this potentially favorable treatment. These include:

- Self-created assets, such as advertising.
- Interests in a corporation, partnership, trust, or estate.

- Films, sound recordings, and similar property not purchased as part of the acquisition of a business. Films, sound recordings, videotapes, and books that are not subject to the new rules will be amortized under rules existing prior to the Clinton Tax Act.

- Computer software. Special rules apply for certain software instead of the general rule for 15-year amortization. Depreciable software can generally be depreciated over a 36-month period. Software purchased with computer hardware is generally depreciated over the same period as the hardware. Other software may qualify for immediate deduction as a business expense.

- Partnership interests. Special rules apply to partnerships. Where you purchase an interest in a partnership, the purchase will be treated as a purchase of intangible assets subject to the new amortization rules, to the extent that the tax basis of partnership assets are increased as a result of the transaction.

- Real estate and rights relating to the use of real estate. Interests in land including mineral rights, easements, air rights, and so forth. Existing leases.

- Other tangible property is not acquired as part of the assets of a substantial portion of an acquired business.

- Debt.

- Sports franchises.

- Mortgage servicing rights. Special rules apply for mortgage servicing rights purchased in a transaction other than the purchase of a trade or business. The cost of these rights is amortized on a straight-line basis over 108 months.

Limitation on Deducting Losses on Qualifying Intangible Asset Acquisitions

If you sell or dispose of a portion of the intangible assets from a particular acquisition, you cannot recognize any tax loss on that portion of assets. Instead, the loss is deducted only over the remaining 15-year amortization period that applied to the group of assets acquired. In other words, the loss not recognized on the sale of some intangible assets, is applied to adjust your tax basis in the intangible assets still owned. The entire loss is only recognized when all intangible assets from a particular acquisition are sold.

When the New Rules Are Effective

Although this new rule is effective for property acquired after the date the Clinton Tax Act was enacted, taxpayers can elect to retroactively apply its provisions to assets acquired after July 25, 1991. The election, however, must apply to all assets purchased since that date. It cannot be made on a selective basis only for certain assets.

> **TIP:** Evaluate whether this election can be beneficial. If you purchased business with substantial goodwill and other intangibles not amortized, the election could be helpful. If you believe your allocations in prior acquisitions were rather aggressive, perhaps the election may be more advantageous than the expense of fighting the IRS on an audit. In other situations, where the purchase was structured with a substantial portion of the cost allocated to covenants not to compete and other assets supporting depreciation or amortization over periods shorter than the new 15-year period, then the election may not be advantageous. If it is, file amended tax returns for the periods affected. Be certain to be alert for IRS pronouncements following the date of the Clinton Tax Act, which explain how to report this election.

If there was a binding contract in effect when the Clinton Tax Act became law, the taxpayers may choose not to have these provisions apply. This permits taxpayers who had a deal in process to try to argue for a shorter amortization period for purchased intangibles under prior law rules.

Antichurning rules, similar to those enacted with other tax laws, seek to prevent taxpayers from qualifying existing assets for this potentially favorable 15-year amortization benefit.

How to Allocate the Purchase Price to Various Assets for 15-Year Amortization and Other Benefits

The determination of the investment (tax basis) in assets subject to the new amortization rules will be based on the residual method that existed prior to the Clinton Tax Act. In this method, both the buyer and the seller use the residual method of allocating purchase price. This is the same method provided for in the regulations for certain stock purchases treated as asset acquisitions. To apply the residual method, you must first identify all the assets you bought or sold. Next, determine the fair market value of each asset. You must then categorize every asset into one of four allocation categories. The first category, Class I assets, includes cash, demand deposits, and similar cash items. The second category, Class II assets, includes certificates of deposit, foreign currency, readily marketable securities, and similar items. The third category, Class III assets, is the catchall category and includes any asset that does not fit into Class I, II, or IV. The final category, Class IV assets, includes intangible assets such as goodwill and going concern value. This is the residual category to be used to determine the basis for amortization under the new rules.

Once you have identified all the assets, their fair market values, and classes, you must determine the total purchase price you will allocate to the assets acquired. The total purchase price, as you would expect, includes the cash paid, the amount of liabilities assumed, the costs of the acquisition, and the fair market value of any property transferred to the seller. This total purchase price is then allocated sequentially to each asset you identified using the procedures described earlier. The purchase price is allocated to Class I assets first. No allocation can exceed the fair market value of any asset. After you have allocated to Class I assets their share of the purchase price, you proceed in a similar fashion through each of the successive classes. Again, no asset in the first three classes can be allocated an amount greater than its fair market value. Whatever is left, the residual amount, is then allocated to goodwill and going concern value in Class IV.

EXAMPLE: Newco buys the assets of Sellco for $400,000 and assumes $600,000 of Sellco liabilities. Newco incurs $30,000 in professional fees to consummate the transaction. Thus, the total purchase price Newco paid was $1,030,000. The basket of assets Newco acquired included cash of $50,000, marketable securities of $90,000, land worth $240,000, and a manufacturing building worth $350,000. Here's how you allocate the purchase price: First, cash, your Class I asset is allocated $50,000; next, the marketable securities, your Class II assets, are allocated $90,000; then the land and building, your Class III assets, are allocated $240,000 and $350,000 respectively. Finally, the remaining purchase price of $300,000 is allocated to the Class IV assets of goodwill and going concern value.

This residual method sounds so simple and mechanical that you may be tempted to think that there need be little planning or concern after the Clinton Tax Act. There still may be, however, implications to the proper identification of each asset identified in the residual class, and the determination of the fair market value for those assets. You may still have to identify carefully such intangible assets as customer lists, franchise and lease agreements, general goodwill, and the like because there could be important tax implications to you as a result of the allocation. Depending on what you plan to do with the various assets, financial reporting requirements could be a consideration, and there could be tax consequences to the seller. The allocation is especially important to the buyer in the event some, but not all, intangible assets are later sold. This is because the allocation will affect the gain or loss on such a sale. Legal considerations could also be important where different assets are subject to different financing, license, or other agreements.

TIP: Even if all Class IV assets are to be amortized over a 15-year period for you as the purchaser, the seller could have different tax or other implications from the allocations. Some assets could generate capital gains, while others might generate ordinary income. The implications to financial ratios, could affect financial reporting, loan covenants, and so forth.

A number of court cases have held that the allocations the buyer and seller agree to in the contract are generally binding. Therefore, when negotiating and drafting the legal agreements for the transaction, it is important to consider the tax consequences.

AMT DEPRECIATION RULES CHANGED

Corporations are subject to a corporate alternative minimum tax (AMT) similar to the AMT affecting individual investors (see Chapter 4). A special tax preference item unique to corporate taxpayers is the adjustment for current earnings (ACE). The rationale for this adjustment is that it prevents corporations from reporting substantial earnings to shareholders while reporting little taxable income to the IRS. The ACE adjustment is based on differences between financial statement and tax earnings—more specifically, 75 percent of the difference between a corporation's alternative minimum taxable income (AMTI) for the tax year, and the corporation's adjusted earnings and profits. One of the major adjustments in determining a corporation's AMTI for purposes of this calculation had been the ACE depreciation deduction. Under prior law, corporations could depreciate personal property for regular tax purposes using a 200 percent declining balance method over the assets recovery period. For AMT purposes, the depreciation deduction would be stretched out by requiring the use of only a 150 percent declining balance method. The period over which deductions had to be calculated using this slower rate was the class life of the asset. These were periods prescribed by the IRS. In general, they would exceed the recovery periods provided for under more recent depreciation legislation.

For property placed in service after December 31, 1993, the depreciation adjustment that had been required for the ACE calculation will be eliminated. This will provide some simplification of this adjustment item.

> **TIP:** The effects of ACE depreciation adjustments on property placed in service in 1993 or earlier are not affected. Therefore, the records and annual calculations relating to these depreciations adjustments must be continued.

RESEARCH TAX CREDIT REINSTATED AND EXTENDED

Tax Benefits of Research Costs Generally

You may qualify for several potential tax benefits if you incur research expenses. Research and experimentation expenses may qualify for a valuable tax credit that was extended and enhanced by the Clinton Tax Act. Research expenses may qualify to be deducted currently (or amortized over 60 months) under another special tax provision where they do not meet the requirements to qualify for the research tax credit (described in the following section). These deductions, however, could trigger a tax preference item under the alternative minimum tax (AMT) (Chapter 4). The increased tax rates affecting the AMT can thus minimize the value of this benefit.

> **TIP:** The definitions of qualifying research and experimentation expenses for purpose of the special deduction can be broader than the definition of qualifying research for the tax credit. Therefore, some expenditures may qualify for the deduction benefit even if they do not qualify for the credit.

General Change Affecting Research Credit

Prior law had included a credit for taxpayers who increased expenditures on certain qualifying research expenditures. This credit expired

July 1, 1992. The Clinton Tax Act retroactively reinstates this tax credit and makes some minor modifications to encourage qualifying expenditures. The reinstated credit will be available for 3 years, until June 30, 1995.

> **TIP:**   If you incurred qualifying costs after June 30, 1992, evaluate whether you should amend your tax return and claim an increased credit.

Overview of Research Credit

The credit is available for incremental research and development costs incurred in a trade or business. The credit consists of two components: 20 percent of the basic research expenditures to qualified universities and 20 percent of the qualified research expense over a base period amount.

The latter portion of the research credit can be generalized in the following steps:

Step 1.   Determine the total qualifying research expenditures in the current tax year. These are expenses intended to discover information that is technological in nature and useful in the development of a new or improved business component. The research must be elements of a process of experimentation for a new or improved function, performance, reliability, or quality. Qualifying expenses include those incurred for in-house research in your own business and 65 percent of the amounts paid for qualified research by third parties. The following types of expenditures will not qualify for the credit: foreign research or research in the fields of art, social sciences, humanities, and so forth. The Clinton Tax Act further defines certain expenditures as not qualifying. Expenditures incurred after commercial production of a product begins do not qualify for the research credit. Market research and testing, and quality control testing costs cannot be included.

Step 2.   Determine the base period amount. The purpose of this amount is to assure that only incremental research costs generate a credit. The base period amount is a percentage of the average annual gross receipts in the 4 tax years prior to the period for which the credit is claimed. This is subject to a minimum: The base period amount cannot be less than 50 percent of the qualified research expense for the current year as determined in Step 1. Under prior law, the fixed base percentage for start-up businesses was set at 3 percent. This applied to businesses that did not have gross receipts in at least 3 years during the period 1984 to 1988. The Clinton Tax Act limits this 3 percent fixed-base percentage to the first 5 tax years after 1993. Thereafter, a start-up business will determine its base period percentage on the ratio of qualified research expenses to the business's gross receipts. This can provide start-up companies with substantial research expenses an opportunity to earn larger credits. The objective is for companies performing research to move toward a fixed percentage based calculated from its actual ratio of qualified research costs to actual gross receipts.

Step 3. Multiply the excess of the current year expenditures determined in Step 1 over the base period amount determined in Step 2 by the incremental research credit percentage. This is generally 20 percent of the excess of qualified research expense for the tax year over a base period amount. Where applicable, 20 percent of university basic research payments are also included in the credit.

Step 4. Reduce your business deduction by the amount of research credit you are entitled to under Step 3. Alternatively, you can elect to take a reduced research credit and not reduce your business deduction for research costs. The reduction is determined by multiplying the maximum corporate tax rate (now 35 percent) by the research credit determined in Step 3.

Step 5. Determine which of the many limitations that could affect the amount of the deductible credit apply. Where the credit is earned by a partnership or S corporation in which you own an interest, the amount of the credit you can claim is limited to the amount of tax attributable to your share of the taxable income from that entity. The limitations on the general business credit described below must be addressed. Other limitations may also apply depending on the circumstances.

Research Credit Is Claimed as Part of the General Business Credit

Where the research and experimentation credit is available, it becomes part of the general business tax credit. The general business credit is the aggregate of various tax credits including the rehabilitation tax credit (available for qualifying expenditures incurred in the rehabilitation of old or historic buildings); the low-income housing credit (see Chapter 10); the research credit; and others. Complex rules help determine the order and availability of the tax credits used. There are also several restrictions on the use of the general business credit and hence the component credits that make up the general business credit.

The general business credit is subject to a limitation that the tax credits cannot be used to offset tax liability of more than $25,000, and 25 percent of any tax liability in excess of that amount.

> **EXAMPLE:**   An investor earned a $53,000 research tax credit. Assuming all the other limitations and restrictions have been dealt with, the following amount of the investor's $56,000 tax liability can be offset in the current year. The first $25,000 of the tax liability can be offset entirely by the credit. Next, 25 percent of the $31,000 remaining tax liability ($56,000 − $25,000) can be offset, or $7,750 ($31,000 × 25%). Thus, a total of $32,750 of the credit can be used. The remaining credit is carried over to future years, subject to the applicable limitations in those years.

Unused credits above this limitation may be carried back to 3 prior tax years and, if not used, carried forward to the next succeeding 15 tax years. If any research credit still remains unused, it can be deducted in the following year.

CONCLUSION

The Clinton Tax Act has made a number of important changes to depreciation and tax credit rules affecting businesses. The results can be either positive or negative depending on the particular business and the types of depreciable assets acquired. In all instances, however, it is important to carefully evaluate depreciation and tax credit implications.

PART SIX

OTHER TYPES
OF INVESTORS

18 Senior Citizens and Retired Investors

Many of the changes in the Clinton Tax Act were targeted at senior citizens. This chapter will highlight some of those changes, including those affecting the taxability of Social Security. Other indirect changes, however, will be just as important. The changes in medicaid planning will affect estate and financial planning for many senior citizens. One hope of the Clinton Tax Act drafters is that the Act should serve to keep downward pressure on interest rates. If this in fact happens (or if the detractors of the Clinton Tax Act are correct in forecasting that it will hurt economic growth), interest rates could remain low. While many other factors affect interest rates, to the extent that the Clinton Tax Act helps hold rates down, it may exact the its biggest burden from senior citizens. Those living on fixed incomes may have little optimism that the low interest rates they are now earning will increase soon.

SOCIAL SECURITY

Older Americans with higher incomes will face tax increases as a result of the higher tax rates and the greater portion of Social Security benefits subject to tax. The law includes a reduction in Social Security benefits for those eligible recipients who work. In 1993, the reduction in benefits works as follows:

Age	Reduce benefits above	By the following ratio
62–64	$ 7,680	$1 for each $2
65–69	$10,560	$1 for each $3
70+	NA	No reduction

TIP: The consequences can be adverse. Social Security recipients lose a portion of their Social Security benefits where their earnings exceed a certain threshold. The combination of this reduction and the new taxes can be extremely burdensome in some cases. Finally, the Clinton Tax Act increases the progressive nature of the tax rate system. The more you make, the higher rate you pay. When combined with the new Social Security tax provisions, the higher tax rates can have yet another negative result for seniors—not only may they pay tax on more income, they may pay some of it at a higher rate. The combination of these three negative factors: lost Social Security benefits, more Social Security benefits taxed, and higher tax rates, can be so costly as to make working hardly worthwhile in some situations.

To be realistic, state and local taxes and employee business expenses such as commuting must also be considered. The net result can be shocking.

The unfortunate consequence of this dilemma is that some able senior citizens who could enhance their lives and income, and continue making a contribution to society, will be severely discouraged from doing so. Others who are in need of money will be driven to work for unreported cash, driving more of the economy underground. The tax system should motivate people to work and contribute to society, not to sit idle because of poorly drafted legislation. Hopefully, Congress will see fit to revise this provision.

It has been estimated, however, that 80 percent of current Social Security recipients who did not pay tax on Social Security prior to the Clinton Tax Act will not be affected.

For those wealthier taxpayers receiving Social Security who face tax increases, this will increase incentives for tax-deferred investments, pension plans, slower distributions from existing pension plans, a greater appetite for tax-free municipal bonds and other investments.

Under prior law, 50 percent of Social Security income could be subject to tax. The Clinton Tax Act increases this to 85 percent for tax years beginning after 1993. This increase, however, will only apply where provisional income exceeds $44,000 for taxpayers filing a joint income tax return ($34,000 for other taxpayers). These amounts are referred to as the threshold amount.

TIP: For married taxpayers filing separate returns, the increased tax on Social Security applies without any threshold amount (where provisions income exceeds zero).

The new tax on Social Security is based on a new tax base: modified adjusted gross income, sometimes referred to as provisional income. This is defined as adjusted gross income, plus tax-exempt income, plus

50 percent of the Social Security benefits you have received (although you're including 85 percent in the calculation). This schematic is shown in Table 18.1.

If you file a joint tax return with your spouse, and your provisional income is more than $32,000, but less than $44,000, then 50 percent of your benefits are included in the calculation. This is the same as under prior law. For taxpayers other than married taxpayers filing joint or separate returns, with provisional income above $25,000 but not more than $34,000, prior law rules will apply and only 50 percent of Social Security benefits are included in the calculation. The calculation is as follows. Include in income, the lesser of the following amounts:

1. 50 percent of Social Security benefits; or
2. 50 percent of the excess of your provisional income over the following threshold amount:
   a. $32,000 if married filing a joint return.
   b. $-0- if married filing a separate return.
   c. $25,000 if filing under any other tax status.

Where your provisional income is above the threshold amount, you must include the lesser of the following two components in income:

1. 85 percent of the provisional income above the threshold amount ($44,000 married filing joint; $34,000 others); or
2. The sum of the following two items:
   a. $6,000 if married filing a joint income tax return or $4,500 if filing under any other tax status; or
   b. The amount of Social Security benefits taxable under current law. This is the same as the amount for taxpayers with provisional income below the threshold amount.

TABLE 18.1   Calculation of Provisional Income

Adjusted gross income (all income less certain deductions such as alimony, etc., but before itemized deductions)

\+

Tax-exempt income

\+

$1/2$ Social Security benefits

=

Provisional income

In no situation will you have to pay tax on more than 85 percent of your Social Security benefits.

TIPS: If your income is likely to exceed the threshold amount in all years, you may benefit from restructuring your investments so that your income fluctuates so that in some years you are below the threshold and only in other years above it. Timing of capital gains may enable you to achieve this. It may pay to reevaluate life insurance type products and annuities. The buildup of value within insurance and annuity products is not subject to current income tax at the new higher Clinton Tax Act rates. Also, this growth is not included in income for purposes of calculating the new Social Security tax. Be cautious, however; insurance and annuity products carry risks, significant fees, and often substantial restrictions. Timing the income you receive (by juggling hours worked if you work part time, or by billing assignments strategically if you are a consultant) can help minimize the effects of the new rule for some.

A special election is provided for taxpayers to treat a lump-sum payment of Social Security as received in the year the benefits relate to. If you receive a lump-sum payment in 1994 or later that in part related to 1993 or earlier, this election could be helpful.

The calculation of the new Social Security tax costs is demonstrated in Table 18.2.

PLANNING FOR THE NEW SOCIAL SECURITY RULES

The following planning ideas can minimize the tax consequences of the new Social Security rules.

Installment Sales

When you sell an asset on the installment method, you receive payments over a number of years rather than all in the year of the sale. A portion of the proceeds received in each year is subject to tax. The use of the installment method can lower significantly the amount of income received in the year the transaction occurs. Properly planned, an installment sale can help you avoid subjecting a large portion of your Social Security payments to tax in that year.

TABLE 18.2   Calculation of Tax on Social Security Benefits

(A) + Taxable Income

(B) + Tax-Exempt Income

(C) = Modified adjusted gross income (AGI)

(D) + Social Security benefits × ¹/₂

(E) = Provisional income—(C) + (D)

(F) − Adjustments to Income

(G) = Income (E) less Adjustments (F)

(H) − Threshold amount: $32,000 if married filing jointly; $25,000 for all others

(I) = Total Adjusted income (G) less threshold amount (H)

(J) Divide (I) by 2 =   . The lesser of (D) or (J) is the taxable benefit under prior law.

(K) Enter smaller of ¹/₂ Social Security benefits (D) or ¹/₂ of adjusted income less threshold amount (J). If provisional income (E) is $44,000 or less (married filing joint) or $34,000 or less for all others, this is the taxable portion of your Social Security benefits. If these amounts are exceeded, continue with item (L).

(L) Provisional Income (E) less $44,000 if married filing jointly; $0 if married filing separately and do not live apart all year; $34,000 for all others

(M) = Multiply (L) by 85% =

(N) + Lesser of (K) or $6,000 if married filing jointly; $0 for married filing separately who do not live apart all year; $4,500 for all others

(O) = 85% provisional income
     (M) + $6,000, $0 or $4,500 (N) =

(P) 85% Social Security benefits

(Q) Lower of (O) or (P) =   . This is the taxable portion of your Social Security benefits.

Lease, Don't Sell

If you sell an asset, the large capital gains could subject a large portion of your Social Security benefits to tax. Consider leasing as an alternative. The lower rent payments received annually may never be sufficient to force any of your Social Security benefits to be taxed.

Invest in Annuities or Insurance Products

The tax-free buildup of cash value inside certain annuities and insurance products is not taxable. Where these products make sense from an investment perspective, this tax-free buildup can add a valuable bonus.

Government Savings Bonds

The interest income on government savings bonds can avoid taxation until the bonds are redeemed. The safety of these bonds can also make them attractive to those living on their savings and concerned about investment risk.

Growth Stocks

Growth stocks currently paying little dividend income can avoid taxation of your Social Security benefits. Unfortunately, for many taxpayers affected by these new rules, current income may be essential so that this strategy, even if appropriate from a tax perspective, would not be feasible.

> **TIP:**   Some utility stocks, mortgage funds (Ginnie Mae's), and annuities make distributions that include a portion of your principal. Thus, only some portion of your monthly or quarterly payment will actually be taxable. These types of investment may offer a compromise—more favorable tax results but cash distributions necessary to meet living expenses.

Withdraw Pension and IRA Monies Last

If you have a choice of withdrawing funds from your IRA, pension plan, or other investments, deplete investments first. The monies remaining in your IRA, for example, will continue to grow tax deferred, and may not trigger an income tax cost if not withdrawn.

> **TIP:**   Watch out for the minimum distribution rules to avoid unexpected and costly penalties if IRA money is not distributed as required once you reach age $70^1/_2$.

RENTAL REAL ESTATE LOSSES AFFECTED BY SOCIAL SECURITY CHANGES

The passive loss limitation rules can prevent an investor, other than an active real estate professional, from deducting losses generated by a rental property. Where your modified adjusted gross income is not more than $100,000, and you meet an active participation test, you may qualify to deduct up to $25,000 of losses against any income without regard to this limitation. To qualify for this real estate loss exception, you must meet both an income and a participation test. When your modified adjusted gross income reaches $150,000, this allowance is eliminated. The modifications of your adjusted gross income include adjustments for individual retirement account contributions, alimony payments, and taxable Social Security benefits. The Clinton Tax Act changes that increase the amount of taxable Social Security could thus have the additional negative effect of reducing a senior citizen's tax benefit on rental real estate investments as well. The $25,000 allowance is phased out for taxpayers with modified adjusted gross income over $100,000 at the rate of 50 cents for each additional dollar of income.

MEDICAID PLANNING OPPORTUNITIES LIMITED

The Clinton Tax Act has made substantial changes to the medicaid qualification rules which will adversely affect many senior citizens attempting to plan their finances and estates to protect some assets for their heirs. Any analysis or planning for the new law, however, must be considered preliminary until the final provisions of President Clinton's proposed health care program are enacted. Major changes in health care could have a substantial affect on this type of planning.

Families facing the possibility of long-term nursing home care have taken steps to safe-guard their life savings by transferring assets to a spouse, children, or special trust. The goal is to permit the family member needing nursing home care to meet Medicaid income and asset tests so that Medicaid, instead of limited family resources, will cover the costs.

Under prior law, if you gave assets to your children in order to protect them from being used to pay nursing home bills (and to thus enable you to meet the income and asset tests) you could have remained ineligible for a period of 30 months. The Clinton Tax Act increases this look-back period to 36 months, and makes several other restrictive changes. If you transfer assets to a trust, the period is extended even further to 60 months. Even trusts established by someone on your behalf (rather than by you) which could only distribute income to you, could be affected. An exclusion can permit you to set up and fund a trust to provide for support of a disabled child. The exact rules are somewhat unclear and either Congress or the IRS may be issuing changes or guidance.

If you are subject to the new rule as a result of making gifts during the look back period, then you must calculate the period for which you will be ineligible for Medicaid. This period is calculated as follows:

$$\frac{\text{Aggregate dollar value of gifts/transfers during look-back period}}{\text{Your state's official rate for average monthly costs of private care}}$$

If your spouse transfers assets, the penalty period determined above will be allocated between the two of you. A limited number of exceptions are also provided. For example, certain transfers to your spouse, a disabled child, or others of your house, may not trigger the disqualification. These more restrictive rules are also applied on a broader basis. Under prior law, your eligibility only affected nursing home care. This has been expanded to include home care benefits as well. Further, states are required to seek reimbursement of nursing home costs from your estate. For these purposes, the definition of what is included in your estate has also been expanded to include non-probate assets. Probate assets are those assets transferred under your will. Non-probate assets include other assets in which you had an interest but which did not pass under your will.

CONCLUSION

In addition to the much publicized increase in taxation of Social Security benefits, the Clinton Tax Act has a host of direct and indirect changes affecting senior citizens and retired taxpayers. Since investment income typically takes precedence over wages in retirement, the many investment changes made by the Clinton Tax Act are vitally important. These are addressed in the next chapter.

19 Stock, Bond, and Other Investors and Dealers

TAX RATES AND OTHER CHANGES AFFECTING INVESTMENT STRATEGIES

The Clinton Tax Act has made several fundamental changes affecting investors in securities. Changes in investment strategy may be indicated by the tax changes. Caution should be in order, however, since taxes are only one component of your total net-of-tax return, and it is rarely appropriate to permit the tax tail to wag the entire dog. While the changes will not cause major shifts in investment strategy, it can be helpful to summarize the possible effects on investments.

> **TIP:** Some mutual fund companies have already started offering new funds, or at least promoting existing funds as designed for the new post-Clinton Tax Act environment. These funds focus on tax-free bonds, and funds designed to maximize after-tax returns by concentrating on a mix of low current income stocks, tax-free bonds, and so forth. Some European stock funds with losses on prior market declines have been suggested to minimize the effect of higher tax rates since future gains may be offset by tax loss carryforwards. More investment products targeted to the new tax provisions are likely to be offered. Exercise caution in investing in such funds, however. The Clinton Tax Act did not change any of the principles of sound investing. Watch out for the hype and stick to a well-designed investment strategy.

Tax-Free Bonds

The higher marginal tax rates make municipal bonds relatively more attractive. This is because a taxable bond will have to have a relatively higher yield to net you the same after-tax return as a tax-exempt bond. Table 19.1 illustrates the after-tax equivalents.

TABLE 19.1   After-Tax Equivalents

Taxable Interest Rate (%)	Taxable Equivalent Percentage	
	Pre-Clinton, 31%	Post-Clinton, 39.6%
4	5.8	6.6
5	7.2	8.3
6	8.7	9.9
7	10.2	11.6

TIP: Your actual tax rate can be noticeably higher than the stated 39.6 percent federal tax rate. The various phaseouts of your itemized deductions and personal exemptions could increase your marginal tax cost. State and local taxes could add on a significantly increased cost. For many high-income investors, overall marginal tax rates could be rather close to 50 percent making the net-of-tax value of tax-exempt interest income double that of non-tax-exempt interest.

Be careful when investing in tax-free bond funds. Some of the distributions may be taxable capital gains distributions. The other new tax rules concerning discounted bonds could also cause some of the income of a tax-exempt bond fund to be taxable.

Growth Stocks

The combination of higher corporate and individual tax rates, coupled with the relatively advantageous treatment of capital gains, suggests an investment strategy favoring growth stocks (and equity mutual funds concentrating on growth stocks), which reinvest funds instead of paying dividends. This type of strategy will minimize individual taxes on dividends currently paid (and for which the corporation does not receive any deduction). The gains ultimately realized will be capital gains on your sale of stock taxed at a maximum 28 percent rate, rather than dividends taxed at a maximum 39.6 percent rate. Effectively, growth stocks, as opposed to income stocks, convert ordinary dividend income into more favorably taxed capital gains.

TIP: The increased tax rates, relatively lower capital gains rates, and other changes made by the Clinton Tax Act make it important to reevaluate the mix of securities you hold, and the types of accounts in which they are held. Long-term growth stocks may be preferable to hold in taxable portfolios while bonds, utility stocks, and other current high-income-oriented investments, would be preferable to hold in a tax-favored account (IRAs, KEOGHs, etc.) where they will not be readily diminished by taxes. Where you have significant trading activity, so that gains and losses are realized currently, these types of investments will be even better off in tax-favored accounts after the Clinton Tax Act than before. This is because the trading volume will frequently trigger the higher tax rates where the securities are held in a non-tax-deferred account.

Series EE Government Bonds

The tax-deferral benefits of United States government savings bonds makes them more appealing following the increased tax rates created by the Clinton Tax Act. While the interest rates on EE bonds may sound low, they can exceed the returns on many bank, savings, and certificate of deposit accounts. The bonus is that the tax on the bonds can be deferred until the interest is withdrawn.

Some lower- and middle-income taxpayers may be able to use savings bonds for educational expenses and avoid any tax on the interest earned. To qualify for this benefit, the bond must be issued to an individual who has reached age 24 before the bond is issued. The redemption proceeds must be used to pay qualified higher education expenses such as tuition and fees at an eligible educational institution for you, your spouse, child, or other dependent. The ability to exclude this interest income is phased out as your modified adjusted gross income exceeds certain levels. Because of these phaseout ranges, taxpayers subject to the highest Clinton tax rates will not be able to take advantage of this tax-planning opportunity.

Bonds and Other Income-Oriented Investments

The new higher Clinton tax rates can make bonds and other income-oriented taxable investments less attractive for those in the highest tax brackets. Depending on your investment strategy and trading patterns, it may be advantageous to direct the income-oriented portion of your investment portfolio into tax-deferred or retirement vehicles to minimize current tax costs.

Stocks with Significant Intangible Value

The Clinton Tax Act permits the amortization of the cost of purchased intangible assets, such as trade names, goodwill, and so forth over a 15-year period. Under prior law, these costs had not been deductible. This can create a tax incentive to corporations spinning off divisions or subsidiaries with valuable intangible asset value, such as a well-known trade name. Such transactions will be designed to realize an increased sales price as a result of the purchaser realizing increased tax benefits of 15 year amortization. Corporations or investor groups with sufficient capital can benefit from acquiring corporations, or their subsidiaries or divisions, with significant intangible assets. The substantial tax benefits that the amortization of these assets can offer at the new higher corporate tax rates could create additional values in select corporations with strong brand names or the ability to capitalize on these benefits.

Reconsider Individual Retirement Accounts

Many people stopped contributing to individual retirement accounts (IRAs) when Congress eliminated the deduction for many taxpayers. If you or your spouse are an active participant in a qualified pension plan (such as one provided by your employer), the contribution to your IRA that can be deducted for tax purposes may be reduced or eliminated. However, IRAs have retained an important benefit, apart from the tax deduction for the contribution. The funds invested grow tax deferred. The new higher tax rates make reconsideration of IRAs, even where the contribution is not deductible, worthwhile for many investors.

> **TIP:** If your investment horizon is very long term, the advantages of tax-deferred growth within an IRA can outweigh the disadvantages.

Maximum Contributions to Employer-Sponsored Plans

If your employer sponsors a 401(k), simplified employee retirement plan (SEP), take maximum advantage of the plan by making the maximum contributions possible. Since the Clinton Tax Act has reduced the maximum amounts which can be contributed to pensions, a greater use of non-qualified retirement plans is likely. These are plans not insured by the Pension Benefits Guaranty Corp. Further, your employer may not even segregate the assets in your non-qualified plan, and they will be subject to the risk of the general creditors of the company. The use of Rabbi trust or independently funded insurance arrangements may minimize some of these risks.

Tax Shelters

Higher tax rates mean the look for shelter is on again. This, however, is not going to mean a return to the pre-Tax Reform Act of 1986 tax shelter heyday. It seems likely that too many investors got too burned to make the mistake of investing in any type of transaction for tax benefits without proper consideration of the economic prospects of the deal. Further, lengthened depreciation periods, passive loss limitations, limitations on tax credits, investment interest limitations, at-risk rules, and a host of other restrictions still exist to prevent the proliferation of the type of tax shelters that existed in the 1970s and 1980s. Low-income housing credit deals are a likely candidate for tax-beneficial investments. The tax credits can be quite valuable, and the transactions are well suited for syndication to passive investors (Chapter 10). The new exclusion for up to half of your gain on the sale of stock in qualifying small businesses (QSB) may spawn investment products to take advantage of this valuable tax break (see Chapter 15). In rehabilitation tax credit deals, where old or certified historic buildings are renovated, a portion of the costs incurred may qualify for a tax credit. Oil and gas partnerships have tax advantages and could, depending on economic and other factors, be encouraged by the tax legislation. Some of the initial costs of these ventures can qualify for favorable tax benefits.

Early Pension Contributions

The earlier in the year you make your KEOGH, IRA, or other pension contributions, the sooner your funds will begin to grow tax free. The higher post-Clinton Tax Act rates make the value of earlier contributions even more valuable than under prior law.

> **TIP:** Investors in the highest tax brackets should exploit opportunities to direct savings that would have been invested in mutual funds and other taxable vehicles into increased retirement accounts. There may be opportunities to increase contributions to 401(k) plans, encourage an employer to start a SEP, and so forth.

Utility Stocks

A combination of factors may suggest that utility stocks are not quite as favorable as prior to the Clinton Tax Act. Higher income tax rates coupled with the taxation of more Social Security benefits make utility stocks less advantageous for high-income senior citizens than previously. On the other hand, from a purely tax perspective, a utility with a high portion of its dividend consisting of return of nontaxable capital may be more advantageous, than one that pays out a purely taxable dividend.

Mutual Funds

Growth, rather than dividend-oriented mutual funds will be more advantageous for high-income investors seeking capital gains rather than more highly taxed dividend distributions.

Low-Income Housing Partnerships

The extension of the low-income housing credit, increased tax rates, and modest easing of the requirements to qualify for the credit should result in increased limited partnership offerings. These offerings may also be helped by the other incentives the Clinton Tax Act has provided for disadvantaged areas. Exercise caution, however; low-income housing deals are complicated and long term, and can be risky.

REITs

Real estate investment trusts received several modest advantages under the Clinton Tax Act. The modification of the passive loss rules for active real estate professionals should have some positive effect on the real estate market, although it is only a modest factor when compared with other factors influencing value. A REIT is not subject to the new higher corporate tax rates. Also, some REIT distributions can be tax-free returns of capital. This means that instead of more highly taxed current dividends, you may realize a larger portion of more favorably taxed capital gains when you sell.

Reevaluation of Insurance Investment Products

Not only can life insurance be an important tool in planning for the new higher 55 percent estate tax rate, but investment aspects of insurance products that offer tax deferral have become more advantageous as a result of the higher income tax rates. This is because of the tax-free buildup of cash values inside the policies. Variable life policies, which permit your investment inside the policy to be directed to stock mutual funds and other investments, can offer particular tax advantages when compared with similar investments outside the structure of an insurance policy.

An incremental advantage for older taxpayers is that this growth is also excluded from the calculation of the new Social Security tax (Chapter 18).

> **TIP:** Be careful in evaluating insurance products. If you do not have pure insurance needs, be certain that the product can still justify the purchase. Carefully analyze the provisions of any insurance proposal, evaluate the fees involved, and consider consulting a fee-only financial or insurance planner to obtain objective advice if the amounts involved warrant it.

Annuities

The higher tax rates make any investment vehicle providing tax deduction or deferral more advantageous. Annuities can be such a vehicle through providing tax-deferred compounding. The tax-deferred buildup of value in an annuity also escapes the tax on Social Security benefits. The Clinton Tax Act increased the progressive nature of the income tax rate. This increases the possibility that you may be in a higher tax bracket now, but a lower tax bracket following retirement when interest will be taxed. This type of shift can further enhance the advantages of annuity investment products.

> **TIP:** Carefully evaluate the policies you are considering. Consider the effect that commissions and other transaction costs will have on your return. Be certain to investigate the consequences of surrender charges, which can be significant in early years, sometimes as high as 7 percent.

Retail Stocks

A number of the tax changes will affect retailers. The repeal of the luxury tax for all consumer goods other than automobiles is beneficial for the manufacturers and retailers of such luxury items. It is unclear, however, to what extent the tax alone determines such luxury consumption. The higher tax rates, the uncertainty about future tax rates, and the status of the economy may outweigh such benefits.

Lower-income taxpayers will see reductions in their tax costs under the Clinton Tax Act. Also, the various credits provided for low-income areas and taxpayers will boost cash flow to low-income taxpayers. A large portion of this increase is likely to find its way into consumption, thus benefiting retailers focusing on this market niche.

SMALL ISSUE BONDS

State and local governmental units may continue to issue certain tax-exempt bonds to finance private agricultural and manufacturing facilities. The Clinton Tax Act has retroactively reinstated this "small issue" exemption to July 1, 1992, and made this benefit permanent. This move represents a continued investment option for investors.

QUALIFIED MORTGAGE BONDS AND MORTGAGE CREDIT CERTIFIED PROGRAMS

Qualified mortgage bond and mortgage certificate programs had assisted taxpayers meeting several requirements to purchase homes. These incentives permitted state and local governments to issue tax-exempt bonds to help finance such residential purchases. Since the bonds were tax exempt, the state and local governments could raise monies at favorable lower interest rates, which could then be passed on to purchasers. These tax incentives expired in 1992. The Clinton Tax Act retroactively reinstated these benefits for bonds issued after June 30, 1992, and made the benefits permanent. Thus, these securities should be more readily available to investors.

PRIVATE ACTIVITY BONDS

Tax-exempt private activity bonds can be issued after 1993 by state and local governments to finance government-owned high-speed rail facilities. These bonds may be issued without regard to the annual limitations on private activity bonds that may apply to each state.

DISCOUNTS ON TAX-EXEMPT BONDS

Where a bond is purchased at a discount, the discount reflects an upward adjustment in the bond's yield—effectively the interest earned until maturity. The market discount on certain bonds issued on or before July 18, 1984, could effectively generate capital gain on sale, even though some portion of the gain was really attributable to discount, which is analogous to interest and should be taxed as ordinary income. The Clinton Tax Act requires that the accrued market discount on tax-exempt and market-discount bonds issued on or before July 18, 1984, when the bonds are purchased after April 30, 1993, be taxed as ordinary income and not capital gains.

> **EXAMPLE:** An investor acquired a discount bond originally issued June 1, 1993, in a transaction on March 15, 1993. The new rules do not apply since the purchase date had to be May 1, 1993, or later.

STRIPPED PREFERRED STOCK SUBJECT TO ORIGINAL ISSUE DISCOUNT RULES

Stripped preferred stock is preferred stock when the rights to the dividends to be paid is separated from the ownership of the preferred stock itself. Preferred stock is stock in a corporation (an ownership interest in a corporation) that usually is entitled to dividend payments before the common stockholders. Preferred stockholders cannot participate in the growth in value of the corporation as do common stockholders, but receive preference over common stockholders if the corporation is liquidated. Many preferred stocks are subject to call features that permit the corporation to redeem them under specified conditions. Some preferred stocks have a cumulative dividend. If a dividend is missed, it accumulates and must be paid in the future. A preferred stock differs from a bond in that it does not have a fixed maturity date.

Effective April 30, 1993, the original issue discount (OID) rules will apply to stripped preferred stock that meets the following requirements:

- It is limited and preferred as to dividends.
- It does not participate to a significant extent in the growth of the corporation.
- The redemption price is fixed.

The OID of the preferred stock is the difference between the stated redemption price of the stock and the purchase price. The OID amount is treated as ordinary income for tax purposes. The amount of OID that must be included in income also increases your basis. This prevents you from being taxed twice on the same income. (The Clinton Tax Act does not fully address the tax consequences to a holder of the dividend rights on stripped preferred stock.)

INVESTMENT INTEREST LIMITATION RULES

In general, interest expense on debt incurred to carry investments cannot be deducted if greater than your investment income. Generally, gain you realize on the sale of investment assets cannot be included in your investment income for purposes of calculating the limitation on deducting investment interest. A special election will permit you to include capital gains in the formula if you subject those capital gains to your maximum tax rate rather than the general 28 percent maximum rate that applies to capital gains. A more general discussion of the investment interest limitation rules appears in Chapter 7. This rule is effective beginning in 1993.

> **TIP:** The interplay of the various phaseouts of personal exemptions and other benefits, the alternative minimum tax, and other tax considerations suggest that for higher-bracket taxpayers a projection of the tax consequences of making the preceding election will be prudent.

ANTICONVERSION RULES THAT PREVENT TURNING ORDINARY INCOME INTO CAPITAL GAINS

Rationale for Anticonversion Rules

The proof that capital gains benefits are back is that Congress was concerned enough about investors trying to convert ordinary income (taxed at rates of up to 39.6 percent) into capital gains (taxed at rate of not more than 28 percent) that it passed additional complex provisions, called anticonversion rules, to prevent abuse.

A transaction is subject to the new anticonversion rules where an investor has two or more positions with the same or similar property and substantially all the investor's return is due to the time value of the investor's net investment in the series of transactions. This is conceptually a series of transactions where your economic position is that of a lender: Your expectation of a return (profit) is in the nature of interest, and your risks are similar to those taken by a lender.

The goal of the anticonversion rules is to prevent you from structuring investment transactions, such as hedges or straddles, that artificially convert what is an interest return (a payment for the time value of money) into a capital transaction (which should really be limited to appreciation of risk capital or an equity interest).

> **EXAMPLE:** An investor purchased a $1,000 bond at par on June 1, 1994, and simultaneously entered into a contract to sell the bond at 105, or $1,050, to another investor on May 31, 1995. Assume market interest rates are 5 percent simple interest. The return realized by the first investor is conceptionally no different than if she had invested the money in a CD. The interest on the CD is a payment for her having tied her money up for an entire year. This is conceptually different from the result she would have realized had she purchased $1,000 of IBM stock on June 1, 1994, and sold it one year later at $1,050 due to appreciation. This latter transaction deserves capital gains benefits because of the equity risks taken, the first transaction does not. This result is the objective of the anticonversion rules.

Transactions Subject to the Anticonversion Rules

The following transactions are subject to the new anticonversion rules:

- The transactions consist of your acquiring property while entering into a substantially contemporaneous agreement to sell the same, or substantially identical, property in the future.
- The transaction is a straddle. In a straddle, you have two or more positions in securities that offset each other. For example, if you realize a tax loss on actively traded personal property, you are not permitted to recognize that loss if you have unrealized gains in offsetting positions for similar property. For stocks, similar rules would apply where you hold options traded on an exchange. Hedge transactions, regulated futures contracts, and other investments are subject to special rules.
- The investment is marketed to investors as a transaction that has the economic characteristics of an interest-like return but can be taxed as a capital gain.

> **TIP:** This is Congress's warning to tax shelter promoters that conversion transactions will not be tolerated.

- Any additional transactions defined as conversion transactions in regulations to be issued by the IRS. Until regulations are issued, this open-ended approach will make it difficult to plan transactions that are not clearly conversion transactions.

Transactions and People Not Subject to Anticonversion Rules

There are some limitations on the anticonversion rules. The new rules do not change the treatment of gain from the sale of property by tax-exempt organizations for purposes of calculating unrelated business taxable income, or for the gross income requirement of regulated investment companies.

Certain active security traders are excluded from the anticonversion rules. Option and commodity dealers and traders who engage in transactions in the ordinary course of their businesses will generally not be subject to these rules. An options dealer is a person registered with the appropriate national securities exchange as a market maker or specialist in listed options. A commodities trader is a person who is a member of a domestic board of trade designated as a contract market by the Commodity Futures Trading Commission. The IRS may expand this in future regulations to include registered persons who are users of memberships (they lease a membership from the owner.) This exception is intended only to benefit active dealers and traders, so limited partners and others in similar positions as passive investors in a partnership or corporation that operates an active business will not qualify. The IRS will issue regulations further clarifying and limiting these definitions.

Tax Consequences of Transactions Subject to Anticonversion Rules

The purpose of anticonversion rules is to require taxpayers to treat a portion of the gain realized on transactions described earlier as ordinary income and not capital gain. This ordinary income is not characterized as interest income. The complex aspect of this rule is to determine the amount of the gain that must be recharacterized. The amount is the interest you would have accrued on your net investment in the transaction at 120 percent of the applicable federal rate (AFR). The AFR is actually a number of different interest rates published monthly by the IRS. The rates are based on current market rates. There is a rate for short-term transactions (not more than 3 years) medium-term transactions (more than 3 years but not more than 9 years) and long-term investments (more than 9 years). Rates are issued for different interest-compounding periods: annual, semiannual, quarterly, and monthly.

Several special rules can modify the preceding general rule. For example, the amount you must report on your tax return as ordinary income under these rules is reduced by the amount you already had to report as ordinary income from the conversion transaction.

SECURITIES DEALERS REQUIRED TO USE MARK-TO-MARKET ACCOUNTING

Security dealers may hold a particular security as either inventory to sell to customers in the ordinary course of their business, or as an investment to be held for appreciation. In calculating income tax under prior law, there were several options for accounting for securities held by a dealer. They could be recorded at cost, which meant that unrealized gains and losses were not recorded. An unrealized gain (loss) occurs where a stock, for example, has appreciated (declined) in value but has not yet been sold so that the gain (loss) has not been converted to cash (realized). A lower-of-cost-or-market method was also used. Under this approach, which was conservative for financial reporting but aggressive for reducing taxes, only unrealized losses, but not unrealized gains were recognized. The Clinton Tax Act changed these rules.

Securities held in a dealer's inventory must now be carried at their fair market value. The Clinton Tax Act permits a limited number of exceptions from this mark-to-market rule. Securities held by dealers as investments may not be marked-to-market values at the end of the dealer's tax year (usually, but not always, December 31) if they are clearly identified when acquired as being held for investment. While financial accounting procedures may help identify securities held as investment assets, accounting procedures alone will not be fully determinative of the proper treatment. Certain rights to income not deemed to be securities in the hands of the dealer will be exempt from these rules. If securities are improperly excluded from these mark-to-market requirements, they will have to be reclassified and marked to market as required. As a penalty, any losses realized on the securities prior to the application of the mark-to-market rules will not be deductible when they are marked to market. Instead, these losses will be suspended until the security is actually sold.

The income, or loss, on these mark-to-market procedures will be ordinary, and not capital. For taxpayers other than C corporations, this means a maximum tax rate of 39.6 percent rather than 28 percent. There are a few exceptions for this rule that gain or loss is ordinary. Where the security is identified as an investment and not inventory, this rule should not apply. Also, the gain or loss realized on the hedge of an item that is not a security under these new rules is excluded.

> **TIP:**   Some dealers were having difficulty meeting initial deadlines for identifying investment securities that are exempt from the new rules. The IRS has provided some leniency in this regard. Because of the complexity of these new rules, there will likely be additional pronouncements from the IRS. Be certain to check with your tax adviser so that you remain current on important changes.

The IRS may require that securities be marked to market more frequently. Regulations are to be issued to provide guidance to minimize the potential accounting burdens of these new rules.

These rules apply to securities held by dealers. Securities are defined in very general terms so that, in addition to items typically considered to be securities, the rules also include partnerships, currency or equity notional principal contracts, evidences of indebtedness, and interests in financial derivatives. A dealer is anyone who regularly offers to enter securities positions with customers in the ordinary course of business or regularly purchases or sells securities.

> **TIP:**   These definitions are quite general. Until regulations are issued by the IRS, it will be difficult to ascertain precisely who will be subject to these rules, and which assets will be deemed securities for this new tax rule.

These rules generally apply to tax years ending on or after December 31, 1993. Since this new rule requires a change in the method of accounting, the cumulative effect of this change is recognized ratably over a 5-year period. An accounting method is the set of rules under which a business or other taxpayer calculates taxable income or loss for a particular period. The most common methods used are the cash basis method (you generally report income in the year you receive the cash, and deductions in the year you pay the expenses) and the accrual method of accounting (you generally report income in the year in which your right to receive it occurs, and expenses are deducted when all the events necessary to establish the amount and liability of the expense have occurred). There are numerous detailed and technical exceptions and requirements for applying a method of accounting; this new change affecting security dealers is just one example.

Special rules are provided for certain financial institutions and floor specialists and market makers.

CONCLUSION

The Clinton Tax Act has made numerous changes affecting investors in stocks, bonds, and other securities. Every investor must evaluate his or her investment strategy in light of the new changes. However, the changes are not so significant that major portfolio restructuring would likely be justified. Sound principles of investment management, such as diversification, liquidity, and so forth, should continue to apply. Finally, the market has likely already anticipated and reflected the effects of the Clinton Tax Act, by the time you are reading this chapter.

20 Divorced Investors

The Clinton Tax Act has numerous implications for divorcing tax-payers. Many changes are indirect and as a result, implications to the divorce-planning process are not always obvious. Therefore caution should be exercised.

SHOULD YOU FILE A JOINT OR SEPARATE RETURN?

When divorce is imminent, it is usually advisable to evaluate carefully the costs of filing separate tax returns. This is important to avoid the risks of joint and several liability from filing a joint return with a person who may soon be an ex-spouse. The joint return should always be a concern because the innocent spouse rules are not a certain protection against the tax problems the other spouse can create. Further, filing separate tax returns avoids the difficulties of having to address who should bear the costs of the audit. These benefits of filing a separate tax return must be weighed against the additional tax costs that both parties may bear to file separately. Several changes in the Clinton Tax Act affect this analysis.

Clinton Tax Act includes several tax rate increases. Married tax-payers filing joint income tax returns are taxed at a 36 percent rate when income reaches $140,000. Married taxpayers who file separate tax returns, however, pay the 36 percent rate when income reaches $70,000. In addition to the increase in top rates, the act also includes a tax surcharge resulting in an effective tax rate of 39.6 percent, which is assessed on all taxpayers at a $250,000 level. However, married tax-payers filing separate tax returns are assessed the highest tax and surcharge rate of 39.6 percent at $125,000 of income. This 39.6 percent rate is the result of applying a 10 percent surtax on taxable income above a specified amount (see Chapter 2).

For purposes of calculating the alternative minimum tax (AMT), the minimum tax exemption amount is subtracted from alternative minimum tax income (AMTI; see Chapter 4). The AMT tax rate and exemption amounts have been changed by the Act. Taxpayers filing joint tax returns are entitled to a $45,000 AMT exemption amount. A single taxpayer is entitled to a $33,750 AMT exemption. But married taxpayers filing separately are only entitled to a $22,500 AMT exemption.

The different manner in which the higher tax rates and AMT exemption amount are applied to married taxpayers filing joint versus separate tax returns could increase the cost of filing separate tax returns. These and other changes will have to be factored into the analysis since you may prefer a tax savings, if significant, to avoiding the potential risk of future audit liability.

MEDICAL CARE PAYMENTS FOR CHILDREN

If a court issues a qualified medical support order the parent's health care plan will have to comply and to continue providing medical care coverage. This rule will make it easier for certain spouse's to force a non-cooperative spouse meet his or her divorce obligations. The IRS will have to issue guidance on how the new rule will be applied by employers, and what steps you may have to take to obtain this benefit. Further, as with all health care related matters, the health care programs being considered at the time of this writing may affect this rule.

RELATIVE ADVANTAGE OF CAPITAL GAINS CAN AFFECT STRATEGY IN NEGOTIATING PROPERTY SETTLEMENTS

When negotiating any property settlement, the value of the assets is obviously the major factor. The inherent tax consequences of the assets are also essential to address. Two assets valued at $100,000 do not have the same net economic value where one has a tax basis of $10,000 and the other has a tax basis of $100,000. The first asset has a potential tax cost if it is sold as a result of the $90,000 of inherent gain. This makes that asset less valuable, potentially $35,640 less valuable after the effective date of the new 39.6 percent marginal tax rate ($90,000 × 39.6%). The Clinton Tax Act has not directly made changes to the capital gains tax rules. However, by increasing the marginal individual tax rate to 39.6 percent while holding the maximum tax on capital gains to 28 percent, it has created an incentive to structure investment and business transactions in a manner that will be characterized as capital gains instead of ordinary income. When negotiating a property distribution, this additional complication should be considered when evaluating the net economic worth of any asset. An asset with a potential capital gains cost will be worth more than an asset with a like amount of potential ordinary income cost.

ESTATE AND GIFT CHANGES

The Clinton Tax Act made several changes to the estate and gift tax, each of which has a potentially substantial cost to the families of wealthy taxpayers. The top tax rates for estate and gift tax purposes have been increased from the 50 percent level they were to have reached in 1993 to rates of up to 55 percent. The phaseout of the graduated tax rates and the unified credit will occur on transfers from $10,000,000 to $21,040,000.

A commonly used estate planning technique when a spouse, say the husband, remarries is to establish a qualified terminable interest property (Q-TIP) trust for the benefit of the new wife. Income from the trust is payable at least annually to the new wife. On the demise of the new wife, the trust corpus passes to beneficiaries designated in advance by the husband, typically the children of his first marriage. If properly structured, this approach enables the husband's estate to avoid any current tax cost. However on the death of the new wife the Q-TIP trust will usually bear a portion of tax as a result of then being taxed in new wife's estate. For wealthy taxpayers planning for divorce, this will affect the planning for distributions to the children of the current marriage since the increase in tax rates could affect the net-of-tax amount they will ultimately receive.

The Clinton Tax Act made several changes that affect the taxation of trusts. Trusts are subject to the same increased tax rates affecting wealthy individuals. However, the tax rate scale for trusts is even more compressed than for individuals so that the higher tax rates take effect at lower income levels. Table 20.1 shows these tax rates.

Trusts are frequently used to protect future payments to children following a divorce. The tax changes will make this a more costly means of ensuring future payments.

TABLE 20.1   Tax Rate Scale for Trusts

Trust/Estate Taxable Income ($)	Tax Rate (%)
-0- to $1,500	15
$1,500 to $3,500	28
$3,500 to $5,500	31
$5,500 to $7,500	36
$7,500+	39.6

MOVING EXPENSE DEDUCTION CHANGED

It is not uncommon for someone undergoing divorce to move during or following a divorce. The tax deduction for moving expenses has been modified. Some of the modifications will significantly reduce tax benefits of a move; others will increase the tax benefits. These should be addressed before relying on any tax benefits. Most indirect moving expenses are no longer deductible. Under prior law, to qualify to deduct any moving expenses, the distance between the location of your new job and old home had to be at least 35 miles more than the distance from the location of your old job and old home. After 1993, the distance is increased to 50 miles.

PASSIVE LOSS LIMITATION RULES

The Clinton Tax Act has at least brought some reasonableness to the application of the passive loss rules by minimizing their impact on active real estate professionals. The result for some taxpayers could be a reduction in tax cost. This simplifying change may also cause changes in transfer pricing, organizational structure, and fee payments for your ex-spouse and entities involved. This should carefully be considered in evaluating any settlement. Further, planning for some couples may involve shifting ownership of real estate assets to the spouse with a limited, or no other work involvement. This change in ownership could affect the dynamics of the divorce process. Pre-nuptial agreements will also have to account for this change in tax planning.

EXPENSING DEDUCTION

The Clinton Tax Act increases from $10,000 to $17,500 the amount of personal property (equipment, removable fixtures, etc.) that can be deducted immediately, under Code Section 179, in the year acquired instead of being depreciated over its regular depreciation period. Employers who operate in any of 95 designated communities will qualify for several new special tax breaks, including an increased expense allowance for writing off purchases of equipment and other qualifying property. The maximum deduction will be the lesser of the cost of the qualifying property placed in service in the tax year, or $37,500. In all instances, this means that the equipment, furniture, and other qualifying property listed on an income tax return could understate by even a greater margin the fair value of a business's asset.

HIGHER CORPORATE TAX RATES

The Clinton Tax Act has changed the relationship between corporate and individual tax rates. This change could have indirect effects on divorce negotiations, including the following: The tax rate on personal service corporations is increased from 34 percent to 35 percent. A personal service corporation is a corporation whose principal activity is the performance of personal services substantially performed by owner-employees in the fields of health, law, engineering, architecture, accounting, actuarial science, performing arts, or consulting. Owner-employees are persons who own more than 10 percent of the stock of the corporation. Personal service corporations do not have the benefit of paying tax at the graduated corporate tax rates ranging from a low of 15 percent to the new high rate of 35 percent. All their income is taxed at a flat 35 percent rate. Most personal service corporations avoid most or all of this high corporate tax through electing taxation as an S corporation so that the income is passed through to the owner-employees, or by paying all corporate taxable income out as salaries to the owner-employees. The Clinton Tax Act, however, will affect this strategy. Since the personal tax rate can reach 39.6 percent, it is nearly 5 percent higher than the corporate rate. Where monies must be retained in the corporation to fund corporate operations, it may be cheaper to have the corporation pay the tax at a 35 percent rate, rather than distribute the monies to the owner-employees as compensation if it will then be taxed at the 39.6 percent maximum rate.

Where funds are needed for corporate investment, the Clinton Tax Act may make the use of a C corporation, which retains income and pays the maximum corporate tax a more favorable option than under prior law where the maximum corporate rate of 34 percent was higher than the maximum stated individual rate of 31 percent. The result is that businesses experiencing a growth phase and requiring significant reinvestment of funds, whose shareholders are high-income earners, may wish to terminate their S corporation status and become C corporations since the tax cost will be lower.

The implication is that these changes have altered the structure used for some professional corporations, and the incentives available for varying types and amounts of payments. If you are involved in the valuation of such businesses, or in negotiating maintenance or other payments based on earnings, you should be alert to this factor when analyzing financial data in future years.

REPEAL OF LUXURY TAX

Prior tax law had included a 10 percent "luxury" tax on certain expensive purchases. Airplanes costing over $250,000, boats costing over $100,000, and jewelry and furs costing over $10,000 were subject to this tax. The Clinton Tax Act eliminated the luxury tax on these items effective January 1, 1993. If your ex-spouse purchased a luxury item in 1993 and paid a luxury tax, he or she may contact the store and request a refund. If the tax was significant, the refund could be an asset worth considering in structuring a settlement.

CONCLUSION

As with all prior tax acts, the Clinton Tax Act has numerous changes that may affect the matrimonial process. Most will have only indirect effects, and thus future regulations and the passage of time will be necessary to identify all the implications.

21 Tax-Exempt Investors

The Clinton Tax Act has made numerous changes affecting the tax consequences of tax-exempt investors (such as pension funds) investing in real estate. Many of these changes are favorable modifications to the rules concerning unrelated business taxable income (UBTI). Taxation of investments of tax-exempt entities in real estate investment trusts (REITs) has also been changed somewhat.

> **TIP:** Tax-exempt investors, charitable organizations, and pension plans can be subject to a host of regulations and restrictions other than the tax laws. For example, the charter (certificate of incorporation) for the tax-exempt organization may prohibit certain types of activities. A pension plan will still be obligated to meet ERISA and other requirements. Before implementing any changes in investment policy as a result of the Clinton Tax Act changes, discuss them with legal counsel. Also, it may be advantageous to have the board of directors or other governing persons or body approve the change formally.

TAX-EXEMPT INVESTORS AND UBTI

Tax-exempt organizations are subject to complex and stringent rules that can cause them to pay tax, like any other taxpayer, on certain income unrelated to their tax-exempt purpose. Tax-exempt investors include pension funds, charitable organizations, and the like. This type of income is called unrelated business taxable income (UBTI). The Clinton Tax Act made these rules easier and more favorable for tax-exempt entities.

UBTI is generally income from any unrelated business regularly carried on by a tax-exempt entity. Pension and other tax-exempt investors, for example, must consider the UBTI rules when making investments. Where real estate had been purchased with debt financing, rents and gains could generate UBTI, taxable to the otherwise tax-exempt organization. Where a tax-exempt entity is a partner in a partnership investing in real estate, special rules can also trigger tax consequences. Partnership allocation provisions must also be considered where taxable partners and tax-exempt partners invest in the same partnership. Finally, depreciation over a 40-year Modified Accelerated Cost Recovery System period can be required to be used by a tax-exempt entity. Investments in master limited partnerships (MLPs), certain options, and assets held primarily for sale to customers as inventory could all trigger tax. The Clinton Tax Act has modified many of these rules.

PARTNERSHIPS WITH TAX-EXEMPT AND NON-TAX-EXEMPT PARTNERS

Equity kicker mortgages can be problematic if the tax-exempt entity is recharacterized as a joint venture partner subject to the potential UBTI problems. The legal documentation should specifically state that the relationship is lender/borrower and that the parties do not intend to be partners. The tax-exempt organization could negotiate a cap on the interest the lender can receive. An unlimited share in profits should be avoided. The organization could also limit its areas of control as the lender.

Where there are both tax-exempt and non-tax exempt partners in the investing partnership (as there often are; e.g., the general partner), additional requirements must be met. These rules require that mixed (exempt and nonexempt) partnerships must have qualified allocations of income and loss among the partners and such allocations must have substantial economic effect. Qualified allocations mean income and loss are allocated to the partners in the same percentages during the entire period the qualified organization is an investor. For example, a transaction could have 99 percent of cash and profits allocated to limited partners until capital and a preferred return are received. Then 50:50 allocation becomes effective. This flip violates the qualified allocation rule. A mixed partnership can meet an alternative test in order not to taint the income of the qualified investor in debt-financed property as taxable UBTI. This alternative requirement permits nonqualified allocations where the tax-exempt investor's allocable share of partnership income doesn't exceed its smallest share of partnership loss. The substantial economic effect test must also be met. As a result, it is recommended, where possible, to structure deals solely with tax-exempt partners, or by using an equity kicker loan arrangement.

EXCEPTIONS TO UBTI RULES

There are several important exceptions from this UBTI rule under prior law. Since many of these rules continue to apply, as modified, being aware of them will help you understand the changes made by the Clinton Tax Act.

Debt-Financed Property

Interest and dividends where the stock, bond, or other asset was not acquired with debt financing are excluded. This permits tax-exempt entities to invest in most stocks, bonds, CDs, real estate investment trusts (REITs), and real estate mortgage investment conduits' (REMICs) regular interests. Special new rules for investments in REITs are discussed later in this chapter. However, if property generating dividend or interest was acquired with debt financing that is outstanding during the tax year, the following amount will be UBTI:

$$\text{Gross Income Receive} \times \frac{\text{Avg. Debt Outstanding in Year}}{\text{Avg. Adjusted Tax Basis of Property}}$$

Requirements for Debt-Financed Real Estate to Avoid UBTI Problems

Rent from real property can be excluded from UBTI (it will not be taxable to the tax-exempt venturer) if certain requirements are met.

Requirement 1.   Rent from personal property is excluded if it is "incidental" to the rental of real property. This means rents can't exceed 10 percent of total rent. This test is applied when the property is first placed into service. However, if more than 50 percent of the rent is attributable to personal property, then rent on all personal and real property is tainted as UBTI.

Requirement 2.   Rent cannot be excluded from UBTI if it is based on income or profits of a tenant. For these purposes, a lease where rent is based on a fixed percentage or percentages of gross revenue (sales) of the tenant will not taint the rental income as UBTI. This percentage rent can even be reduced by a base amount; for example, rent can be 5 percent of gross sales in excess of $150,000. A tenant can also reimburse the landlord for taxes and other common area charges. As a result of this, where a tax-exempt entity wants an equity feature, it can be preferable to favor an equity kicker lending relationship rather than a joint venture partner relationship. An equity kicker loan can be used to give the tax-exempt lender an interest in the rent and profits from the property. However, there are risks that an equity kicker could taint interest income as UBTI.

Requirement 3.   Rent on property acquired or improved with money obtained from nonqualified financing (acquisition indebtedness) will, in part, be tainted as UBTI. The following amount will be taxable to the tax-exempt investor as UBTI:

$$\text{Gross Rental Income} \times \frac{\text{Avg. Acquisition Indebtedness}}{\text{Avg. Adjusted Basis in Property}}$$

Acquisition Indebtedness is debt incurred (1) to acquire the property (including underlying debts on the property); (2) after the acquisition of the property, which wouldn't have been incurred if the property hadn't been acquired, and it was reasonably foreseeable at the time of the acquisition that this debt would have been incurred; or (3) before the acquisition of the property, which wouldn't have been incurred if the property hadn't been purchased.

There were some important exceptions even under prior law: Financing should not taint the rent earned on a property as UBTI where the property use is substantially related to the tax-exempt organization's tax-exempt purpose. Qualified organizations (KEOGHs, pension and profit-sharing plans, but not IRAs) can invest in debt-financed real estate without tainting their income as taxable UBTI if the property is not subject to a sale-leaseback and is not acquired with seller financing, the purchase price was fixed (not contingent) when the property was acquired, and there are only tax-exempt partners in the investing partnership.

The preceding rules governing seller financing of real estate and certain sale-leaseback transactions have been made more favorable by the Clinton Tax Act. Commercially reasonable seller financing will be permitted. However, participating loans are still subject to certain restrictions (although less stringent than those applicable under prior law).

Seller-financed participating loans are permitted where real estate is purchased from a thrift institution or bank in receivership. Participating mortgage financing and contingent purchase prices will be permitted subject to certain restrictions. The principal amount of the loan cannot exceed the debt on the property when the institution acquired the property in foreclosure. Also, the present value of the participating interest cannot be more than 30 percent of the purchase price. A purpose of this new exception is to help relieve the burdens on troubled financial institutions. The objective is to foster purchases by tax-exempt organizations of real estate owned by these thrift institutions.

Some tax-exempt organizations will be permitted to purchase real estate and real estate mortgages from failed financial institutions after 1993 without triggering UBTI. The properties that qualify for this treatment had to have been acquired by the thrift institution in a foreclosure proceeding prior to the time it entered into receivership. To qualify for this benefit, the tax-exempt organization cannot spend more than 20 percent of the price on improvements. Also, no more than one-half of the properties so acquired may be sold by the tax-exempt organization. The properties sold must be identified within 9 months and sold within 30 months.

Requirement 4. The payments must be "rental payments" and not "service payments." Services rendered primarily for the convenience of the occupant and not usually or customarily rendered in connection with the rental of space are considered services and not rentals. For example, an attended parking lot could constitute services.

The rules for investments by a tax-exempt organization in real estate options and deposits have also been made more favorable by the Clinton Tax Act. After 1993, gains and losses from options to buy or sell real estate, or from deposits received for the sale of real estate that were forfeited, will not trigger UBTI.

Sale Leaseback

A tax-exempt entity will now be permitted to purchase property and to lease up to 25 percent of the floor space of the property back to the seller without the transaction triggering UBTI. However, the leaseback must be based on commercially reasonable terms.

> **TIP:** Each time the law requires commercially reasonable terms, taxpayers must exercise caution. The IRS may provide specific guidance as to how this should be demonstrated. Until more guidance is provided, written third-party bids, appraisals or similar reports from brokers, and other corroboration should be obtained at the time the transaction is entered into. This corroboration should be saved with the legal documents for the transaction in the event of a later tax audit.

Inventory

A limited quantity of real estate mortgages and real estate properties purchased after 1993 by pensions and certain other tax-exempt organizations from banks or thrift institutions that are then in receivership or conservatorship can be sold. The tax-exempt organization will not be taxed on UBTI on the sale even though the property sold will be characterized as inventory. Inventory is property held for sale in the ordinary course of a taxpayer's trade or business. The bank or thrift from which the tax-exempt taxpayer acquired the property had to have obtained the properties by foreclosures prior to the time that it entered receivership or conservatorship. Within 9 months after the tax-exempt organization has acquired these properties, it must designate them as qualifying for this special rule. The properties cannot generally be sold more than 30 months after their acquisition. Also, not more than half the value of the properties acquired from a bank or thrift in a single transaction can be sold under this rule. There are also limitations on the amount of improvements that the tax-exempt taxpayer can make to these properties.

TITLE HOLDING COMPANIES

Title holding companies will not endanger their tax-exempt status after 1993 if they receive modest amounts of UBTI incidental to their holding real property. Modest is generally considered to be not more than 10 percent of the gross income of the title holding company. For example, income from operating a parking lot on the premises of a building may no longer be problematic. Under prior law, a tax-exempt title holding company could have lost its tax-exempt status on receipt of UBTI.

TAX-EXEMPT ORGANIZATIONS' INVESTMENTS IN REITs

What Is a REIT?

Real estate investment trusts (REITs) have long been a common form of real estate ownership. The rules for pension funds investing in REITs have been liberalized. To understand these changes, a brief review of the requirements for a REIT is necessary.

A real estate investment trust is a special form of real estate owner-ship that permits an entity (usually a corporation) widely held by a group of investors to own real estate and pass through the income to its owners (shareholders) without the corporation first paying a tax. In a REIT, a large number of investors pool their capital, and the cor-poration invests in a diversified real estate portfolio. Thus, a REIT is to real estate what a mutual fund is to stocks.

To maintain its qualification as a REIT, the entity must meet a number of strict technical requirements. The ownership interests must generally be broadly held. At least 100 persons must own a REIT's shares for at least 335 days during the year. In addition, to assure the diversification of ownership, more than 50 percent of the REIT's shares cannot be owned by five or fewer persons. To maintain REIT status, fully 75 percent of the REIT's assets must be invested in cash, government securities, and real estate. To assure that a REIT invests in passive real estate holdings, at least 75 percent of a REIT's income must be from the following sources: rents from real property, tenants' reimbursements for property taxes and other expenses, real estate tax abatements and refunds, interest on real estate mortgages, distribu-tions from other REITs in which it has invested, and gains on the sale of real estate and real estate mortgages it has held for a required time period. Also, 95 percent of the REIT's gross income must be derived from sources satisfying the 75 percent test—dividends, interest, and gains from the sale of stocks and securities. Finally, less than 30 per-cent of the REIT's gross income must be from the sale of stocks and securities held short term, prohibited transactions, real property held less than 4 years, and interests in mortgages on real property held less than 4 years. The types of real estate rentals a REIT may receive are also restricted to assure that the REIT's rental activities are passive. A REIT must meet strict distribution requirements directed at assuring that the REIT serves as a conduit for the income earned on its real estate investments. Thus, a REIT must distribute at least 95 percent of its taxable income to its shareholders.

The requirement that five or fewer persons cannot own more than 50 percent of a REIT's stock will no longer be as problematic because a pension fund will not be considered an individual owner for pur-poses of this test. However, where a REIT has material (more than 5 percent) income that would be considered UBTI if the REIT were a pension trust, and the pension trust owns more than 10 percent of a REIT's stock (and more than 50 percent of the REIT stock is owned by pension trusts holding such 10 percent or greater interests), a portion of the income from the REIT will have to be treated as UBTI:

$$\frac{\text{UBTI of the REIT}}{\text{Total REIT Income}}$$

The purpose of this rule is to prevent a tax-exempt organization from using investments structured through REITs to circumvent the remaining UBTI rules.

> **TIP:**   Certain tax-exempt organizations will still be subject to nontax restrictions that could affect their investments even after the favorable Clinton Tax Act changes. The Employment Retirement Income Security Act and the tax law prohibited transaction rules may have to be considered.

TAX-EXEMPT ORGANIZATIONS' INVESTMENTS IN MLPs

Where a tax-exempt organization invested in a publicly traded master limited partnership (MLP), its share of income had been treated as UBTI under prior law. The Clinton Tax Act changed this rule. Where a tax-exempt organization invests in an MLP, the sources of the partnership's income will be analyzed to ascertain what portion of the tax-exempt organization's income will be characterized as UBTI. An MLP is a publicly traded partnership that escapes corporate tax treatment only if it meets a series of tests with a strong similarity to the REIT rules (in some cases, they are identical as a result of cross-referencing the REIT provisions). Generally, any publicly traded limited partnership will be taxed as a corporation unless at least 90 percent of its income is passive. Passive income for these purposes is defined as certain interest, dividends, rents from real property, and gains from the sale of certain assets treated as passive, such as real property. For the purposes of this test, however, when real estate is held primarily for sale to customers, gross income is not reduced by inventory costs. Rents from real property are defined by reference to the REIT rules. Therefore, a real estate MLP cannot count rents toward its 90 percent requirement where (1) the rents are dependent on the income of the tenant (percentage rents, however, can be acceptable), (2) the MLP has a 10 percent or greater owner-ship interest in the tenant, and (3) rent attributable to personal prop-erty can't exceed 15 percent of total rent under any lease.

CONCLUSION

The Clinton Tax Act has made several liberal changes to the taxation of tax-exempt entities that should permit them to expand the scope of their investment activities without triggering tax problems.

Glossary

Accelerated Cost Recovery System   Since 1981, the rules for calculating depreciation (annual write-offs) for buildings, furniture, and other assets. The depreciation system after 1986 is sometimes called the Modified Accelerated Cost Recovery System (or MACRS). Depreciation write-offs are technically called recovery deductions. The basic approach to calculating depreciation under these rules is to multiply a percentage provided in IRS charts by the costs (adjusted basis) of the building, furniture, or other assets you are depreciating. The Clinton Tax Act modified these rules by lengthening the depreciation period for certain real estate to 39 years.

Accelerated Expenses   Pay expenses earlier. A common year-end tax planning step to pay for certain expenses prior to December 31, rather than incur them after December 31. This provides the tax benefit of a deduction a year earlier than would be achieved by waiting until January 1 or later to pay the expense. The Clinton Tax Act restrictions and retroactive tax increases make any decision to accelerate or defer expenses complex. Consider the alternative minimum tax before committing to any planning step.

Accrual Method   One of two major sets of rules for determining when a deduction can be claimed and when income must be reported. The simpler rule, which is used by individuals, is called the cash method of accounting. Under the cash method of accounting, you generally report income for tax purposes when you receive it and generally deduct expenses for the year you pay it. Under the accrual method of accounting, used by many businesses, partnerships, and corporations, income is reported and expenses are deducted in the year to which they relate rather than the year when paid.

Acquisition Costs   When buying a business or property, costs that have to be added to (capitalized as part of) the cost (adjusted basis) in the property (e.g., the cost of a title insurance report, legal fees, transfer taxes, accounting fees). Carefully evaluate the acquisition costs to find expenses that you can deduct currently. Plan how you allocate the total acquisition cost between land, building, furniture, and other assets you purchased since land can't be written off (depreciated); buildings can be, and furniture can be written off (depreciated) quickest of all.

ACRS   See Accelerated Cost Recovery System.

Active Income   See Passive Loss Rules.

Active Participation Test   A test to determine whether an investor has sufficient involvement with a rental property to qualify for certain deductions. Qualified investors with income (see Modified Adjusted Gross Income) less than $150,000 can deduct some or all of the tax losses, up to $25,000, from their rental property against any income including wages (active income) and dividends and interest (portfolio income). The amount of the $25,000 loss allowance that can be used is reduced as income exceeds $100,000 and is eliminated entirely when income reaches $150,000. To meet the active participation test, you must own at least 10 percent of the investment, and make management type decisions.

Adjusted Basis   Roughly speaking, an investment, for tax purposes, in certain property that equals the cost paid to buy or build a building (or any other asset), plus the costs to improve it. A casualty loss reduces the adjusted basis. Adjusted basis is used to calculate depreciation (multiply it by the appropriate depreciation or MACRS percentage) and to determine the taxable gain or loss when you sell property (subtract adjusted basis from your net sales proceeds to determine your gain). If you're subject to the alternative minimum tax, your assets may have a different adjusted basis for the regular tax and the alternative minimum tax.

Adjusted Gross Income (AGI)   Total income from whatever source (wages, rents, dividends, profits from a business, and so forth) less certain deductions (trade or business expenses, depreciation on rental property, allowable losses from sales of property, alimony payments, and so forth). AGI is important for calculating the amount of deductible medical expenses and casualty losses. A modified version of adjusted gross income is used to determine taxation of Social Security under the Clinton Tax Act. The $25,000 special allowance to deduct rental expenses when you actively participate is based on modified adjusted gross income, which is adjusted gross income increased by any passive activity losses, certain Social Security payments, and individual retirement account deductions (IRAs).

AGI   See Adjusted Gross Income.

Alternative Depreciation System   Special rules used to calculate depreciation (recovery deductions) for real estate and other property where taxpayer is subject to the alternative minimum tax, the property is financed with tax-exempt bonds, and so forth.

Alternative Minimum Tax   A second parallel tax system that many wealthier taxpayers must consider when calculating tax. The alternative minimum tax (or AMT) is determined by starting with taxable income calculated according to the regular tax rules. Add certain tax preference items and adjustments required by the AMT. Only certain itemized deductions are allowed. Next, subtract an exemption amount. The result is multiplied by either a 26 percent or 28 percent rate for individuals. If the tax due exceeds the tax owed under the regular tax system, the taxpayer must pay the larger alternative minimum tax.

AMT   See Alternative Minimum Tax.

Amortization   Deductions for writing off the cost of intangible property. Internal Revenue Code Section 197 intangible assets acquired when purchasing a business now are amortized over a 15-year period.

Amount Realized   For any property, the money and the fair market value received by the seller. It also includes the amount of any liabilities that are the responsibility of the buyer.

Annual Exclusion   An amount up to $10,000 per year that any person may give away to any other person without incurring gift tax. There is no limit on the number of people to whom you can make these gifts in a year. This exclusion can be doubled to $20,000 per person, per year, if you're married and your spouse consents to join in making the gift. This is called gift splitting.

Anticonversion Rules   A series of rules designed to prevent taxpayer from converting what should be ordinary interest income taxed at the highest marginal tax rates into capital gains. Transactions affected are primarily those where taxpayer's economic position is similar to a lender's.

At-Risk   Rules limiting the amount of tax losses that can be deducted from a business or investment to the amount you have at-risk in that investment. The at-risk amount includes the cash and the fair market value of any property you have invested in the business. The at-risk amount (your deduction limit) also includes debts for which you are personally liable.

Basis   Taxpayer's investment for tax purposes; generally the price paid to acquire property or the costs incurred to build property. See Adjusted Basis.

Beneficiary   A person who receives the benefits of a trust or of transfers under a will.

Bequest   Property transferred under a will.

Bonds   Special tax benefits are afforded by the Clinton Tax Act to investors in certain qualified small issue bonds, qualified mortgage bonds, and mortgage credit certificate programs.

Buy-Sell Agreements   Contractual arrangements governing the transfer of ownership interests (stock or partnership interests) in a closely held business.

Bypass Trust   See Credit Shelter Trust.

C Corporation   A regular corporation that pays tax directly to the IRS. A C Corporation can be contrasted with a S corporation, which generally doesn't pay tax; instead, its shareholders (owners) pay tax on their share of the S corporation's income.

Capital Asset   Anything a taxpayer owns of a permanent nature that can produce income or has a value, such as a building, house, or furniture.

Capital Expenditure   A payment to buy, build, improve, an asset (taxpayer-owned property) that will last for more than one year. Capital expenditures generally can't be deducted in the year paid. Instead, they must usually be added to the investment (adjusted basis) in the asset and then must be written off (depreciated) over a longer period. Examples of capital expenditures include the costs to construct a building, replace a roof and so forth.

Capital Gain   The gain from selling a capital asset that is held for longer than one year. The gain is usually the amount realized (net sales price) less the investment (adjusted tax basis) in the property. Capital gains receive favorable tax treatment in that the maximum rate is set at 28 percent when the maximum tax rate on ordinary income is 39.6 percent. Capital losses can only be deducted in any year up to the amount of capital gains plus $3,000. Special rules, which permit 50 percent of the capital gain to be excluded, apply for capital gains realized on investments in qualified Small Business Stock.

Capitalization   The addition of nondeductible expenses to the investment (adjusted basis) in the property.

Cash Basis Method   A method of determining when income must be reported and when expenses can be deducted used by most individual taxpayers. Certain partnerships, corporations, and other taxpayers may not be able to use the cash method. Under the cash method, income is generally reported in the year it is received and expenses are usually deducted in the year of payment.

Cash Flow   The actual cash received after paying expenses on rental property. Depreciation write-offs are an expense for tax purposes that does not require you to pay cash. So when calculating the cash flow from a property, you must add back depreciation write-offs to the income (or loss) you report for tax purposes on the property.

Casualty Loss   A loss, from a fire, storm, theft, and so forth to real estate investment property or a private dwelling, the damages from which are eligible for a loss deduction. Certain disaster losses may be deducted in the year before they actually occurred. New rules ease the requirements for reinvesting insurance proceeds received as a result of a casualty.

Charitable Remainder Trust   Property or money donated to a charity, reserving to the donor the right to use the property, or to receive income from it for a specified time (a number of years, the duration of the donor's life, or the duration of the donor's life and the life of a second person such as a spouse). When the agreed period is over, the property belongs the charitable organization.

Corporation   A legal entity separate from the individuals who own it (called shareholders). Different types of corporations important to real estate investors include: real estate investment trust, S corporation, C corporation, and cooperative corporation (see C corporation, S corporation).

Credit Shelter Trust   A trust designed not to qualify for the unlimited estate tax marital deduction so that it will use up the lifetime $600,000 exclusion (unified credit). The same as a bypass trust (because such a trust bypasses, is not included in, the surviving spouse's estate).

Dealer   An investor who buys and sells assets, such as real estate, or bonds so often he or she is considered to be in the business of dealing in that asset.

Declining Balance Method   A type of depreciation that is twice as fast as the straight-line (ratable) way of calculating depreciation.

Defer Income   A common tax-planning technique near December 31 that puts off recognizing income until the next year to avoid paying tax on the income for another full year. Examples of income deferral include delaying the sale of stocks or property until January, or selling property on the installment method and not receiving cash until the next year.

Deferral of Estate Tax   Where a sufficient portion of an estate comprises assets in a closely held and active business, its payment of the estate tax attributable to those assets over approximately 14-year period instead of within nine months of the owner's death.

Depreciation   The writing off of an asset's cost over its useful life or using methods prescribed by the tax laws. Depreciation is based on the idea that property wears down over time due to the elements, physical wear and tear from use, and so forth.

Depreciation Convention   An assumption or rule to simplify depreciation calculations. For example, depreciation is not calculated on a daily basis for years when property is bought or sold. For furniture and equipment (personal property), a midyear convention is generally used. This results in taxpayers getting a half year of depreciation no matter when during the year the item is bought or sold.

Depreciation Method   A prescribed approach to calculate depreciation. The straight-line method results in deducting equal or ratable amounts of an asset's cost over the asset's useful life or depreciation (recovery) period. For example, a machine costing $1,000, with a depreciation period of 10 years, would be depreciated at a rate of $100 in each year.

Disaster Area Relief   Special tax relief for insurance proceeds for homeowners and renters whose principal residences and household belongings were damaged in a federal declared disaster area after September 1, 1991.

Donee   A person who receives a gift.

Donor   A person who makes a gift.

Education Assistance   Certain expenses, up to $5,250, paid for an employee educational assistance program before 1995 that are excludable from the employee's taxable income.

Elective Expensing   The opportunity of taxpayers who meet certain requirements to write off up to $17,000 of certain furniture and equipment (personal property) immediately. This amount is increased from $10,000 under prior law. Normally, the cost of furniture and equipment must be written off over 7 years using the 200 percent declining balance method of depreciation.

Empowerment Zone   These are specially designated areas where investors can earn special tax benefits. Employers in any of nine designated empowerment zones will receive a tax credit of 20 percent on the first $15,000 of wages and additional benefits to qualified workers.

Enterprise Communities   These are specially designated communities where investors can earn special tax benefits. Employers who operate in any of 95 designated communities will qualify for several new special tax breaks, including an increased expense allowance for writing off purchases of equipment and other qualifying Code Section 179 property.

Estate Tax   On the death of a taxpayer, a tax due on the transfer of wealth to family and others. Exclusions are provided for transfers to the taxpayer's spouse, charities, and so forth. The tax rate for the estate tax can reach as high as 55 percent. A once-in-a-lifetime credit enables you to pass property worth up to $600,000 to others without having to pay an estate tax.

Estimated Tax   Income taxes paid by certain individuals on a quarterly basis to avoid underpayment penalties. The Clinton Tax Act has provided special rules for the payment of estimated taxes resulting from the retroactive tax increase. The general rules to avoid penalties have also been made more lenient.

General Partnership   A partnership that has only general partners—no limited partners. This is the most common way for a few friends or investors to put their money together to buy a rental property.

Generation Skipping Transfer (GST) Tax   A transfer tax generally assessed on transfers to grandchildren, great grandchildren, and so forth. Each taxpayer is given a $1 million exclusion from the GST.

Gift   If you transfer property without receiving something of equal value in return, the federal government will assess a transfer tax where the value of the gift exceeds the annual exclusion and your unified credit is exhausted.

Gift Tax   A tax that can be due when giving property or other assets away. You are allowed to give away a maximum of $10,000 per person (to any number of people) in any year without the tax applying. Above the $10,000 amount, you have a once-in-a-lifetime exclusion permitting you to give away $600,000 of property without paying any gift tax. The gift tax and the estate tax are coordinated (unified) so that the $600,000 exclusion is only available once between them. The Clinton Tax Acts increased income tax and estate tax rates make the maximum use of this planning opportunity even more important.

Grantor   The name given to an investor who establishes a trust and transfers assets to it.

Gross Estate   The total value of the assets own at a taxpayer's death, or that are included in the estate. The value is determined at the date of death or as of the alternate valuation date, which is six months following the date of death.

Gross Income   A taxpayer's earnings from all sources including wages, rents, royalties, dividends, and interest.

Half-Year Convention   A required method when calculating depreciation on equipment and furniture (personal property), that provides a half year's worth of depreciation deductions in the year the taxpayer buys or sells the property.

Heirs   The persons who receive the assets following a taxpayer's death.

Improvements   Payments for additions or betterment to property that will last more than a year and must thus be added to the investment (capitalized as part of your basis) in the property.

Installment Sale   A sale where taxable gain is recognized over a number of years as the payment for the property sold is received. If you are a dealer in property, you can't use the installment method. See Dealer.

Insurance Trust   An irrevocable trust established to own insurance policies and thereby prevent them from being included in an estate.

Investment Interest Limitation   The limitation interest incurred on debt used to carry investment assets, which can only be deducted to the extent of investment income. The Clinton Tax Act generally prohibits your including gains on the sale of investment assets in this calculation although there is an exception where you make a special election to tax your capital gains at a higher tax rate.

Involuntary Conversion   When property is destroyed (converted) by a casualty loss and an insurance payment is received, the avoidance of a current tax cost by reinvesting the money in qualifying replacement property. The Clinton Tax Act extended the reinvestment period to 4 years after the close of the tax year in which the conversion occurred.

Irrevocable Trust   A trust that cannot be changed after being established. This essential characteristic allows the assets you give to the trust to be removed from your estate.

Kiddie Tax   Unearned income (dividends, rents, interest, and so forth) of a child under age 14 taxed to the child at the parent's highest tax rate. This tax makes family tax planning much harder.

Limited Partner   A partner (owner) in a partnership who can't participate in the management of the partnership's business. The advantage is that lenders and others can't generally sue a limited partner personally if the partnership defaults on its mortgage payments or is sued because someone is injured on the property, and so forth.

Limited Partnership   A partnership with at least one general partner and any number of limited partners. Limited partnerships are one type of vehicle for investing in low-income housing credit deals.

Low-Income Housing Credit   An extremely favorable tax credit obtained when qualifying investments are made in certain low-income housing. The rules for the credit are extremely complex. The Clinton Tax Act made several technical changes to the requirements for the credit, and retroactively reinstated the credit, which had expired.

Luxury Tax   A tax on certain consumer goods deemed luxury items (boats, airplanes, jewelry, and furs) that has been retroactively repealed by the Clinton Tax Act, except for the tax on automobiles.

MACRS   Modified Accelerated Cost Recovery System. See Accelerated Cost Recovery System.

Marital Deduction   The unlimited transfer of assets by either of legally married spouses to the other spouse without incurring any gift or estate tax cost. This is too often used as a simplistic approach to eliminate the entire estate tax on the death of the first of you or your spouse.

Marriage Penalty   The tax cost affecting married couples, compared with the tax cost applicable to two unmarried single taxpayers. The Clinton Tax Act has significantly increased this penalty. The increases are not all obvious and are not only in the regular income tax rate. The alternative minimum tax and various phaseout rules include provisions adding to the marriage penalty burden.

Material Participation   A taxpayer's involvement in a business on a (1) regular; (2) continuous; and (3) substantial basis. The passive activity rules create three general types of income: (1) passive (such as an investment in a limited partnership); (2) portfolio (such as dividends and interest on stocks and bonds); and (3) active income (such as wages and earnings from a business in which you are active). For income to qualify as active, you must materially participate in the business.

Midmonth Convention: In calculating depreciation write-offs for buildings, the entitlement to claim one-half month's worth of depreciation for the month the property is bought and one-half month's worth of depreciation for the month the property is sold.

Modified Adjusted Gross Income   Gross income (wages, dividends, rents, and so forth) less adjustments from gross income (business deductions, rental expenses, alimony, moving expenses after 1993, and so forth) plus certain modifications. The modifications depend on the particular use of the modified adjusted gross income. For example, a modified version of adjusted gross income is used to calculate the taxable portion of Social Security benefits. See Adjusted Gross Income.

Moving Expenses   Qualified deductions when moving to a new home in connection with starting work at a new principal place of work. Deductible expenses may include the costs of moving your household goods, but the Clinton Tax Act eliminated many expenses that had been deductible under prior law. To qualify, your new principal place of work must be at least 50 miles farther from your former home than was your former principal place of work.

Ordinary Income   Income or gain from selling property that is not a capital asset (see Capital Asset). It is taxed at rates of up to 39.6 percent, much less favorable for many taxpayers than capital gains rates of a maximum 28 percent.

Organizational Expenses   Costs to set up a business, partnership, or corporation that can be written off (amortized) over 60 months beginning with the date the business, partnership, or corporation begins to conduct an active business.

Partnership   A syndicate, joint venture, group, or other arrangement, in which two or more investors join their money and skills to carry out a business as coowners and to earn a profit. A partnership is generally treated as a flow-through (conduit) so that each partner reports his or her share of partnership income or loss on a personal tax return. The partnership files a Form 1065 as an information report with the IRS but doesn't pay any tax. An election is available to avoid being taxed as a partnership.

Passive Income   Income earned from rental property or as a limited partner investor. Passive losses (tax losses from rental property or from investments made as a limited partner) can only be applied to offset passive income. If you qualify as actively participating in a real estate rental, you may be able to deduct up to $25,000 of your passive tax losses against any income without regard to this limitation.

Passive Loss   Tax losses from rental real estate properties (e.g., as a result of depreciation write-offs) or from investments as a limited partner. Passive losses can generally be used only to offset passive income.

Personal Property   Furniture, equipment, and other movable property and assets. Buildings and land are not personal property—they are real property.

Preferred Stock   Stock that has a preference over common stock for the payment of dividends and that generally has only a limited, if any, participation in the future economic growth of the corporation. Preferred stockholders also receive preference over common stockholders if the corporation is liquidated. Many preferred stocks are subject to call features that permit the corporation to redeem them under specified conditions. Some preferred stocks have a cumulative dividend. If a dividend is missed, it accumulates and must be paid in the future. A preferred stock differs from a bond in that it does not have a fixed maturity date.

Present Interest   A gift's capacity to be enjoyed by the beneficiary immediately; a requirement for the gift to qualify for the annual $10,000 gift tax exclusion.

Qualified Terminable Interest Trust (Q-TIP)   A trust that qualifies for the unlimited marital tax exclusion. Therefore, there will be no estate tax on the value of the property transferred to the surviving spouse in a Q-TIP trust. The spouse must receive all income at least annually. The Q-TIP enables the spouse to obtain income and other benefits, the estate avoids tax, and the grantor can designate who will receive the property remaining on the spouse's death.

Research Credit   A tax credit available for increases in qualified research expenses and basic research payments to universities and other qualified organizations. The Clinton Tax Act retroactively reinstated this credit, which had lapsed.

S Corporation   A corporation whose income is generally taxed to its shareholders thus avoiding a corporate level tax.

Second-to-Die Insurance   Insurance for a couple that pays a death benefit only on the death of the last spouse. This payment method makes the cost of such insurance less than insurance on just one person's life. This type of insurance is designed for an estate plan where on the death of the first spouse many assets are given tax free to the surviving spouse using the unlimited marital deduction. On the death of the second spouse, the insurance benefit is paid and provides the cash to pay the estate tax. It is also called survivors insurance.

Section 6166 Deferral   An Internal Revenue Code provision permitting an estate to defer the estate tax. The higher estate tax rates make this planning benefit more important to consider.

Self-Employed Health Insurance   A deduction retroactively reinstated by the Clinton Tax Act for a portion of the health insurance premium payments by self-employed persons.

Small Business Investment Company   Gain on the sale of securities can be reinvested on a tax-free basis in qualifying small business investment companies.

Small Business Stock   With reference to taxation, the exclusion of up to half the gain on the sale of certain small business stock. This benefit can effectively reduce the capital gains cost on qualifying investments to a 14 percent level.

Stripped Preferred Stock   Preferred stock where the future right to dividends has been separated from the stock itself. The Clinton Tax Act extended the original issue discount rules to these investments.

Targeted Jobs Credit   A credit of up to 40 percent of the first $6,000 of wages ($3,000 for summer youth) paid to members of certain disadvantaged groups.

Taxable Estate   The gross estate reduced by expenses and debts and charitable contributions.

Trust   Property held and managed by a person (trustee) for the benefit of another (the beneficiary). The terms of the trust are generally governed by a contract that the grantor prepares when establishing the trust.

Unified Credit   A total of $600,000 of transfers that every taxpayer is allowed to exclude from estate and gift tax. The Clinton Tax Act has increased the marginal estate tax rate and has changed the phaseout of this unified credit.

Uniform Gifts (Transfers) to Minors Act (UGMA or UTMA)   A method to hold property for the benefit of another person, such as a child, which is similar to a trust, but is governed by state law. It is simpler and much cheaper to establish and administer, but is far less flexible than a trust.

Unrelated Business Taxable Income (UBTI)   Certain income earned by otherwise tax-exempt organizations from activities unrelated to their tax-exempt purpose that may be subject to taxation. The Clinton Tax Act liberalized these rules.

Index